New Testament Commentary

I & II Thessalonians

New Testament Commentary

I & II Thessalonians

William Hendriksen

THE BANNER OF TRUTH TRUST

THE BANNER OF TRUTH TRUST
78b *Chiltern Street, London* W1M 1PS

*

© 1955 *William Hendriksen*
First British edition 1972

*

*

Printed by offset lithography in Great Britain
by Billing & Sons Limited, Guildford and London

TABLE OF CONTENTS

LIST OF ABBREVIATIONS

The letters in book-abbreviations are followed by periods. Those in periodical-abbreviations omit the periods and are in italics. Thus one can see at a glance whether the abbreviation refers to a book or to a periodical.

A. *Book Abbreviations*

A.R.V.   American Standard Revised Version
A.V.   Authorized Version (King James)
B.D.B.   Brown-Driver-Briggs, *Hebrew and English Lexicon to the Old Testament*
Gram.N.T.   A. T. Robertson, *Grammar of the Greek New Testament in the Light of Historical Research*
H.B.A.   Hurlbut, *Bible Atlas* (most recent edition)
I.S.B.E.   *International Standard Bible Encyclopedia*
L.N.T.   Thayer's *Greek-English Lexicon of the New Testament*
M.M.   *The Vocabulary of the Greek Testament Illustrated from the Papyri and Other Non-Literary Sources,* by James Hope Moulton and George Milligan (edition Grand Rapids, 1952)
N.N.   *Novum Testamentum Graece,* edited by D. Eberhard Nestle and D. Erwin Nestle (most recent edition)
N.T.C.   W. Hendriksen, *New Testament Commentary*
R.S.V.   Revised Standard Version
W.D.B.   *Westminster Dictionary of the Bible*
W.H.A.B.   *Westminster Historical Atlas to the Bible*

B. *Periodical Abbreviations*

BTr   *The Bible Translator*
EQ   *Evangelical Quarterly*
ExT   *Expository Times*
Int   *Interpretation*
JBL   *Journal of Biblical Literature*
RB   *Revue biblique*
RHPR   *Revue d'histoire et de philosophie religieuses*

Please Note

In order to differentiate between the second person singular and the second person plural, without reverting to the archaic "thou" and "ye" except where it is proper to do so, we have indicated the former as follows: "you"; and the latter as follows: "y o u."

Introduction
to
I and II Thessalonians

I. Reasons for Studying These Epistles

We are about to study certain epistles written by a man who, with the aid of his associates, "turned the world upside down." Interest in Paul never lags.[1]

This interest is varied. Some focus their attention particularly upon Paul *the theologian*. They ask such questions as, Was Paul the constructor of a doctrinal system or was he a disciple of Jesus? What were his views with respect to various doctrinal themes? Should the Church of the present day allow itself to be guided by these views or should it regard them as being without normative value?

Others, again, sketch a portrait of Paul *the man*. Their main interest may be called *psychological*. These ask, How can we account for his seemingly boundless energy? Was he normal or abnormal? Can his experience on the way to Damascus be explained psychologically or did something of a supernatural character occur? Was he fearless or fearful? Was he cold or sympathetic?

Finally, there are also those for whom Paul is, above all, *the missionary*. In this group there are some who stress the idea that Paul is the missionary whom we should copy. They argue that however great his advantages may have been, they cannot have been so great as to rob his example of all value for the present day and age. They conclude that *Paul's* methods should be *our* methods. If he believed in the indigenous (self-supporting, self-propagating, self-governing) church, so should we. Others, however, while going along with this view to a considerable extent, are not so sure that Paul's principles and methods are applicable today without extensive

---

1 Thus, among the important works either newly published or appearing as reprints during the single decade 1940-1950 were the following:

R. M. Hawkins, *The Recovery of the Historical Paul*, Nashville, 1943.

C. W. Quimby, *Paul for Everyone*, New York, 1944.

John Knox, *Chapters in a Life of Paul*, New York and Nashville, 1946.

E. J. Goodspeed, *Paul*, Philadelphia, Toronto, 1947.

R. Machen, *The Origin of Paul's Religion*, reprinted Grand Rapids, 1947.

F. Postma, *Paulus*, Pretoria, 1949.

W. Ramsay, *St. Paul the Traveler and the Roman Citizen*, reprinted Grand Rapids, 1949.

W. Ramsay, *The Cities of St. Paul*, reprinted Grand Rapids, 1949.

W. J. Conybeare and J. S. Howson, *The Life and Epistles of St. Paul*, reprinted Grand Rapids, 1949.

A. Barnes, *Scenes and Incidents in the Life of the Apostle Paul*, reprinted Grand Rapids, 1950.

modification. They call attention to the greatness of *this* missionary, his extraordinary charismatic gifts and qualifications. They also emphasize the fact that times and circumstances have changed, and consequently, that often that which was the right thing to do for Paul is the wrong thing to do for us.

Thus we have the *theological,* the *personal or psychological,* and the *missionary* interest in Paul (to say nothing about the various ways in which these interests blend and combine).

Now it is a fact that these three lines converge beautifully in the two epistles to the Thessalonians. To begin with the *theological* or *doctrinal* interest: to be sure, there are epistles that are more consistently doctrinal, yet nowhere do we find so much source-material for the doctrine *of the last things* ("eschatology") as in these eight chapters. It is a well-known fact that *in I Thessalonians every chapter ends with a reference to the second coming.* See 1:10; 2:19, 20; 3:11-13; 4:13-18; 5:23, 24. Also II Thessalonians abounds in eschatological material; see especially 1:7-10 and 2:1-12. For information on such subjects as "the rapture" (in whatever sense one conceives of it), the time of Christ's return, the great apostasy or "falling away," "the man of sin," "the one who (or: that which) restrains," "the mystery of lawlessness," and "the manifestation of his (Christ's) coming" — we naturally turn first of all to I and/or II Thessalonians.

Again, though it is certainly true that other passages in Paul's epistles and in Acts may be regarded as windows which afford a look into the heart of the great apostle, none are more revealing in this respect than I Thess. 2:1-12; 3:1-10; 5:12-24; and II Thess. 3:7-10. Here truly is a portrait of Paul *the man.* In these two epistles he stands out "in all the charm of his rich and varied personality" (George Milligan, *St. Paul's Epistles to the Thessalonians,* London, 1908, p. xliii).

And as to Paul *the missionary,* his "strategy" — proclaiming the message in the great centers, making use of the synagogue, basing his argumentation upon the prophecies of the Old Testament, etc. — is as clearly evident at Thessalonica as anywhere else. In fact, special studies devoted to this subject refer again and again not only to Acts 17:1-19, which contains a brief report of the work at Thessalonica, but also to I Thess. 1:8-10, which tells us something about the contents and amazing success of Paul's missionary message. Cf. also Phil. 4:16.

I and II Thessalonians may be regarded therefore as an important source for the subsequent formulation of doctrine, as an indispensable guide for the study of the man Paul, and as an important chapter in a handbook for missionaries. What is offered in these two short epistles is all this *and more.* It is above all a part of God's infallible special revelation, which comes *to every believer* with absolute, divine authority, and shows him what he should believe and how he should live.

II. The Founding of the Church

The evangelization of Europe began in earnest when Paul set his foot on what is today the long and narrow stretch of N.E. Greece. Here was Philippi, situated about ten miles inland from the Aegean Sea. It was "a city of Macedonia, the first of the district, a (Roman) colony" (Acts 16:12).

To this city came Paul, Silas — the companion whom he had chosen for this journey (Acts 15:40) —, Timothy as assistant (Acts 16:3), and Luke the beloved physician (Acts 16:10). In Philippi a church was established which Paul afterward called "my joy and crown" (Phil. 4:1). Here Lydia was converted, and she and her household were baptized (Acts 16:14, 15). The masters of a girl who had a spirit of divination became angry when Paul expelled the demon. They reasoned that "the hope of their gain" was gone. As a result Paul and Silas were imprisoned and beaten with rods. About midnight God sent an earthquake which opened the prison-doors. The jailer was converted and "was baptized, together with all his, immediately" (Acts 16:16-34). After an honorable release from prison, Paul and Silas "entered into the house of Lydia: and when they had seen the brothers, they encouraged them and departed," leaving the town (Acts 16:40). Luke stayed behind, as is clear from the fact that in relating further events he no longer says "we" (as in Acts 16:16) but "they" (Acts 17:1). From the fact that Timothy's name is not mentioned again until Acts 17:14 is reached some infer that he also remained for a while in Philippi, and that he did not rejoin the other two (Paul and Silas) until they, having labored for a while in Thessalonica, had reached Berea. Others, however, believe that Timothy too had traveled from Philippi to Thessalonica (either in the company of the others or a little later). They are of the opinion that this may be safely inferred from the fact that his name, together with that of Paul and Silas, is included in the salutation of both of the epistles (I Thess. 1:1; II Thess. 1:1). This view, as I see it, deserves the preference. It is not so strange that the youthful (cf. I Tim. 4:12) assistant Timothy is not always mentioned along with the others. Even today the newspapers in reporting that the president made a trip to California usually omit the names of most of the members of his entourage. But that does not mean that they were absent.

From Philippi a person could travel on one of the most famous of Roman military roads, the Egnatian Way. When completed it extended all the way from Byzantium (= Constantinople = Istanbul) on the Bosporus to Dyrrhachium situated straight west on the Adriatic (in what is now Albania). Thus it formed the connecting link with Rome. It was of sturdy construction, well kept, relatively safe, and marked by milestones (as Strabo informs us). The missionaries took this road, first to Amphipolis, called thus because the river Strymon flowed *around* it, and then to Apollonia. They continued on to Thessalonica. Altogether the distance of actual travel from Philippi to Thessalonica was about a hundred miles, comparable to that from: Detroit to Lansing (Mich.); Detroit to London (Ont.); Grand Rapids to Flint (Mich.); Atlanta to Columbus (Ga.); Los Angeles to San Diego (Cal.); London to Bristol (England); or Amsterdam to the Belgian border near Eindhoven (The Netherlands).

Of all the cities and towns on this great highway, Thessalonica, situated on what is now called the Gulf of Salonica, and built in the form of an amphitheater on the slopes at the head of the bay, was the largest and most influential. The road ran through the heart of the city, just as a remnant of it does even today. In Thessalonica it is still called by the ancient name, The Egnatian.

The city had been founded in 315 B. C. by Cassander, on or near the site of ancient Therma. This Cassander had been an officer under Alexander the Great. Having killed the latter's mother Olympias because she opposed him, and having crushed her army, Cassander subsequently for political reasons married Alexander's half-sister. Her name was Thessalonica. Convenient to bear in mind is the following:

Paul wrote a letter to the church at *Philippi*. That place was founded (about 358 B. C.) by *Philip* II of Macedon. The apostle also wrote two letters to the church at *Thessalonica*. This city was named in honor of *Philip's daughter Thessalonica*.

When the Romans, having conquered Macedonia, divided it into four parts, Thessalonica was made the capital of one of these. Later — about 146 B. C. — it became the capital of the entire province of Macedonia. In the struggle between Pompey and Caesar, Thessalonica became one of the former's chief bases, but soon afterward — 42 B. C. — it sided with Anthony and Octavian. The loyalty of the city was not left unnoticed. The great emperor Augustus rewarded it by making Thessalonica a free city. Thus it obtained a considerable measure of "home rule," self-government in internal affairs. It chose its own magistrates, who were called "politarchs."

Although most of the Thessalonians were Greeks, sothat the culture of the city was basically Hellenic, yet there were also some Romans and many Orientals. It is hardly necessary to add that the commerce of the city also attracted many a Jew. The presence of these Jews and their missionary activity exerted a measure of influence upon pagan religion, causing some of the Gentiles to attend the synagogue and to become "God-fearers."

Under the Romans the city enjoyed great prosperity. In the days of the Byzantine Empire it ranked second only to Byzantium.

In the history of the Church there is especially one event which made Thessalonica famous. A. D. 390 the emperor Theodosius the Great caused the massacre of no less than seven thousand of its citizens on account of

6

a riot which had occurred there. He ordered them to be put to death regardless of rank, sex, or degree of guilt. It was then that the great bishop Ambrose, wishing to vindicate the rights of the moral law — and incidentally the rights of the Church over against the State — refused him communion. It was only after the emperor had submitted to public penance, had begged for pardon, and had made certain definite promises, that absolution was finally granted.

The city figures prominently in the history of the Crusades. It came under more or less stable Ottoman rule in the year 1430. The Turks had held it before but had lost it again. From 1430 until 1912 they kept it. In 1912 it was reconquered by the Greeks. During World War I the Allies began their *Salonica* (as the city got to be called) *Campaigns* here, and during World War II it suffered considerable damage. Having always been a center of trade, the city attracted many Jews.

Today Salonica is next to the largest city in Greece, having a population of about a quarter of a million. It is the heart of a district which produces textiles, leather goods, machine tools, and cigarettes. It is connected by rail with Athens. In fact, owing to its strategic location, it is a center of road, rail, sea, and air-transportation. It trades in such commodities as tobacco, livestock, wheat, cotton, silk, and vegetables. Its university was opened in the year 1926. Among the famous churches which one can find here today are Hagia Sophia, St. George, and Demetrius. One of its most famous ancient relics is the triumphal arch of Emperor Constantine.

Paul's activity in Thessalonica was twofold: a. he earned his living by working with his hands for his daily bread (I Thess. 2:9; II Thess. 5:8), and b. he preached the Gospel (Acts 17:2; I Thess. 1:5; 2:2, 8, 11, 12; 4:1, 2). He did the former in order that he might not burden anyone and in order that it might be clear to everyone that he was not to be classified with traveling philosophers whose aims and interests were often selfish.

Paul remained in Thessalonica at least three weeks. The three week figure is mentioned in Acts 17:2, but it should be noted that it probably merely indicates the duration of his teaching *in the synagogue*. If it be borne in mind that a church of considerable size was established here (implied in I Thess. 5:12), that many of the citizens of Thessalonica turned from the worship of idols to serve the living God (I Thess. 1:9), that this spiritual awakening was so far-reaching that its report spread in every direction, and especially that during the "campaign" in this city Paul twice received a bounty from the church at Philippi (Phil. 4:16), the conclusion lies ready at hand that the *total* period of time which the missionaries spent in founding the new church was somewhat longer than three weeks.[2]

---

[2] Thus also L. Berkhof, *New Testament Introduction*, Grand Rapids, 1915, pp. 222, 223; F. W. Grosheide, *Handelingen* (in *Korte Verklaring*), Kampen, second

The preaching (teaching and exhortation) began in the synagogue. That was in line with Paul's custom. As already suggested, it was probably continued elsewhere. According to some "the house of Jason" was used for this subsequent preaching-activity. Others, however, are of the opinion that this house served as lodging-place for the missionaries and as Paul's workshop (cf. in this connection Acts 18:2, 3).

The inspired sources do not give us a complete and detailed survey of the contents of Paul's message at Thessalonica. A few important matters are mentioned however. Thus we learned that he taught that the Messianic prophecies had attained their fulfilment in Jesus, he being the Christ; that he suffered, died, was raised from the dead, and will come again, all this according to the Scriptures; that by his work he delivered from the wrath to come all those who trust in him; that idol-worship is evil; and that believers, having been called into his glorious kingdom, should live a life of sanctification so as to please the God who saved them, and should be orderly in their daily conduct in the midst of a wicked world ("If any man will not work neither let him eat"). See Acts 17:3; I Thess. 1:9, 10; 2:12; 4:1-3; II Thess. 3:10.

On one point — namely, the Lord's return and the events that will precede it — Paul had given somewhat detailed instruction while he was with the Thessalonians (II Thess. 2:1-5). It is not improbable that the teaching on other doctrinal themes had been just as thorough.

The circumstances under which all this evangelistic activity was carried on were partly discouraging, partly encouraging. Paul had "suffered" and had been "shamefully treated" in Philippi (I Thess. 2:2). Hence, it took courage to enter a new field after such experiences. On the other hand this labor was not in vain. Moreover, as already remarked, there was encouragement from Philippi.

Paul's heart was in his message. He preached "straight from the shoulder." There never was any attempt at flattery. Nevertheless, the truth was spoken in the spirit of tender affection and gentleness. Thus with the warmth of inner conviction, deeply persuaded of the supreme importance of his message, the great missionary, dealing with *each man* as a father with his children, taught, exhorted, and encouraged. See I Thess. 1:1-5; 2:4, 5, 7, 8, 10, 11.

And the Holy Spirit applied the message to the hearts of several of the hearers (I Thess. 1:5). Many were converted. They accepted the message as being the word not of men but of God (I Thess. 2:13). From that moment on they sought, with the help of the Spirit, to please God (I Thess. 4:1). Love ruled the brotherhood (I Thess. 4:9, 10). A church was estab-

---

edition 1950, p. 55; George Milligan, *op. cit.*, p. xxviii; but not R. C. H. Lenski, *The Interpretation of the Acts of the Apostles*, Columbus, Ohio, 1944, p. 693.

lished. Its membership was filled with contagious enthusiasm. In every heart there was a song, on every lip a testimony.

It is clear both from the book of Acts and from the epistles that most of the converts were from the Gentiles: "some" Jews and "a great multitude" of Greek proselytes (who were in the habit of attending the Synagogue) were persuaded, as were also many of the city's women, those of the upper class, wives of leaders (Acts 17:4). Many pagan idol-worshippers, having listened to the Gospel as proclaimed by Paul and his associates, experienced a fundamental change, a transformation of mind and heart (I Thess. 1:9; cf. 2:14 and Acts 20:4).

Paul never forgot the extraordinary response which his message had received in Thessalonica. When a little while later he writes a letter to this church, he makes mention of the joyful and enthusiastic manner in which the word had been taken to heart (I Thess. 1:6), and of the fact that this congregation had become an example to all believers in Macedonia and Achaia (I Thess. 1:7). He even adds that whenever people talk about him they describe him as the man through whose preaching a mighty spiritual change had been brought about in Thessalonica. The great missionary feels very happy about this, for it makes his work easier. Wherever he goes the fame of his message has preceded him. Indeed, the new converts have not kept quiet. See I Thess. 1:6-10.

It is not at all surprising that Paul's "success" made the Jews who were not converted very jealous and angry. With the help of certain street-loafers they hurried to the house of Jason where they expected to find the proclaimers of the new message. Failing to find them there, they dragged Jason and some other converts off to the "politarchs" (city-magistrates [3]) and shouted, "These fellows, who have turned the world upside down have come here also, and Jason has welcomed them. And they are all acting contrary to the decrees of the emperor, saying that there is another king, Jesus" (Acts 17:6, 7). The people and the politarchs were disturbed when they heard this, and "when they had taken security from Jason and the rest, they let them go" (Acts 17:8, 9).

The brothers immediately sent Paul and Silas away by night to Berea. The Jews here were "more noble" than those of Thessalonica, and eagerly welcomed the message, making a daily study of the Scriptures to see whether what Paul proclaimed were true. But when everything was going splendidly, the Jews at Thessalonica, hearing about the success which the missionaries were having, came to Berea in order to stir up a riot against

---

[3] The word "politarch" (Acts 17:6, 8) was at one time considered an error on the part of Luke. However, the discovery of seventeen inscriptions at Salonica containing this very term has proved that Luke was right and that the critics were wrong. See J. P. Free, *Archaeology and Bible History*, Wheaton, Ill., third printing 1952, p. 321.

them. The result was that, while Silas and Timothy were left behind in Berea in order to give spiritual support to the infant church, Paul himself, escorted by some of the brothers, made his way to the coast. Those who conducted Paul brought him as far as Athens. As they were leaving, he told them to ask Silas and Timothy to come to him as soon as possible (Acts 17:10-15).

There followed an interesting ministry at Athens. Read about it in Acts 17:16-34. However, the response here was not nearly as favorable as at Berea. Meanwhile Paul was anxiously awaiting the arrival of Silas and Timothy with tidings from Macedonia. From I Thess. 3:1, 2 it may be safely inferred that Timothy left Berea and found Paul while the latter was still in Athens. It is probable (though not certain) that also Silas rejoined Paul at Athens. One fact, however, is clear: Paul was deeply concerned about the recently won converts whom he had left behind in Thessalonica. Twice (once while at Berea and once while at Athens?) he made a plan to revisit them, but by a method which is not indicated, Satan prevented him from carrying out these plans (I Thess. 2:17, 18). Meanwhile his anxiety persisted. Finally, when he could stand it no longer, he (or he and Silas) decided to be left at Athens alone, and sent Timothy to strengthen and encourage the brothers at Thessalonica (see comments on I Thess. 3:1, 2). If Silas spent any time with Paul at Athens, he must have returned to Macedonia soon (perhaps to Philippi), for it is clear that both he and Timothy "came down from Macedonia" to Corinth after Paul had begun his labors in that city (Acts 18:1, 5; cf. I Thess. 3:6).

III. Paul's Purpose in Writing

A. *I Thessalonians*
Corinth was the commercial and political metropolis of Greece. Its name was a synonym for licentiousness. For a while the great missionary labored alone here. He struck up an acquaintance with Aquilla and Priscilla, driven from Rome by the edict of Emperor Claudius (who ruled from A. D. 41-54), and stayed with them because he was of the same trade, a tentmaker. He first preached in the synagogue, but afterward in the house of a Gentile who lived next to it.

It seems probable that while Paul was alone at Corinth — i.e., before Silas and Timothy had returned from Macedonia — he received some very disquieting news from the churches at Galatia. He heard that the Judaizers had been at work and had succeeded all too well in their attempt to destroy the edifice which he had reared with so much suffering and patience. Accordingly, the apostle wrote his Epistle to the Galatians.

Meanwhile the young church of Thessalonica was also on his mind. He feared lest, as a result of his very brief stay and sudden departure, of his inability to return personally, and of the scoffing and ridicule which the Macedonian church-members would have to endure from their relatives and neighbors, the temptation to drift back into paganism or Judaism might prove to be overpowering (I Thess. 3:5). To be sure, *some* of the Jews had accepted the Gospel, but how would they fare at the hands of those Jews — by far the majority — who had *not* accepted it? The answer to this question was not difficult to surmise. Paul knew all about the assault upon the house of Jason. Moreover, in addition to the hostile Jews there were the Judaizers who, according to the latest reports, were doing such damage in Galatia. Were they going to enter and ruin Macedonia also? Again, a great many of the devout Greeks and not a few of the leading women had been converted; but what about the proselytes who had *not* been converted, and especially . . . what about the *husbands* of the converted women? The very thought of what these husbands might do to their wives in attempting to force them to give up their faith in Christ was disconcerting. True, in the little while which Paul had spent in Thessalonica multitudes of pagans had renounced their idolatry and accepted the new religion; but was this faith firmly-rooted and genuine? Would it be able to endure persecution from the side of the wicked rabble, the same rabble which always stood ready to be bribed into deeds of violence? The Thessalonian believers (only a few of whom are mentioned by name: Jason, Aristarchus, Secundus, Acts 17:5-9; 20:4) were still so immature, so deficient in religious knowledge and experience! Also, on the whole they were poor (II Cor. 8:2, 3). Would Timothy, who at this very moment was working among them, be able to cope with the situation which he found? Would he come back safely, and if so, what news would he bring? In this connection, it is interesting to note that a very similar concern was going to fill the heart of Paul on his *third* missionary journey. *Then* conditions at *Corinth* — the very church where Paul was now laboring — would fill his mind with distress, and *then* the helper whose return was anxiously awaited would be *Titus* instead of Timothy. Read about it in II Cor. 2:12, 13; 7:5-15. Truly, in addition to dangers from without — and these were many! — there was that which oppressed the apostle daily, namely, "anxiety for all the churches" (II Cor. 11:28).

Great was Paul's relief when Timothy returned (Silas also came back from Macedonia, Acts 18:5). The report which he brought from the church at Thessalonica was so encouraging that the heart of the great missionary was filled with joy and thanksgiving. "Now I (really) *live*," said Paul, as Timothy brought him the wonderful news of the undiminished faith and love of the infant church (cf. I Thess. 3:8). Not only did the arrival of Silas and Timothy and the information which they conveyed add zest to his preaching (Acts 18:5), but he also decided to express his feeling of gratitude in a letter to the Thessalonians. This was to be a letter of encouragement, the tenor of which would be "Y o u're doing fine, continue to do so more and more (cf. I Thess. 4:1). Do not let persecutions get y o u down. These are necessary; also, they are to be expected, just as I told y o u when I was still with y o u (cf. I Thess. 3:2-4)."

Mingled with the good news which predominated in the report which Timothy brought there was some bad news. Base opponents, filled with prejudice and hatred, were casting insinuations at the character and ministry of Paul (I Thess. 2:3-10), and were trying thus to undermine his influence and destroy the comfort which his message had brought. And comfort was badly needed, comfort blended with further instruction. This was true especially with respect to one important matter. Some members of the church had "fallen asleep." Would they share in the glory of Christ's return? See I Thess. 4:13 ff. Moreover, if this return was imminent, why work any longer? Why toil for the things which were soon to perish? (cf. I Thess. 4:11).

It is clear that Paul was filled with deep concern and warm affection for this church, so recently established. He writes his letter in order:

a. to meet head-on the whispering campaign with reference to his "personality" and motives (see chapters 1 and 2),

b. to express his joy and gratitude because of the good news which Timothy had brought (see chapter 3),

c. to shed further light upon the question which had arisen with respect to those who had fallen asleep (see 4:13-18) and the related question of the manner of Christ's return (see 5:1-11), and

d. to give exactly such directions as could be expected from a missionary who is writing to men who have just recently been drawn out of the kingdom of darkness (idolatry, immorality, etc.) into the kingdom of light (see 4:1-12; 5:12-28). Thus he stresses the fact that the new faith demands a complete break with the immoral conduct which characterizes heathendom (I Thess. 4:1-8), and he emphasizes the need of proper respect for the offices, of love and peace among all the brothers, of readiness to help those in distress, and of orderly conduct in the sight of the world (I Thess. 5:12-14).[4]

---

[4] The question with reference to the purpose of I Thessalonians has recently been revised with respect to one particular point, namely, whether the apostle in this epistle is trying to give an answer to a letter from Thessalonica which Timothy presumably had brought with him. One can find something on this topic in the older commentaries, but see especially the recent discussion by Chalmer E. Faw, "On The Writing of First Thessalonians," *JBL* 71 (December 1952), 217-225. Faw presents strong (yet, as I see it, not wholly convincing) arguments for the position that there was such a letter *from* Thessalonica, and that the apostle, in addition to expressing his reaction to an oral report which Timothy had brought him, takes up the various items mentioned in this letter, shedding light on matters with respect to

which the church at Thessalonica (particularly its leaders) desired further instruction. Faw's arguments may be summarized as follows:

a. Expressions such as these: *"Now concerning* love of the brothers" (I Thess. 4:9), *"now concerning* (notice, however, word-transposition in the original) those that have fallen asleep" (4:13), *"now concerning* the times and the seasons" (5:1) reveal a pattern which in Paul's epistles has its parallel *only* in I Corinthians ("*Now concerning* virgins," "*now concerning* the things sacrificed to idols," "*now concerning* spiritual gifts," "*now concerning* the collection for the saints" — see I Cor. 7:25; 8:1; 12:1; 16:1), and which in *that* epistle is introduced by the phrase, "Now concerning *the matters about which y o u wrote*" (I Cor. 7:1). Hence, if this literary pattern (of introducing several items in a series by using the phrase *now concerning*, with similar variants in both I Thessalonians and I Corinthians) when used in I Corinthians indicates that the apostle is giving a seriatim answer to *a letter*, why should we not reach the same conclusion with respect to its use in I Thessalonians?

b. The abrupt manner in which some of these matters are introduced (here in I Thessalonians) confirms the position that Paul has before him *the letter from the Thessalonians*, on which he is commenting item by item.

c. The fact that Paul seems to be reluctant to write on certain subjects (see I Thess. 4:9; 5:1) but does so anyway, though hesitantly, points in the same direction.

Though, as I see it, Faw's article is well written and conveys much valuable information, and though his theory — that here in I Thessalonians Paul is answering a letter — *may* be true, this article and this theory have failed to convince me that this is the only possible conclusion, and this for the following reasons:

a. The solitary parallel of I Corinthians is too flimsy a ground for such a conclusion. After all, as Faw's article clearly shows, the New Testament contains other instances of the use of the phrase *now concerning*, instances in which it clearly does *not* introduce a reflection on an item in *a letter* (Mark 12:26; 13:32; John 16:11; Acts 21:25).

b. In one respect I Corinthians is not a parallel, for *there* (I Cor. 7:1) Paul specifically informs us that he is taking up the matters *about which they had written*. *In I Thessalonians he makes no mention of any letter which the Thessalonians had written!* It is even possible that they did not deem it necessary to write such a letter, seeing that Timothy could be trusted to give a full oral report.

c. Faw's second and third arguments do not prove that Paul had before him *a letter* from the Thessalonians. A memorandum carefully prepared by Timothy himself or even a systematic oral report fills all the requirements. As to the third argument it should not be immediately assumed that the manner in which Paul phrases I Thess. 4:9 and 5:1 indicates real *reluctance* on his part. Another explanation is also possible. See comments on these verses.

Anyone who is interested in this subject should read (in addition to Faw's article of recent date) what the following have to say respecting it:

Bacon, B. W., *An Introduction to the New Testament*, New York, 1900, p. 73.

Barnett, Albert E., *The New Testament, Its Making and Meaning*, New York, 1946, p. 37.

Frame, James E., *A Critical and Exegetical Commentary on the Epistles of St. Paul to the Thessalonians* (in The International Critical Commentary), New York, 1912, pp. 9, 157, 178.

Harris, J. Rendel, "A Study in Letter Writing," *The Expositor* Series 5, Vol. 8 (September, 1898), 161-180.

Lenski, R. C. H., *op. cit.*, pp. 318, 319.

Moffatt, James, *An Introduction to the Literature of the New Testament*, New York, 1917, p. 67.

Plummer, Alfred, *A Commentary on St. Paul's First Epistle to the Thessalonians*, London, 1916, p. xviii.

Smith, David, *The Life and Letters of St. Paul*, New York, 1920, pp. 152-166.

Van Leeuwen, J. A. C., *Paulus' Zendbrieven aan Efeze, Colosse, Filemon, en*

B. *II Thessalonians*

We can imagine with what joy I Thessalonians was read by the members of the newly-established congregation. Yet, it soon became apparent that a second letter was necessary. Tidings reached Paul — by means of the very men who had delivered the first letter to its destination and had now returned? — that believers in Thessalonica, while experiencing spiritual growth, were still being persecuted, in fact more than ever. Also with respect to the second coming of Christ, on which the apostle had written such comforting words, there was still some confusion: some were thinking that the Lord's *sudden* coming, of which Paul had written (I Thess. 5:3), implied his *immediate* coming. There was need not only of further instruction on this point but also of an admonition that the church adhere to the teaching which it had received previously. In this connection it seems that someone claimed to have (or to have heard about) a letter, coming or purporting to come from Paul; and this too had had its damaging effect. The notion that the Lord was most certainly going to return "any day now" may have encouraged disorderly conduct (cf. I Thess. 4:11, 12) to continue and increase. This matter had to be dealt with. There was also the question, "What must be done with those who do not obey the instructions which they receive? Just how must the church deal with these disobedient ones?" And finally Paul himself (and those with him in Corinth), experiencing many difficulties, felt the need of asking for the prayers of the Thessalonians.

Accordingly, Paul's purpose in writing II Thessalonians is as follows:

a. To express his gratitude for the spiritual growth (increase in faith and love) which believers in Thessalonica are experiencing even in the midst of persecution, and to encourage them with the assurance that *at Christ's second coming* their enemies would be punished and they themselves would be glorified (see chapter 1),

b. To calm those who had become excited and confused with respect to *the second coming,* and to inform them that certain events must take place before that *second coming* occurs (see 2:1-12),

c. In this connection, to exhort all to keep clinging to the traditions which they had been taught whether by word or epistle, to warn against imaginary or spurious letters that distort the truth regarding *the second coming,* to admonish the disorderly (who seem to have given up their occupations because of fanaticism with respect to *the second coming*), and to give directions with respect to those who do not obey the instructions which they have received (see 2:13-4:18; cf. 2:2).

Interspersed with these thoughts are passages in which the believers at

---

Thessalonika (in *Kommentaar op het Nieuwe Testament*), Amsterdam, 1926, pp. 359, 360.

INTRODUCTION

Thessalonica are asked to remember Paul and his associates in prayer, and in which they are committed to God's loving care, that their hearts might be established, and that they might receive good hope through grace, peace at all times in all ways, the love of God, and the patience of Christ.

From this brief purpose-summary it is evident that this is clearly a *Second Coming* epistle.

IV. The Time and the Place

Of late an attempt has been made to invent an entirely new chronology of the life of Paul.[5] But in view of the fact that this attempt is based on the opinion that the book of Acts is not entirely reliable, it is not necessary to enlarge on it (see, however, the note). Turning, then, to Acts and to the two epistles now under study, we find a very noticeable parallel. *This parallel indicates, without a shadow of a doubt, that I and II Thessalonians were written while Paul was on his second missionary journey. The probable place of writing is Corinth.*

We base this conclusion on the following considerations:

(1) According to Acts 16:11-40 the apostle on his second missionary journey worked in Philippi. From there he went to Thessalonica and Berea, and from there to Athens (Acts 17). From Athens he proceeded to Corinth (18:1). For a while he was at Athens alone, but when he reaches Corinth, Silas and Timothy arrive from Macedonia (18:1, 5). The order of places is therefore: Philippi, Thessalonica, Berea, Athens, Corinth. Now this corresponds with what is found in I Thessalonians. Here too we meet a Paul who had been in Philippi (I Thess. 2:2), and who from there went to Thessalonica, and from there (via Berea, which is not mentioned here) to Athens (I Thess. 3:1). When, in addition, we read that Timothy had now arrived (I Thess. 3:6), the natural inference is that this refers to the same

---

[5] I refer to the attempt by John Knox; see his *Chapters In A Life Of Paul*, New York and Nashville, 1946. Here the reliability of Acts is attacked (e.g., p. 35). The author has apparently joined the list of those who regard Luke as a more or less biased writer, who overemphasized the role of Jerusalem in the early history of the church. (*Essentially* the position of these authors has been refuted adequately by J. G. Machen, *The Origin of Paul's Religion*, Grand Rapids, Mich., 1947 reprint.) Especially important from the point of view of chronology is Knox's opinion that the letters of Paul reveal not the slightest awareness on his part that he was engaged in great journeys (p. 40). Naturally, if the three missionary journeys described in the book of Acts are not allowed to stand, the entire chronology changes. To see the difference between the old and the new (Knox's) chronology one should consult *Contemporary Thinking About Paul*, edited by Thomas S. Kepler, cf. the tables on pp. 158, 159 with the one on p. 169. But is it true that Paul's epistles fail to indicate any consciousness that he was engaged in great journeys? I do not see how this can be maintained, especially in view of the following passages: Rom. 1:15; 15:24, 28; I Cor. 16:5; II Cor. 1:15, 16, 23; 2:12, 13; 7:5-15; 9:2; 10:16; 12:14; 13:1; Phil. 4:15, 16.

arrival of which Acts speaks, and that Paul, accordingly, is now in Corinth.

(2) From the salutations (I Thess. 1:1; II Thess. 1:1) it appears that *Silas* (also Timothy) was with Paul when he wrote the epistles to the Thessalonians. And according to the book of Acts, Silas accompanied Paul on his *second* missionary journey (after Acts 18:5 Luke does not refer to him again), *not on his first, nor on his third.* Although this is not positive proof, nevertheless it definitely points in the direction of the conclusion that I and II Thessalonians were written on Paul's *second* missionary journey.

Is it possible to fix the date even more precisely? In this connection mention is often made of the fact that in the year 1909 near Delphi a gray limestone inscription was found which perpetuates a letter of the emperor Claudius to the citizens of Delphi, and contains the name of Gallio and an important date. This date clearly indicates that Gallio, before whose tribunal Paul was brought while in Corinth (Acts 18:12-17) was proconsul for either a one-year or a two-year term sometime during the period A. D. 51-53.[6] From the fact that Paul had been in Corinth *alone* before he wrote I Thessalonians, and that when he wrote it Silas and Timothy had joined him, it is clear that we cannot place this epistle at the very beginning of the period 51-53. From the fact that a sufficient period must have intervened before I Thessalonians could be followed by II Thessalonians, it is also clear that the first letter cannot be placed at the end of that period. If, therefore, we accept a date for the two epistles "about the year A. D. 52" (or simply "sometime during the period 51-53"), we cannot be far from the truth.

In the aforegoing we have been assuming that the order in which Paul's two epistles to the Thessalonians follow each other in our Bibles is the correct one, that is, that what we now call I Thessalonians was actually written before what we now call II Thessalonians. A careful and unbiased perusal of the two letters seems to establish the correctness of this view. Reasons:

(1) Although I Thessalonians contains many references to the fact that Paul has had *personal* contact with the church in question, a contact the memory of which is still very vivid (cf. 1:5; 2:1-16; 3:4) and which must have been very recent, this letter does not contain a single reference to an earlier *letter*. But II Thessalonians does contain a clear and definite reference to an earlier letter, for Paul says: "So then, brothers, stand firm and hold to the traditions which y o u were taught by us, either by word of mouth *or by letter*" (II Thess. 2:15).

(2) In I Thess. 1:6; 2:13 Paul indicates that the Thessalonians have accepted the Gospel by a true and living faith. In II Thess. 1:3 he expresses his gratitude with reference to the fact that this faith *is growing*. Similarly,

---

[6] See: Millar Burrows, *What Mean These Stones*, New Haven, 1941, p. 86.

in the first letter (3:12; 4:10) he exhorts believers to increase in love for one another, and in the second (1:3) he rejoices over the fact that this gradual increase in love has become a fact.

(3) In I Thess. 4:17 the apostle predicts the "rapture" (the being caught up in the clouds to meet the Lord in the air); in II Thess. 2:1 he clearly assumes that the readers have received previous instruction with reference to this subject.

(4) From I Thess. 1:6; 2:14; 3:3 it is evident that from the very beginning believers in Thessalonica suffered persecution. From II Thess. 1:4, 6 it is evident that this grievous trial of their faith has not subsided. If there has been any change at all, it would seem that it has been for the worse.

(5) The first letter contains several injunctions (4:1-12, 5:12-28). In the second some of these injunctions are more sharply expressed (particularly the one with respect to idle and disorderly persons), and the church is given explicit direction how to deal with the disobedient (3:6-15).

(6) In the first letter the sudden and unexpected character of Christ's second coming is set forth (cf. 4:13-18; 5:1-11; note especially the phrase "as a thief in the night"). In the second it is clearly pointed out that this sudden coming does not imply an immediate coming (2:1-12).

(7) In the second letter Paul warns against imaginary or purported, and possibly even against spurious letters (2:2), and in appending the greeting he writes, "This is the mark in *every* letter of mine" (3:17), which is easier to understand if this were a *second* than if it were a *first* letter.

For these reasons we cling to the priority of I Thessalonians. II Thessalonians, as has been shown (see points 1-7 above), presupposes that those addressed are acquainted with I Thessalonians. This also shows that the view according to which I Thessalonians was directed to the "Gentile" community, and II Thessalonians to the "Jewish" community in Thessalonica is uncalled for. Both epistles are directed to the same group of readers, namely, "the church of the Thessalonians" (I Thess. 1:1; II Thess. 1:1).[7]

---

[7] Lyle O. Bristol in an article, "Paul's Thessalonian Correspondence," *ExT* 55 (1944), 223, regards the priority of II Thessalonians probable because: a. it is shorter than I Thessalonians; b. when I Thessalonians was written some members of the Thessalonian church had already died; and c. the organization which it presupposed in I Thess. 5:12, 13 implies a longer time-interval than is possible if I Thessalonians was written first.

But none of these reasons is strong enough to prove anything. Why the first of two letters should necessarily be the shorter one is not clear. It is not at all surprising that in an interval of a few months, with a fierce persecution taking place in Thessalonica, some deaths had occurred. Finally, there had been ample time to organize the church, either during Paul's own ministry or subsequently (for example, after Timothy's arrival in the city; in that case Titus 1:15 would supply an interesting parallel). Paul was a great organizer (Acts 14:23).

Another article is that by Edward Thompson, "The Sequence of the Two Epistles

V. Authorship

A. *Of I Thessalonians*

The authenticity of I Thessalonians is today accepted on nearly every side. Nevertheless, there have always been those who disagree with this well-nigh unanimous opinion, and who consider this epistle to be, either as a whole or in part, the work of a forger.[8]

Their arguments may be summarized as follows:

(1) *This epistle is far less doctrinal than those which are known to have been written by Paul. It is rather insignificant in contents.*

But why must all the writings of the great apostle be equally doctrinal in character? Paul's epistles arose out of certain concrete situations. These situations naturally differed. In one church it was clarification of doctrine that was needed most; in another admonition, exhortation, rebuke, or at

---

to the Thessalonians," *ExT* 56 (1945), 306, 307. This writer defends the priority of I Thessalonians. Among other things he points out that nothing in ancient tradition supports the priority of II Thessalonians, that the more Jewish character of II Thessalonians (discussion of Jewish apocalyptic) does not imply the priority of that epistle, and that it is not true that Paul's allusion to his autograph (II Thess. 3:17) proves that II Thessalonians was written first, for a similar allusion is found in I Cor. 16:21 though a previous letter had been written to the church at Corinth (see I Cor. 5:9).

For the view of A. Harnack and Kirsopp C. Lake (II Thessalonians was directed to a Jewish community, I Thessalonians to a Gentile community) see the latter's chapter in *Contemporary Thinking About Paul* (edited by Thomas S. Kepler), New York, Nashville (no date), pp. 234-238.

[8] For the arguments against the authenticity see especially F. C. Baur, *Paulus*, Stuttgart, 1845, pp. 480 ff. (For an even earlier criticism see Schrader, *Der Apostel Paulus*, V, 1836, pp. 23 ff.) Baur's criticism was the most serious and effective. He convinced some: Noack, Volkmar, Holsten, etc. Cf. also Vander Vies, *De Beide Brieven aan de Thessalonicenzen*, 1865, pp. 128-164. But Baur's denial of the Pauline authorship of I Thessalonians is vitiated by the Hegelian bias upon which it rests. For Baur the question whether an epistle is characterized by the anti-Judaistic line of argumentation seems to settle everything. Thus, all of Paul's thinking and writing is forced into one groove. This is manifestly unfair.

In recent literature a somewhat similar subjectivism is at times apparent. An author starts from the presupposition that whatever is apocalyptic is un-Pauline, and that Paul taught salvation by means of identification through faith with a dying and rising Christ. As a result, certain passages and even entire paragraphs of I Thessalonians are rejected: 1:10; 2:14-16; 4:13-18; 5:1-10; and, for similar reasons the following sections of II Thessalonians are regarded as not genuine: 1:5-10; 2:1-17. Cf. R. M. Hawkins, *The Recovery of the Historical Paul*, Nashville, Tenn., 1943; see especially pp. 234, 241, 292.

However, Paul was a Hebrew of the Hebrews. Now, Hebrew thought has always been characterized by the presence of eschatological and apocalyptic ideas. Paul must have been acquainted with the book of Daniel and with many similar trends of thought in other Old Testament writings (to limit ourselves to canonical scriptures). Moreover, there are similar ideas in the teachings of Jesus (Matt. 24, 25; Mark 13; Luke 21). The total absence of such ideas from Paul's epistles would have been surprising.

times consolation was called for. Besides, it is not true that I Thessalonians is doctrinally insignificant. It sheds needed light on the doctrine of the Second Coming.

(2) *This epistle does not attack the idea that justification is by the works of the law.*

But was Paul a man with one, and *only one,* idea? The situation in Thessalonica was not the same as that in Galatia!

(3) *It is impossible that within a period of a few months the Thessalonian converts could have exerted an influence for good as intensive and extensive as that which is pictured in I Thess. 1:7, 8; 4:10.*

Our answer is: Why not? In fact, it so happens that exactly this bit of information which is furnished by *the letter* is confirmed by that which is supplied by *the narrative in Acts* (17:6). Even the enemies of Paul and of his companions considered the work of the missionaries to be so effective in character that they spoke of "the men who have turned the world upside down." When the Holy Spirit operates in the hearts and lives of consecrated ministers and of converts filled with the enthusiasm of a real, inner conviction, things actually begin to happen!

(4) *The "strong language" which in I Thess. 2:14-16 is used with reference to the Jews could not have been employed by one who in his genuine epistle to the Romans states, "I could wish that I myself were anathema from Christ for the sake of my brothers."*

But why should it be impossible for an inspired author, on the one hand to reveal a terrible reality (namely, the outpouring of God's wrath upon a disobedient people), and yet, on the other hand, in a very touching manner, to express his own genuine sorrow and pain of heart with respect to this reality which concerned his kith and kin? Besides what is taught in I Thess. 2:14-16 does not differ materially from that which is taught in Rom. 9:22; 10:21; and 11:22, 25.

(5) *This epistle is too Pauline! It contains too many passages that resemble those in Paul's genuine epistles (especially I and II Corinthians). Hence, it is clear that a forger is at work.*

But this type of reasoning is the very opposite of that which was followed in arguments (1) and (2) above. *There* I Thessalonians was rejected because it was too un-Pauline. *Here* it is attacked because it is too Pauline! The two arguments cancel each other. Besides, it is not immediately clear why Paul cannot have been the author of an epistle which contains Pauline passages!

On the positive side, there is first of all *the evidence supplied by the epistle itself. This definitely points to Paul as the author* (though two others join him in sending greetings and in confirming whatever he writes). Note the following:

(1) *The epistle presents itself as a letter from Paul* (1:1; 2:18).

(2) *Those who are represented as being with the author as he sends this letter are known (from the book of Acts) to have been with Paul on his second missionary journey.*

They are Silvanus (i.e., Silas) and Timothy (1:1; 3:2, 6); cf. Acts 15:40; 16:1-3, 19; 17:4, 10, 14; 18:5.

(3) *The letter has the typical Pauline form; that is, it has the epistolary structure which characterizes Romans, I Corinthians, II Corinthians, and Galatians, the writings which are ascribed to Paul even by most of those who reject the authenticity of I Thessalonians.*

This letter-plan is as follows (with minor variations): the mention of the writer's name (often: *and* office), the designation of those to whom the letter is addressed (sometimes with brief description), the salutation, the thanksgiving or doxology, the body of the letter (argumentation, admonition, exhortation, consolation, instruction, etc.), the concluding salutation (not always present; when present not always equally circumstantial) and benediction.

(4) *The vocabulary is definitely that of Paul.*

More than 4/5 of the words used in I Thessalonians are found also in the four so-called major Pauline epistles (Romans, I Corinthians, II Corinthians, and Galatians). If we include the prison-epistles (Ephesians, Philippians, Colossians, and Philemon) among those that must be regarded as being genuinely Pauline, we find that almost 9/10 of the words employed by the author of I Thessalonians occur also in these eight letters (the four major and the four prison epistles). And if the pastoral epistles (I Timothy, II Timothy, Titus) are also added, the percentage becomes even a little higher.[9]

(5) *Not only the single words point to Paul as author but so do also many of the characteristic phrases, phrases that are elsewhere found only in Paul.*

a. Phrases[10] found in I Thessalonians (not in II Thessalonians); elsewhere only in the epistles of Paul:

---

[9] In order to reach these percentages I carefully jotted down for myself on cards and in alphabetical order every word found in I Thessalonians (and I did the same for II Thessalonians), and, using *Moulton and Geden's Concordance* to the Greek Testament, I checked the use of these words in Paul's major, prison, and pastoral epistles. It was on that basis that I drew my conclusions. As these conclusions agree, in the main, with those drawn by J. E. Frame, *A Critical and Exegetical Commentary on the Epistles of St. Paul to the Thessalonians* (in The International Critical Commentary) a reference to the pages of that work should suffice (pp. 28-32).

[10] These phrases (in Greek) are found also in Frame (*op. cit.,* pp. 32-34), but he omits the references to the major epistles. I have given a reference also in such cases (for a complete list *Moulton and Geden's Concordance* should be used). Furthermore, I have given the English equivalents, and have re-arranged the phrases according to their chapter and verse sequence.

1:2 in our prayers;	Rom. 1:10
1:3; 3:11, 13 our God and Father	Gal. 1:4
1:5, 6; 2:2, 17 in much (ἐν πολλῇ)	Rom. 9:22
2:4, 15 pleasing God	Rom. 8:8
2:5, 10 God is (my) witness	Rom. 1:9
2:12; 5:24 who is calling y o u	Gal. 5:8
2:12 in order that y o u should live lives worthy of God	Col. 1:10
2:18 once and again	Phil. 4:16
3:2 God's fellow-worker	I Cor. 3:9 (pl.)
3:2 the Gospel of Christ	Rom. 15:19
3:5 in vain (εἰς κενόν)	II Cor. 6:1
3:8 y o u stand firm in the Lord	Phil. 4:1
4:1 in the Lord Jesus	Rom. 14:14
4:11 working with y o u r hands	I Cor. 4:12
4:1 we do not want y o u to remain ignorant	Rom. 1:13
4:15, 17 we who are alive	II Cor. 4:11
4:17 be with the Lord	Phil. 1:23
5:9 through our Lord Jesus Christ	Rom. 5:1
5:10 live together with him	II Cor. 13:4
5:18 in everything (ἐν παντί)	I Cor. 1:5
5:24 who is calling y o u	Gal. 5:8
5:26 holy kiss	Rom. 16:16

b. Phrases found in I Thessalonians and II Thessalonians; elsewhere only in the epistles of Paul:

I Thess.	II Thess.		
1:5	2:14	our Gospel	II Cor. 4:3
2:9	3:8	in order that not (πρὸς τὸ μή w. inf.)	II Cor. 3:13
2:9	3:8	labor and toil	II Cor. 11:27
4:1	3:1	for the rest, brothers	II Cor. 13:11
5:6	2:15	So then (ἄρα οὖν)	Rom. 5:18

Besides these there are several phrases which, though found here and there outside of Paul, occur *chiefly* in those epistles which are generally ascribed to the apostle. It is certainly true that there are also many phrases which may be called *unique* (occurring in I Thessalonians and/or II Thessalonians but nowhere else in the New Testament or nowhere else in Paul's epistles). The difference in subject-matter as well as the natural tendency of almost any author (and particularly of a versatile writer like Paul) to vary his expressions when he writes letters to different people under wholly different circumstances cause us to expect this. The very considerable number of phrases which are either exclusively or chiefly Pauline certainly points in the direction of Paul as the author.

(6) *The epistle clearly reflects the character of Paul.*

Here, as elsewhere in the epistles commonly ascribed to Paul, we are brought face to face with a man who is so very deeply interested in those whom he addresses that he is ever thanking God for them and making mention of them in his prayers (1:2 ff; cf. Rom. 1:8, 9); is anxious to see them (2:17, 18; cf. Rom. 1:11; Phil. 2:24), and when he is unable to do so, sends one of his associates (3:2; cf. Phil. 2:19-23). He takes delight in showering praise upon the readers whenever this is possible, and in imparting encouragement (1:3, 6-10; cf. II Cor. 8:7; Phil. 4:15-17). In this connection note close resemblance between 2:19, 20 and Phil. 4:1. Nevertheless, this praise never ends in man. The writer is always quick to ascribe whatever is good in the believer to the sovereign grace of God, viewing it as an evidence of the believer's election and of the presence of the Holy Spirit in his heart (1:4, 5; cf. Rom. 8:28-30; 8:23; Gal. 5:22-25; Phil. 1:6). He does not hesitate to defend his motives in preaching the Gospel, whenever these motives are attacked, and in doing so he likes to review his manner of entrance among the people who now constitute the church (2:1-12; cf. I Cor. 2:1-5; 3:1, 2). He shows great tact in admonishing (4:9, 10; cf. Philemon 8-22), but is never afraid to assert his authority (5:27; cf. I Cor. 16:1). He takes up, one by one, subjects of special interest to the readers, matters on which they need (or have requested) further instruction (4:13; 5:1, 12; cf. I Cor. 7:1, 25; 8:1; 12:1; 16:1).

The more one studies this *intensely personal* side of the epistle, the more one also becomes convinced that only one man could have written it, namely, Paul!

(7) *There is nothing in this epistle which is not in complete harmony with the doctrine proclaimed in Paul's major epistles* (to say nothing about the prison epistles and the pastoral epistles):

Although, barring the exception already noted (see p. 4), this epistle is not pre-eminently doctrinal, nevertheless it everywhere presupposes the Pauline emphasis on important doctrinal points. Thus, the writer of I Thessalonians teaches us that by nature man is headed straight for the revelation of God's wrath (1:10; 5:9; cf. Rom. 1:18; 2:8; 9:22); he is under the rule of darkness (5:5; cf. Rom. 2:19; 13:12; II Cor. 6:14). But out of this fallen mass God, of sovereign mercy, has elected some (1:4; cf. Rom. 9:11; 11:5, 7). This election has as its purpose the believers' sanctification, his assurance, and his final, complete salvation, to God's glory (1:3-5; 3:13; 4:3, 7; 5:23; cf. Rom. 6:1, 22; 11:36; I Cor. 1:30; 10:31). It was the Lord Jesus Christ who died for believers (5:10; cf. Gal. 2:20), that they might live with and for him. While the believer is in this life, he is being tempted by Satan, who tries to lead him astray (3:5; cf. Rom. 16:20; I Cor. 7:5; II

Cor. 2:11; 12:7). But God preserves him until the day of the glorious mani-festation of the Lord Jesus Christ from heaven, when forever the believer will be with Christ (1:10; 2:19; 3:13; 3:17; 5:23; cf. Rom. 8:18, 19; I Cor. 15:50-58; 16:22).

The testimony of the early church is in harmony with the conclusion which has been derived from the epistle itself. Thus Eusebius, having made a thorough investigation of the literature at his command, states:

"But clearly evident and plain (πρόδηλοι καὶ σαφεῖς) are the fourteen (letters) of Paul; yet it is not right to ignore that some dispute the (letter) to the Hebrews" (*Ecclesiastical History* III. iii. 4, 5). Obviously Eusebius, writing at the beginning of the fourth century, had never heard of anyone who doubted the authenticity of I and II Thessalonians.

Before him Origen (fl. 210-250) again and again refers to (and quotes from) these epistles and definitely ascribes them to Paul. He is especially fond of quoting from II Thess. 2.

From Origen we can go back still farther, to his teacher, Clement of Alexandria (fl. 190-200). He too is well acquainted with the epistles to the Thessalonians, and ascribes them to Paul. The following are some of the references to (or quotations from) I Thessalonians in the works of Clement:

I Thess.

2:4	The Stromata (Miscellanies) VII. xii
2:5-7	The Stromata I. i
2:6, 7	The Instructor (Educator, Pedagogue) I. v
4:3-8	The Stromata IV. xii
4:9	The Instructor I. vi
4:17	The Stromata VI. xiii
5:5-8	The Instructor II. ix
5:6-8	The Stromata IV. xxii
5:13-15; 19-22	The Instructor III. xii

About this same time Tertullian, writing *Against Marcion,* and definitely mentioning Paul by name and "all his apostolic writings" (V. i) not only quotes I Thess. 2:15 (V. xv) but also implies that Marcion and other heretics, about the middle of the second century, considered I Thessalonians to be an authentic epistle of the apostle to the Gentiles, a fact which can be gathered also from other sources. Tertullian refers to (and quotes from) I and II Thessalonians (especially II Thess. 2) again and again.

Clement's contemporary was Ireneus. Because of his many travels and intimate acquaintance with almost the entire church of his day, what Ireneus says about the authorship of I and II Thessalonians must be con-sidered of great significance. His voice in a matter as important as this may be considered the voice of the church. Now in his work *Against Heresies* (V. vi. 1) he not only quotes I Thess. 5:23 but also clearly assigns it to Paul. He also refers to (and quotes) other passages from both epistles to the Thessalonians.

The Muratorian Fragment, an incomplete list of New Testament books, written in poor Latin and deriving its name from Cardinal L. A. Muratori (1672-1750) who discovered it in the Ambrosian Library at Milan, may be assigned to the period 180-200. It contains the following:

"Now the epistles of Paul, what they are, whence or for what reason they were sent, they themselves make clear to him who will understand. First of all he wrote at length to the Corinthians to prohibit the schism of heresy, then to the Galatians against circumcision, and to the Romans on the order of the Scriptures, intimating also that Christ is the chief matter in them — each of which it is necessary for us to discuss, seeing that the blessed apostle Paul himself, following the example of his predecessor John, writes to no more than seven churches by name in the following order: to the Corinthians (first), to the Ephesians (second), to the Philippians (third), to the Colossians (fourth), to the Galatians (fifth), to the Thessalonians (sixth), to the Romans (seventh). But . . . he writes twice for the sake of correction to the Corinthians and to the Thessalonians. . . ." Both I and II Thessalonians are also contained in the Old Latin and Old Syriac versions.

It is true that before the time of the witnesses which have thus far been mentioned there are no quotations that are either definitely said to have been derived from Paul's letters to the Thessalonians or can be derived from these letters *with certainty*. This, of course, is not surprising. The writings which can be confidently ascribed to that early period are very few. Moreover, the letters to the Thessalonians are small and (with the exception noted; see p. 4) contain little doctrinal material. They were probably not as well known as, for example, Romans or I Corinthians.

It is possible, nevertheless, that certain expressions in I and II Thessalonians find an echo in the literature of the sub-apostolic age. This can be neither proved nor disproved. Cf. the following:

I Thess. 1:6	Ignatius, *To The Ephesians* X. iii
"Y o u became imitators of us and of the Lord."	"Let us be eager to imitate the Lord."
I Thess. 2:4	Ignatius, *To The Romans* II. i
"not as pleasing men but God who proves our hearts."	"I would not have y o u be men-pleasers but God-pleasers."
I Thess. 4:9	Barnabas, Epistle of, XXI. vi (cf. IV. ix)
"Y o u yourselves are taught of God."	"Be taught of God" (God-instructed).

I Thess. 4:16	The Teaching (Didache) of the Twelve Apostles XVI. vi
"For the Lord himself shall descend from heaven with a shout, with the voice of the archangel, and with the trump of God; and the dead in Christ shall rise first."	"And then shall appear the signs of the truth. First the sign spread out in heaven, then the sign of the sound of the trumpet, and thirdly the resurrection of the dead."

I Thess. 5:13	The Shepherd III. ix. 10
"Be at peace among yourselves."	"at peace among themselves."

I Thess. 5:17	Ignatius, To The Ephesians X. i
"Pray without ceasing."	"Pray without ceasing."

This evidence does not constitute absolute proof for the position that at the end of the first and beginning of the second century A. D. Paul's letters to the church at Thessalonica were being quoted in writings that have come down to us. The expression "taught of God" (I Thess. 4:9; cf. Barnabas XXI. vi) was a very common one, which may have been derived from the Old Testament as well as from Paul. The following passages immediately occur to the mind: Is. 54:13; 60:2, 3; Jer. 31:33, 34; Joel 2:28; Mic. 4:2; Zeph. 3:9; and Mal. 1:11. Jesus quotes it (see John 6:45) as an expression that is "written in the prophets." Similarly, the passage about the signs (I Thess. 4:16; cf. The Teaching XVI. vi) may possibly go back to a saying of Jesus which is also reported by Matthew (24:30, 31). The passage about being at peace (I Thess. 5:13, cf. The Shepherd III. ix. 10) may have been derived from the saying of the Lord reported by Mark (9:50). On the other hand, if in each instance quoted we have before us the genuine text of Ignatius, it would seem that his use of I Thessalonians may be considered as *probable* (though not *certain*).

The important point is this: nowhere in early literature (not even in the writings of the heretics!) is any doubt cast on the Pauline authorship of I Thessalonians! Whenever the epistle is ascribed to anyone, it is always ascribed to the apostle Paul (thus Origen, Tertullian, Clement, Ireneus, etc.). And this external testimony, as has been pointed out, is in perfect agreement with the internal, the evidence supplied by the epistle itself. The only reasonable conclusion is that Paul was, indeed, the author.

B. *Of II Thessalonians*

The arguments of those who reject, either as a whole [11] or in part,[12]

---

[11] See especially Kern, "Ueber II Thess. 2:1-12, Nebst Andeutungen über den Ursprung des zweiten Briefes an die Thessalonicher," *Tübinger Zeitschrift für Theologie* (1839 Zweites Heft), 145-214. Cf. also the conclusion reached by Mayerhof, Baur, Weizsäcker, Wrede. The argumentation varies.

[12] One of the most recent is R. M. Hawkins, *The Recovery of the Historical Paul,*

NEW TESTAMENT COMMENTARY

the Pauline authorship of II Thessalonians are, with individual variations, as follows:

(1) *II Thess. 2:1-12 is an apocalyptic passage. It fixes the attention on Christ's future glory when he shall vanquish his enemies. This representation is in sharp contrast with Paul's emphasis on the necessity of growth in faith, hope, and love, here and now.*

This wholly subjective argument has already been answered. See footnote 8. The passage (2:1-12) is entirely natural, as recent studies in apocalyptic literature have shown. To reject it because it is apocalyptic is arbitrary.

(2) *If Paul wrote I Thess. 4:13-18; 5:1-11, he cannot also have written II Thess. 2:1-12; for while the first views Christ's coming as imminent, the second regards it as non-imminent.*

The fact is that the first epistle represents Christ's second coming as *sudden*, the second as *non-imminent* (preceded by certain events). These two ideas are not mutually exclusive. Certain signs will precede Christ's return. Yet when it occurs, it will take people by surprise. This representation, moreover, is in line with such passages as Dan. 11:1-12:3; Matt. 24:1-44; and Luke 17:20-37.

(3) *The passage 2:1-12 refers to Nero (the man of sin), reportedly dead but here represented as actually hiding and about to return (according to others, as really dead but about to arise), and to Vespasian (the restrainer); or (according to still others) it refers to the days of Trajan and to the advancing tide of gnosticism. This shows that Paul (who was no longer alive during the reigns of Vespasian and of Trajan) cannot have written it.*

Nothing in the context supports this interpretation. See on 2:1-12.

(4) *The rigorous predestinarianism of 2:11, 12, 13 is un-Pauline.*

But why could not he who wrote Rom. 8:28, 39; 9:10-24; Eph. 1:4, 11; 2:10 also have written II Thess. 2:11, 12, 13? In justice to those who urge argument (4) it must be admitted, however, that they would also scrap the predestinarian passages from Romans and Ephesians, viewing also them as being un-Pauline. The objection to this procedure is that the doctrine of predestination harmonizes with the entire course of reasoning in Paul's epistles. Wherever it is not definitely stated, it is presupposed. It is, *in a sense*, the keystone of the theology of the man who taught that "of him and through him and unto him are all things" (Rom. 11:36). To be consistent, the critics should also reject that passage and many others with it. What, if anything, would be left? (And is not also the Gospel of John, which

Nashville, Tenn., 1943, pp. 262-269, 292. Earlier interpolation theories (according to which II Thessalonians is partly genuine, partly spurious) were held by J. E. C. Schmidt (1801), who subsequently rejected the entire epistle as un-Pauline, Paul Schmidt (1881), and several others. Some regard 2:1-12 as spurious; others view it as the only genuine part of the letter.

records the teaching of Jesus, predestination from start to finish? [13]) There is, however, nothing *rigorous* with reference to this predestinarianism. Ample provision is always made for the factor of human responsibility. For the rest, see on 2:11, 12, 13.

(5) *To a very large extent II Thessalonians is a repetition of I Thessalonians. Clearly, a forger is at work!*

Actual comparison — let anyone check this! — shows that the new material in II Thessalonians (new as compared with the first letter) comprises about two-thirds of the letter. That there should be a certain amount of overlapping is exactly what one can reasonably expect when it is considered that *the same* author writes to *the same* church during *the same* period of time (only a few months intervening between the two letters) and under *the same* circumstances (by and large).

(6) *II Thessalonians differs in too many respects from the genuine Pauline epistles to be regarded as a product of Paul's "pen." Specifically, it is much "cooler" (less friendly, more "official") and also much more "Jewish" in coloring than I Thessalonians.*

It was especially Wrede who, in *Die Echtheit des zweiten Thessalonicherbriefs,* enlarged on this. But to some extent arguments (5) and (6) cancel each other. For the rest, the close relationship between the two letters has been shown. See pp. 16, 17; and see what is said about the resemblance between II Thessalonians and other Pauline epistles (pp. 21, 28).

(7) *The salutation (3:17) looks suspicious. It is clearly a deliberate attempt by a forger to make the letter look authentic.*

The answer to this is that in view of the item of information which 2:2 conveys — see on that passage — the autographic conclusion of 3:17 is altogether natural.

The same internal evidence that has been adduced to prove the authenticity of I Thessalonians establishes that of II Thessalonians. See pp. 22, 23. Hence, in view of what has been said in connection with the first letter a brief statement will suffice:

This second epistle (as well as the first) represents itself as having been written by Paul (1:1; 3:17), with whom are associated the men who are known to have accompanied him on his second journey (1:1). Here too the usual Pauline epistolary form is present, with interesting variation in detail. The vocabulary is definitely Pauline, the percentage of words which the second letter has in common with other epistles that are ascribed generally to Paul being even slightly higher than the percentage of words common to the first letter and the other epistles.

---

[13] See *New Testament Commentary* (hereafter referred to as N.T.C.), John's Gospel, Vol. I, p. 46.

To the list of phrases which II Thessalonians has in common with other Pauline epistles *and which are also found in I Thessalonians* (see p. 21) may now be added those which are found in the second letter and in others generally ascribed to Paul *but not in I Thessalonians.*

Note the following:

II Thess.	
1:1 God our Father	Rom. 1:7
1:8 obey the Gospel	Rom. 10:16
1:10 was believed in (ἐπιστεύθη with impersonal subject)	Rom. 10:10
2:2 as that (or: as if ὡς ὅτι)	II Cor. 5:19
2:3 let no one (μή τις with aor. subjunctive)	I Cor. 16:11
2:7 forward position of the word *only* (μόνον)	Gal. 2:10
2:10 those that are perishing	I Cor. 1:18
2:17 comfort y o u r hearts	Col. 2:2
3:4 have confidence in the Lord	Phil. 2:24
3:13 be not weary in well-doing	Gal. 6:9
3:14 our word	II Cor. 1:13
3:17 the greeting of Paul, with my own hand	I Cor. 16:21

Here, just as in the first letter, the personal character of Paul is reflected. (For the passages in the other epistles of Paul which reflect these same traits see p. 22.) In II Thessalonians we are face to face with a person who *is deeply interested in his readers* (1:3, 11, 12) and *displays warm affection* for them. He shares (*has fellowship* with) their experiences, and *is fond of commending* whatever is good in them (1:4; 3:4). Nevertheless, he *ascribes their virtues to the proper source:* God and his sovereign election (2:13). He *shows great tact* in admonishing them (3:4, 6-15), and *takes up matters of special interest to them* (2:1-12; 3:6-15). His *tender fatherly concern* for the readers is evident also in this, that when he describes the day of the revelation of God's wrath, he immediately adds that this wrath is only for the enemies of the church ("to repay with affliction them that afflict y o u"), and that believers (among whom he also counts the readers) will receive nothing but glory when Christ returns (1:3-10; 2:8-14).

The kind of character which is displayed in this letter points unmistakably to Paul. Nevertheless, at this point we must be careful. Some of the traits revealed in these two letters and in those by the same author occur also in the writings of other apostles. It is therefore not so much *the fact* that they do occur here as *the manner in which they are expressed* (the specific style) that points to Paul as the author. This is often overlooked. Take, as an example, *the sense of fellowship* (with the readers) of which we spoke. The apostle makes mention of the fact that the saints at Thessalonica have become imitators of Paul (and of his companions, yea of the

Lord himself!) in their afflictions (I Thess. 1:6); and that they will again be associated with Paul in the blessed rest which awaits them "at the revelation of the Lord Jesus from heaven" (II Thess. 1:7). However, this amiable way of addressing the readers in order to gain their full confidence and to make them feel that the writer is standing on common ground with them is just as Johannine as it is Pauline, as the beautiful expression in Rev. 1:9 shows.[14] It is the mark of the Christian, not just the mark of Paul! But the manner of expressing it differs: Paul's *y o u with* (and *of*) *us* becomes John's *I with y o u*. Paul tells the readers that *they* have become *imitators* (a noun not found anywhere in John's writings). John states that *he* has become a *fellow-partaker*. (Paul in a similar context also uses this term but with characteristic difference, Phil. 1:7: "*y o u* are fellow-partakers *with me*." Same term, but different context: Rom. 11:17; I Cor. 9:23.) Similarly, when Paul commends the virtues of the readers, he is simply doing what according to the book of Revelation, the great Church-Visitor also does (Rev. 2:2, 3, 13, 19, etc.). But here again the manner of expression is entirely different. The solemn and oft-recurring phrase, "I know thy works, etc." characterizes the book of Revelation, not Paul.

As to external evidence, for the testimony of Eusebius, Origen, Tertullian, and the Muratorian Fragment, in favor of Pauline authorship see pp. 23, 24.

Clement of Alexandria (fl. 190-200) in *Stromata* V. iii quotes II Thess. 3:1, 2. Ireneus, his contemporary, quotes from this epistle again and again:

II Thess.	Against Heresies
1:6-8	IV. xxxiii. 11
1:6-10	IV. xxvii. 4
2:4	III. vi. 5
2:8	III. vii. 2 (cf. V. xxv. 3)
2:11	IV. xxix. 1

He, moreover, makes it very clear that "the apostle" whose passages he quotes is Paul. See IV. xxiv. 1; xxxiii. 11. Though some see possible references to II Thessalonians in *The Epistle of Vienne and Lyons* (as quoted in Eusebius, *Ecclesiastical History* V. i) or in Ignatius, The *Teaching (Didache)*, or Barnabas, such conclusions appear to be rather far-fetched. A mere phrase or a very common saying proves nothing. We seem to be on somewhat firmer ground in finding a reference to II Thess. 2:3 in Justin Martyr's *Dialogue with Trypho* (Cx; cf. XXXII): "the man of apostasy who speaks strange things against the Most High." See the entire context

---

[14] See my *More Than Conquerors* (Interpretation of the book of Revelation), Grand Rapids, Mich., seventh edition 1954, p. 69.

in the Thessalonian passage. Clearest of all is a reference in (the Latin version of) Polycarp's *Epistle to the Philippians* (XI. iii), cf. II Thess. 1:4: "he glories about y o u in all the churches," and another reference immediately following (hence, Polycarp, *Philippians* XI. iv), cf. II Thess. 3:15: "and yet count them not as enemies." Not only does Polycarp quote from II Thessalonians, but he does so in a context in which he definitely mentions "the blessed Paul." Polycarp was very fond of "the blessed and glorious Paul" (see his *Philippians* III. ii).

What has been presented in support of the Pauline authorship of II Thessalonians may be summarized as follows:

(1) II Thessalonians was known in the early Church, the testimony going back from Eusebius and Origen all the way to Polycarp (about 135 A. D.).

(2) Whenever the letter was ascribed to anyone, it was ascribed to the apostle Paul. Ireneus, whose testimony being of a representative character, is especially valuable, nowhere casts any doubt on the position that the great apostle to the Gentiles was the writer of II Thessalonians.

(3) The internal evidence is in complete agreement with the external.

VI. General Contents

A. *Of I Thessalonians*

Many Bible-books, including several epistles, have definite themes. They cover a specific, well-defined subject. A little study reveals the nature of this central theme.[15] This, however, is not true with respect to *every* Bible-book. It is not true either with respect to every communication written today. Letters differ. You have heard that a friend has suffered a grievous loss. So you write him in order to comfort him. Your letter throughout dwells on that *one* theme, for you are aware of the fact that right now it would not be wise to bother him with many other matters. But a year later when time and reflection on God's promises have performed their work of mercy and when circumstances have returned to normal again (as far as this is possible), you write another letter. This is a message filled with news, advice, questions, etc. You communicate with your friend *about various matters.* Now it certainly would be arbitrary for anyone who subsequently examines this your second letter to try to crowd all your thoughts under one central theme (unless you make that theme so very broad in scope and so indefinite that it is a *caption* rather than a definite, specific, material *theme*). Now if attempts to deal thus arbitrarily with uninspired documents are wrong, it is even more wrong to treat Paul's divinely inspired

---

15 As I have shown in *Bible Survey*, Grand Rapids, Mich., third edition (fourth printing), 1953, pp. 36, 37.

epistles in that manner. What results is a merely imagined unity. Often, as a consequence of trying to get everything under one central theme, this or that very important matter is omitted completely from the theme and/or from the Outline under it.[16]

It stands to reason that, in view of the various purposes which the apostle (and his associates) has in mind in writing this letter (see the section on *Purpose,* above), he comments on various subjects. Hence, in this case a rather general and comprehensive caption will have to take the place of a definite, unified, material theme. The caption and subjoined division which I have chosen match what has been said about Paul's *purpose* in writing this letter (see p. 12).

Paul [17] Writes To The Thessalonians

chapters 1 and 2 or 1:1-3:5 — *Reminding Them,* in connection with his *Thanksgiving* for Them, How the Gospel Had Come to Thessalonica, as a Genuine Work of God and Not as a Product of Human Deception; [18]

chapter 3 or 3:6-13 — *Informing* Them How He *Rejoices* over Timothy's Report of Their Continued Spiritual Progress Even in the Midst of Persecution;

4:13-5:11 — *Instructing* Them How Christ Will Come Again, namely, *with impartiality* toward *all* believers, sothat survivors will have no advantage over those who have fallen asleep; and *with suddenness,* sothat people will be taken by surprise; and accordingly:

4:1-12 and 5:12-28 — *Exhorting* Them How They Should Conduct Themselves, living sanctified lives with respect to all classes and at all times.[19]

---

[16] It is for that reason that I cannot agree with the theme and the outline that has been suggested by Edward P. Blair in his article "The First Epistle to the Thessalonians," *Int.* Vol. II, Number 2 (April, 1948), 209-217. Where, either in the theme which he suggests or in the outline (see p. 216 of that article), is anything said about the important section on Christ's second coming? Will anyone who looks at the theme or at the outline as given by Blair know that a considerable portion of Paul's letter deals with a specific problem that had arisen with respect to the Lord's Return? — For the rest, I gladly admit that the article itself is splendid in many ways, and on several points contains exactly the advice which everyone who proceeds to study a Bible-book should heed. Because of its excellence it deserves careful study!

[17] Or more fully: Paul, Silvanus, and Timothy write, etc. But Paul, at any rate, is mainly responsible.

[18] This is the Apostle's *Thanksgiving* and his *Defence* by means of Reminiscence.

[19] I realize that this broad caption and subjoined division is too lengthy for

Thus, in general, there are four divisions (Thanksgiving and Defence, Expression of Joy, Instruction, and Exhortation), but these divisions are not rigid or clearcut (see on 4:1). Thoughts already expressed in one section recur in the next. Besides, the fourth division — Exhortation — comprises both 4:1-12 and 5:12-28. Hence, the four divisions really become five:

Thanksgiving and Defence
Expression of Joy
Exhortation
Instruction
Exhortation.[20]

B. Of II Thessalonians

This epistle is considerably shorter than the first. Its material is more definitely organized around one central theme, even though the theme is not introduced immediately, as in a formal essay on a definite topic, but rises to the surface gradually. Thus, in the first chapter it becomes clearly evident when we reach verse 5, and stays with us for six entire verses (verses 5 through 10). Though it seems to subside somewhat in the last two verses (11 and 12), it is still presupposed, for the prayer contained in that little closing paragraph is uttered "with a view to" the realization of the expectations mentioned in verses 5-10. The theme mentioned in this chapter is "The Revelation of the Lord Jesus from heaven" (verse 7).

That this theme is continued in chapter 2 requires no argument, for this chapter is immediately introduced by the words, "Now concerning the coming of our Lord Jesus Christ and our gathering (to meet) him."

Not every interpreter is ready to grant that the thought of this second coming also underlies chapter 3. Some deny any connection between disorderliness, treated in that chapter, and ideas with reference to the return of the Lord. Yet, a comparison of several passages in both epistles would seem to indicate that there is this connection. It is true, of course, that I Thessalonians is not II Thessalonians, and that the circumstances underlying the second epistle are *not exactly* the same as those presupposed or described in the first. The evil had become aggravated when the second letter was written. Nevertheless, it is hard to imagine that the disorderly persons mentioned in the first letter were such for an *entirely* different reason than those characterized similarly in the second (cf. I Thess. 5:14

---

memorization, particularly if one is trying to commit to memory the themes or captions or brief outlines of all the Bible-books. Hence, for such practical purposes I have suggested a shorter caption and division; see my *Bible Survey*, pp. 340, 341; cf. p. 37.

[20] Approximately this fivefold division is also given in my *Bible Survey*, pp. 340, 341, where three of these five are grouped together under one larger division, and two under the other.

INTRODUCTION

with II Thess. 3:6). If then we may assume that *in general* the same evils prevailed and for the same reason, we get the following picture (combining references in both epistles):

The Thessalonians were shaken from their normal state of mind (II Thess. 2:1, 2), were not calm (I Thess. 4:11), because of their erroneous views regarding Christ's return. This is plainly stated as the reason in II Thess. 2:2. They thought that the day of the Lord had arrived already. It was this disturbed condition which caused them to leave their daily occupations and to become disorderly (I Thess. 4:11; cf. 5:14; then II Thess. 3:6), even to the extent of depending on others for physical sustenance (II Thess. 3:7, 8).

If this position be correct, then also chapter 3 presupposes the same theme as that which controls chapters 1 and 2. Hence, the following theme and outline are suggested:

The Revelation of the Lord Jesus from Heaven

chapter 1   has a twofold purpose
chapter 2   will be preceded by the falling away and by the revela-
(or 2:1-12)   tion of the lawless one
chapter 3   is a firmly anchored hope whose contemplation should
(or 2:13-3:17)   result not in disorderliness but in calm assurance, sted-
                   fast endurance and strength-imparting peace.

As indicated on pp. 14, 15, also in this case there are important interspersions.

Commentary

on

I Thessalonians

Summary of I Thessalonians 1, 2 (or 1:1-3:5)

Paul Writes to the Thessalonians

Reminding Them, in connection with his Thanksgiving for Them, How the Gospel Had Come to Thessalonica, as a Genuine Work of God and Not as a Product of Human Deception.

This Section Comprises the *Apostle's Thanksgiving and his Defence by means of Reminiscence.*

In Chapter 1 the Thanksgiving Predominates, but there is an Undertone of Defence against the Slander of the Adversaries. In Chapter 2 the Defence Predominates, although the Thanksgiving Continues.

The Section, accordingly, may be summarized as follows:

1:1 Names of Senders and Addressee, Salutation

1:2-10 Thanksgiving with Undertone of Defence
    1:2, 3 *Immediate* reason for thanksgiving
        the presence of fruits of the Spirit in the lives of the Thessalonian believers, their:
            work resulting from faith
            exertion prompted by love
            endurance inspired by hope
    1:4-10 *Ultimate* reason for thanksgiving (in which an undertone of defence can easily be detected)
        their election from eternity. Proof:
    objectively, the *trustworthiness* of the message and of the messengers
    subjectively, the admirable manner in which this message and these messengers had been received and the new faith had been spread, a sign of the Spirit's *operation* in the midst of the church, which, in turn, is proof of divine election
    Let not the adversary deny either this trustworthiness or the genuine character of this operation.

2:1-20 (or 2:1-3:5) Defence with Continuing Thanksgiving
    2:1-16 *Apologia pro Vita Sua,* that is, Paul's defence of his manner of life in Thessalonica, defence of his message, motive, and method (with note of thanksgiving to God for the way in which the message had been accepted by those who turned to God)
    2:17-20 (or 2:17-3:5) *Apologia pro Absentia Sua,* that is, Paul's defence of his sudden departure and continued absence from Thessalonica

CHAPTER I

1 1 Paul and Silvanus and Timothy to the church of the Thessalonians in God the Father and the Lord Jesus Christ; grace to y o u and peace.

2 We give thanks to God always for y o u all, making mention (of y o u) in our prayers, 3 continually bearing in mind y o u r work resulting from faith and (y o u r) exertion prompted by love and (y o u r) endurance inspired by hope [21] in our Lord Jesus Christ in the presence of our God and Father; 4 knowing, brothers beloved by God, y o u r election, 5 inasmuch as [22] our gospel did not come to y o u in words only but also in power and in the Holy Spirit and full assurance, just as y o u (well) know what kind of men we became among y o u for y o u r sake. 6 And y o u became imitators of us and of the Lord, when amid great tribulation y o u welcomed the word with joy imparted by the Holy Spirit, 7 so that y o u became an example to all the believers in Macedonia and Achaia. 8 For, from y o u the word of the Lord has echoed forth not only in Macedonia and Achaia, but in every place y o u r faith (directed) toward God has gone forth, so that it is not necessary for *us* to say anything; 9 for they themselves are reporting about us, what kind of entering in we had among y o u, and how y o u turned to God from those idols (of y o u r s), to serve God, the living and real One, 10 and to await his Son out of the heavens, whom he raised from the dead, Jesus, who rescues us from the wrath to come.

1:1-10

1:1. In our day when you write a letter, you first of all address the person to whom you are sending it; for example, Name of Addressee; then,

"Dear Friend:"

At the conclusion of the letter you write your own name; thus:

"Yours truly,

John Brown"

In Paul's time, however, a letter would begin with the name of the sender. This would be followed by the name of the person(s) addressed, to which, in turn, would be appended the customary greeting. Examples

---

[21] Literally: *y o u r work of faith and exertion* (or: *labor*) *of love and endurance of hope;* but such language conveys little meaning in English.

[22] The sense of this statement is: "for . . . that y o u were chosen (elected) we know *from the fact that* our gospel," etc.

are Acts 15:23 and 23:36. So also this epistle: **Paul and Silvanus and Timothy.**

Since the great apostle was mainly responsible for the present letter, he first of all writes his own name, then the names of those who had been associated with him in bringing the Gospel to the Thessalonians, and who were with him now in Corinth as this letter was being written.

The apostle's Jewish name was Saul. This Hebrew name was very appropriate because its bearer belonged to the tribe of Benjamin from which centuries earlier king Saul had arisen (Phil. 3:5; cf. I Sam. 9:1, 2). Its meaning is *asked of God*. But as the apostle was a Roman citizen by birth (Acts 22:28), it is not strange that at the time of his circumcision (cf. Lk. 1:59) he had been given a Roman (Latin) name (Paulus, cf. our: Paul) in addition to the Jewish name (Saul).

Now the Roman name somewhat resembled the Jewish in sound, though not in meaning.[23] The meaning of the Roman name — Paul-us, also written Paullus, (for paurulus; cf. parvus), whence Greek Paul-os (cf. παῦρος) — is *little*. There are those who see special significance in the meaning of this name, or make certain comments about it. Thus, for example, Augustine, playing on the apostle's Roman cognomen, styles him *paullum modicum quid*, and Chrysostom calls him, "the man three cubits tall." The *Acts of Paul and Thecla* describe him as follows: "baldheaded, bow-legged, strongly built, *a man small in size*, with meeting eyebrows, with a rather large nose, full of grace, for at times he looked like a man and at times he had the face of an angel." Others point out that whatever may have been Paul's physical stature (cf. II Cor. 10:10), spiritually he was destined by God's sovereign grace to regard himself as very *little* or *insignificant:* "less than the least of all saints" (Eph. 3:8). Be that as it may — and neither Paul in any of his epistles nor Luke gives definite indication of attaching any value to the meaning of the name, whether Hebrew or Latin —, *one* fact at least is certain, and it is that fact upon which the emphasis should fall, namely, that although here in I Thess. 1:1 Paul does not immediately add to his name the appositive "an apostle" (as he does when he writes to places where his office was in dispute), he is, nevertheless, writing in that capacity. As has already been pointed out (see p. 22), while he writes, he is conscious of his *authority*.

Associated with him, fully endorsing everything he says, are Silvanus and Timothy. Silvanus is a Roman proper name. Originally it was the name of the god of the woods (cf. our adjective *sylvan* and cf. *Pennsylvania:*

---

[23] The question might be asked, "But why did not the apostle simply keep his Hebrew name with Grecianized ending to be used in a Greek-speaking environment? In other words, why was he not simply called Saul-os (instead of Paul-os)?" This, however, would not have been very pleasant. Who likes to be called *loose, wanton, straddling, waddling* (σαῦλος)?

Penn's woods). The name as such bears no relation to the character or personality of this fellow-soldier nor to the place where he was born. It is merely a matter of sound-transposition. From what was probably originally an Aramaic name (with a meaning the same as Saul) comes the Greek Silas, and (without any similarity in meaning, only in sound) the Latin Silvan-us (though the Greek ending is, of course, -os). While Luke uses the name Silas, Paul very naturally refers to the same person as Silvan-us (-os), just as he calls himself Paul-us (-os). A comparison of the passages in Paul's letters with those in Acts makes it altogether probable that by Silas and Silvanus the same person is meant. He figures prominently in the proceedings of the council of Jerusalem (Acts 15:22, 27, 32), and was sent with Paul to Antioch to communicate the council's decision to that city. It has already been indicated (see pp. 5, 16) that after the argument between Paul and Barnabas with reference to John Mark, whom Paul refused to take with him on his second journey, the apostle chose Silas, that is, Silvanus, to accompany him and to carry out special missions; and that after the second journey the book of Acts contains no further reference to him. Also in the epistles of Paul the references to Silvanus always point to the second journey (II Cor. 1:19; I Thess. 1:1; II Thess. 2:1). The question whether the Silvanus mentioned by Peter (I Peter 5:12) was the same person, and in exactly what relation the former stood to the latter and to his letter need not detain us here.

If the mention of Silas, as associated with Paul in the sending of the letter, is not surprising, the mention of Timothy is even less so. The reason for our belief that he as well as Silas had labored with Paul in Thessalonica has already been stated (p. 5). But in addition to laboring there with Paul, Timothy had been sent back to that field afterward and had just now reported his findings (I Thess. 3:1, 2, 6).

We know much more about Timothy than about Silas. But the information furnished will be summarized in the proper place; see N.T.C. on the Pastorals.

The order in which the three names are mentioned is the one which we would expect: first Paul, because he is, in the fullest sense of the term, the apostle. It is he who writes (i.e. dictates) the letter. Next mentioned is Silvanus, who in all probability was the older of the two companions and who had been with Paul from the very beginning of the journey during which the Thessalonians had received the Gospel. Last of all is Timothy, who seems to have been the youngest and who had been added to the little mission-band while the journey was already in progress (Acts 16:1-3). The three are writing (and in the immediate context are transmitting [24] a salu-

---

[24] τῇ ἐκκλησίᾳ is sometimes called the dative of transmittance.

tation) **to the church of the Thessalonians.** The term translated *church* [25] is *ecclesia* (cf. the adjective *ecclesiastical*). Originally it indicated *the popular assembly,* as for example in Athens, in which every free citizen could vote. In the LXX (Greek translation of the Old Testament) it refers to *the community of Israel* (whether or not viewed as assembled for any particular purpose). In the New Testament it refers to *the company of those whom God has called out of darkness into his marvelous light* (cf. I Peter 2:9), whether, a. as here, they be viewed as constituting a *local congregation,* b. as in Eph. 1:22, *the whole body of believers,* or c. as in I Cor. 11:18, *a gathering for worship.*

It is not clear just why Paul employs the expression "of the [26] Thessalonians" instead of "at (or in) Thessalonica" (which is the more usual form; cf. Rom. 1:7; I Cor. 1:2; II Cor. 1:1; Phil. 1:1; Col. 1:2). It is certain, however, that the expression *the Thessalonians* indicates all the members of the church which had very recently been established **in** (and was still in existence by virtue of its vital union with) **God the Father and the Lord Jesus Christ.** The combination of both terms (a. God the Father, b. the Lord Jesus Christ) after one preposition (*in;* that is *grounded in*) would seem to indicate that the two are entirely co-ordinate, that is, that the reference is to the first and to the second person of the Holy Trinity.[27] Note also the trinitarian character of verses 3-5. Hence, the third person (Holy Spirit), mentioned in verse 5, is implied already in verse 1. Paul often mentions the three together in series of closely connected passages (II Thess. 2:13, 14; I Cor. 12:4-6; II Cor. 13:14; Eph. 2:18; 3:2-5; 3:14-17; 4:4-6; 5:18-20). In referring to the second person the full name is used here: the Lord Jesus Christ.

In the LXX the name *Lord* (κύριος) translates *Jehovah,* the God of Israel. It is more often the rendering of Jehovah than of anything else. (At times it is the equivalent of Adon, Adonai, Baal, etc.) Now the Jews were strict monotheists. Yet Paul, though himself a Jew, again and again gives to Jesus the title *Lord.* This shows that, in the thinking of the apostle, Jesus is just as fully divine as is God the Father: one and the same essence is

---

[25] Our English word *church* (cf. German *Kirche,* Dutch *kerk*) is also, in all probability related to the Greek κυριακός-ή-όν, and means "that which is the Lord's."
[26] It is probably best not to look for any profound reason why the article is omitted in the original. Some, nevertheless, suggest that the reason might be that not *all* but only *some* of the inhabitants of Thessalonica had been converted. Far more simple is the explanation given by A. T. Robertson and others, namely, that *Thessalonians,* being a proper name, is definite even without the article. In line with A.V., A.R.V., R.S.V., etc., we abide by the usual rendering "of the Thessalonians."
[27] Thus also in II Thess. 1:2. If the idea were: "from the triune God through Jesus Christ" we would have expected two prepositions, namely, ἀπό and διά. I agree with Lenski (*op. cit.,* p. 219) and others that the expression *God the Father* (I Thess. 1:1; II Thess. 1:1, 2) refers here to the first person as such. Cf. A. M. Perry, "Translating The Greek Article," *JBL* 68 (Dec., 1949) 329-334.

possessed by the Father and by the Son (also by the Spirit, II Cor. 13:14). For Paul, Jesus is our Lord because: a. he is the second person in the Holy Trinity (I Cor. 13:3; Phil. 2:11), the highly exalted One, rightful object of worship, b. he has made us (Col. 1:3, 16), and c. he has bought (redeemed) us with his precious blood (Col. 1:3, 14); hence, we belong to him according to body and soul, in life and death and throughout all eternity. We owe him our full allegiance. This description of Jesus as *Lord* was not derived from the pagan world nor necessarily from the Christian communities in such cities as Antioch, Tarsus, and Damascus. No, Paul "received" it from the original disciples. The early church at Jerusalem (the Aramaic-speaking and then also the Greek-speaking believers) already used the title with reference to Jesus (cf. Gal. 1:18, 19; I Cor. 16:22: "Maranatha," meaning "Our Lord, come," or simply "Lord, come"; [28] John 20:28. Acts 6:1 shows that the early Jerusalem church was bilingual).

To the title *Lord* Paul adds the name *Jesus*. Our English word *Jesus* is really Latin from the closely resembling Greek name ('Ιησοῦς). This, in turn, is the hellenized form of the late Hebrew *Jeshua* (see post-exilic historical books; e.g., Ezra 2:2), the contracted form of *Jehoshua* (cf. *Joshua*, Josh. 1:1; Zech. 3:1). This has been interpreted to mean *Help of Jehovah*. By another approach it has been explained as indicating: *he will certainly save* (this agrees with Matt. 1:21). Accordingly, by giving this name to the Mediator, God meant to indicate that a. no one can save himself, b. salvation ever comes from God, c. this salvation is bestowed through the person and work of him who according to his divine nature is the Son of God, and according to his human nature, the son of Mary, d. it is he who saves, and *he alone*. No one else in all the wide world has been appointed to perform this task.

Anyone can arrive at this meaning by carefully reading the following four passages:

Matt. 1:21: "You must call his name Jesus, for *he* will save his people from their sins."

Matt. 11:27-30: ". . . No one knows the Son except the Father, and no one knows the Father except the Son and anyone to whom the Son chooses to reveal him. Come to me, all who labor and are heavily burdened, and I will cause y o u to rest."

John 14:6: "I am the way and the truth and the life; no one comes to the Father but by me."

---

[28] The latter, if the original meaning of the suffix had been obscured, which is possible. On the use, derivation, and meaning of the word κύριος see especially J. Y. Campbell, art. "Lord," in *A Theological Word Book of the Bible* (edited by Alan Richardson), New York, 1952; also J. G. Machen, *The Origin of Paul's Religion*, Grand Rapids, 1947 (reprint), chapter 8; and G. Vos, *The Self-Disclosure of Jesus*, New York, 1926, chapter 9.

Acts 4:12: "And not by anyone else is there this salvation; for neither is there under heaven any other name that has been given among men by which we must be saved."

Finally, to the title *Lord* and the personal name *Jesus* is added the official name *Christ*.[29] This is the Greek equivalent of the Hebrew Messiah. It is clear, therefore, that for Paul the One here indicated was the fulfilment of prophecy, God's *anointed* (*ordained* and *qualified* by God to carry out the task of saving his people).

By combining these three appellatives into one glorious designation, "the Lord Jesus Christ," Paul indicates that the One thus named, together with God the Father, is able to be and actually is the source of the blessings contained in the salutation which is now pronounced: **grace to y o u and peace.** This form of salutation may have been suggested by the combination of the ordinary Greek and Hebrew greetings. Paul, however, deepens and spiritualizes both.[30] The apostle uses the term *grace* (χάρις) about a hundred times in his thirteen epistles. In the Old Testament it indicates gracefulness, beauty (Prov. 31:30), favor (Gen. 6:8). The various shades of meaning which this word acquires in Paul's epistles should be distinguished, somewhat as follows:

(a) *A quality or attribute of God or of the Lord Jesus Christ: his kindness.* In this connection II Cor. 8:9 is often referred to: "For y o u know the grace of our Lord Jesus Christ." (However, in connection with this passage, meaning (b) might also be considered.)

(b) The *favor* toward his people which results from this kindness of disposition and which manifests itself a. in their deliverance from the guilt and punishment of sin, b. in the *dynamic,* transforming operation of the Holy Spirit in their hearts, and finally, c. in their entrance into glory. On God's part, this favor is entirely *sovereign and unconditional;* on man's part, it is completely *unmerited.* Cf. Eph. 2:8; "For by grace have y o u been saved through faith, and that not of yourselves; it is the gift of God." Salvation by grace stands in opposition to salvation by the works of the law.

(c) The state of salvation, the sum-total of the blessings of salvation, or, at times, any particular blessing or endowment, viewed (in each case) as *the free gift of God.* Cf. Rom. 5:2: "this grace wherein we stand." Eph. 4:7: "But to each one of us was this grace given according to the measure of the gift of Christ."

(d) The *gratitude* which is the believer's reaction when, led by the Spirit, he focusses his attention upon his own unworthiness and upon the greatness of God's goodness toward him. Cf. II Cor. 2:14: "Thanks be to God . . ."

In the present passage (I Thess. 1:1) meaning (b) would seem to be the

---

[29] On this name see G. Vos, *op. cit.,* chapter 8.
[30] See M.M., p. 685.

most fitting. Paul takes the "greetings" (χαίρειν) of the ordinary letter in the Greek-speaking world (cf. also Acts 15:23; 23:26; Jas. 1:1), deepens it into "grace" (χάρις): God's love for the undeserving, his unmerited favor in operation in the hearts and lives of his children, and then adds *peace*.

This addition is natural, for when grace is received, there is *peace* (εἰρήνη) in the heart, *the consciousness of having been reconciled with God through Christ*. Grace is the fountain, and peace is the stream which issues from this fountain (cf. Rom. 5:1). It can hardly be doubted that this *peace* is closely related to the Hebrew *shalom* (cf. Judg. 19:20): wholeness, prosperity, welfare; here (I Thess. 1:1), spiritual welfare. It is the peace of which Jesus spoke in John 14:27 (see on that passage). Paul uses the word more than forty times.

This grace and this peace have their origin in God the Father, and have been merited for the believer by the Lord Jesus Christ.

Just what is the character of this salutation? Is it an exclamation, a declaration, a mere wish? Some consider it to be an exclamation. They are of the opinion that no verb is even implied.[31] Many, however, are not able to follow this reasoning. When a man says to his neighbor, "More power to you!" he is uttering an exclamation, and he does not use any verb. Yet, everyone immediately understands that a verb is implied, the sense being: "May you receive more power!" And so also in the present case. Paul, however, never *uses* a verb in his salutations. John employs the future *indicative* (II John 3: "Grace, mercy, peace *shall be* with us"). In a context which closely resembles Paul's style in Ephesians, Peter employs the *optative* (I Peter 1:2). Compare:

Eph. 1:1-3	I Peter 1:1-3
"Paul, an apostle of Christ Jesus . . . to the saints. . . . Grace to y o u and peace from God our Father and the Lord Jesus Christ. Blessed be the God and Father of our Lord Jesus Christ. . . ."	"Peter, an apostle of Jesus Christ . . . to the elect . . . Grace to y o u and peace *be multiplied*. Blessed be the God and Father of our Lord Jesus Christ. . . ."

From the similarity in the general structure and context of these salutations it may be safely inferred that Paul's implied verb resembles Peter's expressed verb. See also II Peter 1:2 and Jude 2 where the same form of the verb (optative mood) is used. Accordingly, A.V. is probably not in error when it inserts a verb and translates the salutation:

---

[31] See R. C. H. Lenski, *Interpretation of Galatians, Ephesians, Philippians*, Columbus, Ohio, 1937, p. 27.

"Grace *be* unto you, and peace.[32]

However, exactly at this point a question arises. Is it not true then that those are right who contend that the salutation is *a mere wish?* And must we not, in all honesty, conclude that the traditional position of the church with respect to the salutation, as pronounced at the beginning of the service in public worship, is wrong; and that those authorities in Liturgics who contend that the salutation is an act of God whereby he bestows his grace and peace upon those who are ready to receive it by faith,[33] are also wrong?

We believe, however, that this conclusion by no means follows. The traditional position of the church is entirely correct. It has grammar on its side.[34]

The question, in the final analysis, is not: Does the traditional view with respect to the nature of the salutation (as being an actual declaration that God imparts his favor, and that he places his blessings upon the congregation) harmonize with my notion as to what a service of the Word should be? Does it tally with my opinion of the office of the minister? It is this: What is the real sense of Scripture? Then, if the teaching of the Bible happens to go contrary to my way of thinking, let me try to change not the teaching but the way of thinking. And if I am not willing to do this, I should say very plainly, I do not agree with the Bible.

---

[32] The addition "from God our Father and the Lord Jesus Christ" is not supported by the best texts (but see II Thess. 1:1).

[33] Cf. Andrew W. Blackwood, *The Fine Art of Public Worship*, Nashville, 1939, p. 153. (He is referring to the benediction at the conclusion of the service, but with respect to the point at issue this makes no essential difference.) See also W. Heyns, *Liturgiek*, Holland, Mich., 1903, p. 150: "It (the salutation) is a declaration of God that he dwells in the midst of the congregation in order to bless it with his grace and peace"; and A. Kuyper, *Onze Eeredienst*, Kampen, 1911, p. 196: "It is not the cordial wish of that man in the pulpit, who prays that whatever is good, including grace and peace, may come your way; but 'it is God Triune, who pronounces his grace and peace upon you, and who for that purpose uses his servant."

[34] To say that an implied optative indicates that the salutation "amounts to the expression of a *mere* wish" is an indication of a superficial and altogether too limited view of the meaning of the optative mood *in certain specific connections* in Biblical (LXX and New Testament) Greek.

A few examples will make this clear. According to Mark 11:14 Jesus said to the fig tree that produced nothing but leaves:

"Forevermore may no one eat fruit from you again." The verb (may eat) is in the optative mood. But this optative did not express "a *mere* wish." On the contrary, the wish was *effective.* It amounted to nothing less than pronouncing an effective curse upon that tree. As they passed by the next morning, the disciples saw the fig tree completely withered, to its very roots (Mark 11:20).

More to the point, we have a similar use of the optative in connection with the Aaronitic benediction (Num. 6:24-26). The *jussive* of the verbal forms in the Old Testament passage ("let it come to pass") very appropriately indicates *effective impartation*, not *mere* wishing but *effective* wishing. Note the optative mood in the LXX translation of this passage. See Gesenius-Kautzsch, *Hebrew Grammar*, Oxford, 1910, p. 321.

Now the fact that the traditional view is correct is clear both from the Old and from the New Testament. Note the following:

Num. 6:24-26:

Immediately after the words of the Aaronitic benediction we read, "So shall they put my name upon the children of Israel; and I will bless them." Hence, the act of pronouncing the benediction was viewed as an effectual *putting* of the name of Jehovah upon Israel, sothat his blessing would actually result.

Luke 10:5, 6:

"And when y o u enter into any house, first say, 'Peace to this house.' And if a son of peace be there, y o u r peace shall rest upon him; but if not, it shall turn back to y o u."

II John 3:

"Grace, mercy, and peace will be with us . . ." As was indicated earlier, the indicative mood is used. It is a declaration of something that will actually happen. This harmonizes completely with the idea of the expressed optative (Peter and Jude) or implied optative (Paul), when the latter is viewed as expressing an *effective* (not a *mere*) wish.

What Paul, writing officially as Christ's apostle, meant here in I Thess. 1:1 may, accordingly, be summed up as follows:

"May grace and peace rest upon y o u all. As God's official representative I (together with my associates Silas and Timothy) declare that this is what will actually happen."

Two objections should be answered:

(a) "But is it not true that God's grace and his peace *always* rest on the church?" True, indeed, but the effective wish or the declaration is that this grace and this peace shall be applied abundantly especially in connection with this particular service of public worship (for example, when this letter or any part of it is read).

(b) "Is not this a mechanical view?" Indeed not! These blessings are bestowed upon those — and *only* upon those — who are ready to receive them by faith. Read Luke 10:5, 6 quoted above.

2, 3. In letters written by men who were Paul's contemporaries the greeting is often followed by a statement which indicates that the person(s) addressed is being remembered in prayer to *the gods*. Hence, it is not surprising that Paul's epistles contain a similar item. (See also Rom. 1:8; I Cor. 1:4; Phil. 1:3; Col. 1:3; II Thess. 1:3; II Tim. 1:3; Philem. 4.) The resemblance, however, is in form but not in essence. The readers, many of whom were recent converts from the pagan world, must have been impressed by the fact that *this* letter is different. Paul and his companions have excluded the idol-gods from their letter as decisively as the Thessalonians had ex-

45

pelled them from their homes. The thanksgiving is here, but it is addressed to the one true God: **We give thanks to God always for you all.**

The verb "we give thanks" (εὐχαριστοῦμεν) is related to the noun "grace" (χάρις; see on 1:1, meaning d.). Paul and his companions thank God for the fruits of grace that were found in the hearts and lives of the church-members. They do this continually, never skipping a single day. They recognize the unity of faith, love, and hope which characterized the membership: "for y o u *all*."

The main clause, "We give thanks," has three participial modifiers, as follows:

verse 2b: "making mention (of y o u) in our prayers"
verse 3: "continually bearing in mind y o u r work. . . ."
verse 4: "knowing . . . y o u r election . . ."

The first and the second of these clauses indicate the accompanying circumstances of the thanksgiving; that is, they show what Paul, Silas, and Timothy did when they gave thanks for the Thessalonians: how they would mention them by name, and would specify the spiritual fruits which adorned their lives (work resulting from faith, exertion prompted by love, endurance inspired by hope). The second clause, however, does more than this. It also begins to indicate *the reason why* the missionaries are so thankful. They express their gratitude because of these fruits! That is the *immediate* reason. But there is also an *ultimate* reason, which is expressed in the third participial modifier: "knowing y o u r election."

Beginning with the first of these modifiers, Paul says: **making mention (of y o u) in our prayers.** It would seem that the missionaries prayed *unitedly* (in addition, of course, to praying individually). They may have taken turns in leading the devotions. These prayers were not marked by any vagueness. On the contrary, the needs of the various churches were mentioned one by one, as the occasion demanded. The thought is not excluded that individual members may have been mentioned by name.

Now such prayers consisted not only in a series of petitions, but also in thanksgivings, praises, words of adoration. God was given the honor that was due to him in view of the marvelous things he had done. In fact, that is exactly the point which receives the emphasis here, as is indicated in the second participial modifier: **continually bearing in mind y o u r work resulting from faith and (y o u r) exertion prompted by love and (y o u r) endurance inspired by hope in our Lord Jesus Christ in the presence of our God and Father.**

With respect to the meaning of this beautiful passage commentators differ widely.[35] This is the first time the series *faith, hope, and love* occurs in

---

[35] The main theories are best represented by the various renderings which have been suggested, of which we shall mention three:

Paul's epistles. Here hope is mentioned last (faith . . . love . . . hope) in order to link it with "in our Lord Jesus Christ in the presence of our God and Father." In an epistle which deals so extensively with the subject of the confident expectation of (or the "waiting for") Christ's Return, it is

---

"remembering without ceasing" (or a similar clause):
(1) "your work of faith
    and labour of love
    and patience of hope."
We reject this for the simple reason that it makes little or no sense. What is "patience of hope" anyway?
(2) "your work, namely, faith
    and labor, namely, love
    and patience, namely, hope."
Aside from doctrinal objections, we reject this because, though it is grammatically possible, it can hardly be said to be true to the Pauline emphasis. Also, the concept, "patience, namely, hope," is difficult.
(3) "your active faith
    and industrious love
    and tenacious hope."
But this places the emphasis where, according to the original, it does not belong. The words stressed in the original are not faith, love and hope, but work, exertion (or labor), and endurance.
As we see it, the grammatical construction of the clause is as follows:
The nouns *work, exertion,* and *endurance* are object-genitives after the verb *bearing in mind* (being mindful of).
The word y o u r modifies all three, hence, y o u r work, y o u r exertion, y o u r endurance.
Each of these nouns has a modifier in the genitive. It matters little whether this is called "adjectival" or "descriptive" or "subjective" genitive or genitive "of source." All four terms have been used, but basically the idea is the same (though with a slight variation in emphasis). The idea is that the work is definitely *faith*-work, that is, it is work which springs from, is accomplished by, and reveals *faith*. Were it not for the presence of living faith, this work would not be in evidence. And so with the other modifiers: the exertion is prompted by (and reveals) love; and the endurance is inspired by (and gives evidence of) hope.
We construe *Lord Jesus Christ* to be objective genitive (hence, "in our Lord Jesus Christ") after the noun *hope*, which stands closest to it. That is the most natural construction, yields an excellent meaning, which, moreover, is in harmony with parallel passages (cf. 4:13; 5:8, 9; II Thess. 2:16). The fact that, thus construed, the third element in the series (work . . . exertion . . . endurance . . .) is of greater length than the other two does not worry us in the least. Paul is no lover of *"rigid* symmetry." He frequently lengthens (or at least varies) the last of several elements in a series. That makes for progression in thought. Note, for example, how in this very letter when the series "faith, love, hope" is mentioned in 5:8, the apostle enlarges on *hope* ("the hope of salvation, for . . ."). For the opposite view (according to which "our Lord Jesus Christ" belongs to all three items in the series, so that the meaning becomes: work . . . labor . . . hope, all three embracing him, or centering in him) see Lenski's diagram on p. 221 of his Commentary; and see Van Leeuwen (*Kommentaar,* p. 300; *Korte Verklaring,* pp. 15-17).
We do not see any need of linking "in the presence of" (ἔμπροσθεν) with the remote participle "bearing in mind" (μνημονεύοντες). Much more natural is the construction of this preposition with the immediately preceding words, just as in 2:19 and 3:13.

natural that the term *hope* is placed in a climactic position; just as it is natural that in I Cor. 13 *love* is stressed.

Paul thanks God for *the work* accomplished by these recent converts to the Christian religion. He does not immediately reveal what is meant by this *work*. It is probably best not to restrict the meaning too rigidly. Caring for the sick, comforting the dying, instructing the ignorant, all this and much more occurs to the mind. Yet, in view of verses 6-10 of this chapter, it would seem that the apostle (and those with him) is thinking especially of the work of making propaganda for the gospel, and doing this even in the midst of bitter persecution. This, indeed, was work *resulting from faith*. In fact, it was exertion (labor) *prompted by love*. Had there been no love in return for the love of which they were the objects, these Thessalonians would never have been able to accomplish what they did. That they did accomplish the almost unbelievable will be pointed out in connection with verses 6-10.

When we speak of love-labor, we are prone to look only for deeds that can be seen, weighed, and measured. But *suffering* for the name and sake of Christ also falls under the heading of "exertion prompted by love." It implies *endurance*. A person who suffers such persecution is willing, if need be, to *remain under* (cf. the verb ὑπομένω) stress and strain, *confidently expecting* that *in the very presence of the God who will one day judge all men* he will find a safe shelter with his *Lord Jesus Christ* (on this designation see 1:1); in other words, his endurance is "inspired by hope in our Lord Jesus Christ in the presence of our God and Father." (On God the Father — here *our God and Father* — see 1:1.)

4. knowing, brothers beloved by God, your election . . .

In the final analysis, the reason for the joy and gratitude which fill the hearts of the missionaries is the fact that they know that (speaking by and large) the members of the Thessalonian church are God's *chosen* ones. Paul, Silas, and Timothy actually *know* this. They *know* (knowing εἰδότες, is the participle used) it because the facts speak so clearly that the conclusion is inevitable, direct, immediate. This passage is a most forceful repudiation of the position of those who say that one can never really know whether he or whether anybody else is included in God's eternal decree of election. The missionaries had become acquainted with the readers in the recent past. After a very brief stay among them, they had been forced to move on. Nevertheless, they do not hesitate to state, "The ultimate reason why thanksgiving fills our hearts is that *we know* that you were chosen (from eternity)." [36]

---

[36] Excellent are the practical remarks with reference to this in the book by H. Veldkamp, *In De Schemering Van Christus' Wederkomst*, Kampen, 1928, pp. 20-25.

The noun *election* also occurs in the following passages of Paul's epistles: Rom. 9:11; 11:5, 7, 28 (cf. II Peter 1:10).

The apostle, who was himself an "elect vessel" (Acts 9:15), dwells on the theme of sovereign election in such passages as the following (in addition to those already mentioned): Rom. 8:33; 11:29; 16:13; I Cor. 1:27, 28; Eph. 1:4-6; Col. 3:12-17; II Tim. 2:10, 19; Titus 1:1. There are several additional passages which, though not containing the word *elect,* are of value for the study of this subject; e.g., Rom. 8:28-30; I Cor. 4:7; Eph. 2:8; Phil. 4:3.[37]

On the basis of all these passages, Paul's teaching on election can be summarized as follows:

(1) It (election) is from eternity (Eph. 1:4, 5).

(2) It becomes evident in life (I Thess. 1:4). This does not mean that anyone has the right to assign his neighbor to hell or to call him a reprobate: *God* sees the heart; *we* do not. Also, *we* are not infallibly inspired, as Paul's teaching was. There may be a death-bed conversion.

(3) It is sovereign and unconditional; that is, it is not conditioned on foreseen works or foreseen faith (I Cor. 1:27, 28; 4:7; Eph. 1:4; 2:8). See also *Canons of Dort,* I, ix, x.

(4) It is just (Rom. 9:14, 15).

(5) It is not limited to Gentiles; in every age a remnant of the Jews is also included (Rom. 11:5).

(6) It is immutable and effectual; the elect actually reach heaven at last. They obtain salvation (Rom. 11:7). God's "chain" cannot be broken (Rom. 8:28-30; cf. 11:29; II Tim. 2:19).

(7) It affects life in all its phases, is not abstract. Although election belongs to God's decree from eternity, it becomes a dynamic force in the hearts and lives of God's children. That is clearly also the meaning here in I Thess. 1:4; see verses 5-10. It produces such fruits as adoption as sons, calling, faith, justification, etc. (Rom. 8:28-30, 33; Eph. 1:4, 5; Titus 1:1). *The proposition: "If a man has been elected, he will be saved regardless of how he lives (e.g., whether or not he believes in Christ, whether or not he gives evidence of possessing the fruits of the Holy Spirit)," is wicked and absurd. No true and sane believer of any denomination, whether he be Methodist, Baptist, Calvinist, Lutheran, or whether he belongs to any other denomination or religious group, will ever subscribe to it. Everyone should read and reread the beautiful description of the truly elect person which is found in Col. 3:12-17.*

---

[37] See also N.T.C. on John 15:19; H. Bavinck, *The Doctrine Of God* (translated by W. Hendriksen), Grand Rapids, Mich., 1951, pp. 337-407; and L. Berkhof, *Systematic Theology,* Grand Rapids, Mich., 1949, pp. 109-125. The term *elect* does not always refer to the divine decree; see Luke 10:42; John 6:70; Acts 1:24; 6:5, cf. Deut. 4:37; 7:6-8; I Sam. 10:24, etc.

(8) It concerns individuals (Rom. 16:13; Phil. 4:3; cf. Acts 9:15).

(9) It comprehends these individuals "in Christ," sothat they are definitely viewed as one body (Eph. 1:4; II Tim. 2:10).

(10) It is an election not only unto salvation but definitely also (as a link in the chain) unto service (Col. 3:12-17; cf. Acts 9:15, 16).

(11) It is taught not only by Paul, but also by Jesus himself. See N.T.C. on John 6:39; 10:11, 14, 28; 17:2, 9, 11, 24.

(12) It has as its final aim God's glory, and it is the work of his delight (Eph. 1:4-6).

The elect are called "brothers beloved by God." Paul loves the designation *brothers,* using it again and again (I Thess. 1:4; 2:1, 9, 14, 17; 3:7; 4:1, 10, 13; 5:1, 4, 12, 14, 25, 26, 27; II Thess. 1:3; 2:1, 13, 15; 3:1, 6, 13; and many times in the other epistles). In the present instance he adds the beautiful description "beloved of God" (cf. II Thess. 2:13; further also Rom. 1:7; 11:28; 12:19; 16:8, 9, 12; I Cor. 4:14, 17, etc.). Because of its combination with the word "of God" it would seem probable that the deepest and fullest sense must be ascribed to the participle (pl. mascul., perfect passive) *beloved.* See N.T.C. on John 21:15-17. This love of God extends backward to eternity, as the preceding context clearly implies. It also extends forward and is still continuing (as is implied in the tense of the participle). No one can ever separate believers from the love of God in Christ. Moreover, as the parallel passages indicate, *God's* beloved ones are also *Paul's* (and Silas' and Timothy's) beloved ones.

5. But how is it to be explained that the missionaries have a right to be so convinced about the fact that these Thessalonians are God's elect? The reason is given in the verses which follow, which should be considered as a unit (verses 5-10); to begin with: **inasmuch as our gospel did not come to y o u in words only but also in power and in the Holy Spirit and full assurance.**

The meaning is: "that y o u were chosen (elected) we know from the fact that our gospel did not come to y o u in words only," etc.

As we see it, the sense of the entire passage (verses 5-10) can be summarized as follows: "Do not be deceived by the enemies of the faith who are trying, by means of an attack on our integrity, to undermine y o u r faith and y o u r assurance of salvation. Our behavior among y o u was proof of our integrity and of the reliability of our message. Y o u r own joyful acceptance of the gospel which we preached, sothat y o u began to spread the news everywhere, and turned away from those idols of y o u r s to serve the living God and to await his Son from heaven, clearly indicate that what happened (and is happening) in Thessalonica was (is) wrought by the Holy Spirit and was (is) the fruit of election. Any doubt about the genuine character of y o u r faith was removed by Timothy. (See on 3:5.) So continue stedfastly."

In order to confirm the faith of the Thessalonians Paul, accordingly, does two things: he shows:

a. that the message which they had received and the messengers who brought it could be trusted. See verse 5.

b. that the manner in which they received it was proof of the operation of the Spirit of God. See verses 6-10.

Just as at Corinth (I Cor. 2:4), where Paul was carrying on his missionary activity while he was writing this letter, so also at Thessalonica, he was not interested in mere *words* (I Cor. 2:4) but in a genuine demonstration of the Spirit. To this the people addressed will readily testify. The original has the singular — "in *word,* in a mere *discourse.*" There was spiritual *dynamite* (δύναμις) in the message, enough dynamite to demolish the idol-gods (verse 9). In fact, the dynamite *of the Spirit* was of a different kind than physical dynamite, for whereas the latter is limited to *de*structive operations, this dynamite was also *con*structive ("to serve God, the living and real One," etc.). Notice how the concepts *Spirit* and *power* go together here, as so often (see Rom. 1:4; 15:13, 19; I Cor. 2:4; Gal. 3:5; and cf. Rom. 1:4, II Tim. 1:7, 8). This is in accordance with Christ's promise (Acts 1:8. Cf. also Luke 1:17, 35; 4:14; Acts 10:38). The reason why there was such power in the message was because when *Paul* (and those associated with him) spoke, *God* was speaking. This also accounts for the fact that the missionaries had spoken *with full assurance* (a word — used also in Col. 2:2; Heb. 6:11; 10:22; cf. the verb in Luke 1:1; Rom. 4:21; 14:5; Col. 4:12; II Tim. 4:5, 17 — which without even the addition of an article is linked immediately with *the Holy Spirit,* for the full assurance is an immediate effect of the Spirit's presence and power in the hearts of the ambassadors). Because of the immediately preceding and the immediately following context, it would seem that those commentators are wrong who confine this assurance to *the Thessalonians.* The reference here is (at least primarily) to the full assurance *of the missionaries* as they spoke the word.

Paul appeals to the memory of those addressed when he adds: **just as y o u (well) know what kind of men we became among y o u for y o u r sake.** All kinds of traveling philosophers were roving about in the world of that day. They plied their trade for their own sake, in their own interest. Paul, Silas, and Timothy were different. They carried on their difficult tasks for the sake of the people, that they might be saved. In that spirit and frame of mind they had entered Thessalonica, and the experiences which they had endured there had added to their spiritual vigor (hence, it is not at all necessary to weaken the sense of the verb "became"). The obverse side of the events that had recently transpired at Thessalonica (the side which shows how the good news had affected *the Thessalonians*) is shown in the verses which follow.

6, 7. And y o u became imitators of us and of the Lord.

The genuine character of the religious experience of the Thessalonians is portrayed here. They had become *imitators* (μιμηταί, our word *mimickers* is from the same root), not merely *talkers*. Cf. I Thess. 2:14; then also I Cor. 4:16; 11:1; Eph. 5:1; Heb. 6:12. Paul is not afraid to say, "Y o u must be imitators *of me*" (I Cor. 4:16). He dares to say this because, by sovereign grace, he is able to add, ". . . as I also am *of Christ*" (I Cor. 11:1). And those who are imitators of Paul and of Christ are also imitators *of God* (Eph. 5:1). Thus the arrow points back from Paul (and his associates), to Christ, to God. That is the logical order. That is also why here in I Thess. 1:6 "of us" precedes "of the Lord." The missionaries had been physically present with them. Even before any conversion had taken place, the earnestness, devotion, enthusiasm, willingness to suffer for Christ, etc., of the missionaries could be seen and watched. These missionaries, in turn, pointed to and spoke about *the Lord* (see on I Thess. 1:1 for the title).

Now it is not possible to imitate Christ in every respect. For example, in his capacity as the Savior of men he cannot be imitated. But *the third of comparison* (the point with reference to which both the missionaries and the Christ who commissioned them can be imitated) is clearly stated in the words: **when amid great tribulation y o u welcomed the word with joy imparted by the Holy Spirit.** Rejoicing amid *tribulation* (for the meaning of the term see N.T.C. on John 16:33) was something about which Paul and Silas could tell a very touching story! And the story had reference to an event that had occurred just before the missionaries had wended their way toward Thessalonica. At Philippi they had been cast into a dungeon, their feet fastened in the stocks. But about midnight Paul and Silas had been singing hymns to God! And this is only one illustration of their rejoicing amid tribulation. Jesus, too, had rejoiced in the midst of tribulation. See N.T.C. on John 12:20-36 and on 16:33. Hence, when amid similar pressure (see p. 9) those who are here addressed had *welcomed the word* (the gospel of salvation) with Spirit-wrought joy, they had given unmistakable evidence of being imitators of the missionaries and of Christ himself. (In this connection read the beautiful passage: Acts 5:41.) They had proved themselves to be *God's elect*. The connection with I Thess. 1:4 must not be lost sight of.

Now *imitators* become *examples*. There is a kind of *circle* here: first, God performs his works on earth: the Father elects; the Son (and also his special ambassadors) gives an example of rejoicing amid suffering; the Holy Spirit imparts joy. Then the Thessalonians believe, welcome the word, become imitators. They, in turn, carry the good news to others, whose praises (after also *they* have experienced the great change) glorify God in heaven. Thus the circle has been completed. The Thessalonians, as it were, stand in the middle: the word of the Lord came to them, and they, having accepted it by faith, have sounded it forth sothat others also might hear and believe. That this is the right interpretation is shown by what follows immediately: **sothat y o u became an example to all the believers in Macedonia and in Achaia.** One who is not an *imitator* cannot become an *example* (τύπος, derived from τύπτω; hence, the *mark* of a blow, the *figure* made by it; see N.T.C. on John 2:25; further, *image*, Acts 7:43; *mould*, Acts 23:25; and thus *model* or *pattern* for imitation, Acts 7:44; Phil. 3:17). To all believers in the two Roman provinces of *Macedonia* (here, besides Thessalonica itself, was Philippi and Berea) and *Achaia* (here was Athens and Corinth) the Thessalonian converts had become an example. The reason, in exact correspondence with the preceding, is set forth in the following words:

8. For, from y o u the word of the Lord has echoed forth. We repeat what was said in connection with verses 6 and 7: the Thessalonians stood in the middle. They are here compared to a parabolic arch or a sounding-board which re-inforces sounds and causes them to travel in various directions. The arch or the sounding-board does not of itself create the sounds. It occupies a middle-position, receiving them, re-inforcing them, and sending them on. Thus also the word of the Lord, having been received by those people in Thessalonica who are here addressed, had been re-inforced by their own joyful experience in accepting it, and, thus strengthened, had been *echoed* forth (the verb is ἐξήχηται; our word *echo* is related to it), and this **not only in Macedonia and Achaia** [38] **but in every place y o u r faith toward God has gone forth, sothat it is not necessary for us to say anything.** When Paul says, "in every place," he must mean "also in regions outside of Macedonia and Achaia"; hence, probably also *at least* in Palestine, Syria, and Asia Minor. It should be borne in mind that the populous trading-center, Thessalonica, was so located (on the Egnatian Highway, thus linking the East with the West, and at the head of the Thermaic Gulf, thus connecting it with harbors all over the then-known world) that news could spread very quickly to regions far and near. All the believers at Thessalonica had to do was avail themselves of the opportunities which their strategic location afforded. Now the point certainly is not that merely the rumor with reference to the great change at Thessalonica had been spreading, but rather that the believers there, in the enthusiasm of a great discovery, actively propagated their "faith toward God." The preposition *toward* (πρός; see also N.T.C. on John 1:1) prepares us for the prepo-

---

[38] Perhaps here viewed as a unit; we might say: *Greece,* but the correct reading is somewhat uncertain: it cannot be established with certainty whether the definite article here in verse 8 also precedes Achaia.

sition *from* in the next verse: they had turned *from* idols, *toward* God. There had been a complete turn-about in the direction of their lives.

But how did *Paul* know all this? It must be assumed that he had by this time received messages from these various centers. That is not strange at all. Good highways connected the cities of the Roman world, and travel, though slow compared to our own day and age, was not nearly as retarded as some commentators (who reject Thessalonians because of the facts related here in verses 7-10) seem to think. Paul naturally was anxious to relate to all who came to him what great things God had accomplished in Thessalonica. But before he could even get started, the visitors were telling him what they had heard! Well, Paul did not mind that at all. He rather enjoyed it, as is clear from the words:

9. for they themselves are reporting about us, what kind of entering in we had among y o u, and how y o u turned to God from those idols (of y o u r s), to serve God, the living and real One.

Paul and his companions do not need to report. People *are doing* (note present continuative tense) this for them. The missionaries hear the report. Others also hear it. The missionaries hear that others hear it. It is the great news about Paul, Silas, and Timothy ("about *us*") and what God has accomplished through them. The tidings, coming from all the regions which had been penetrated by the faith of the Thessalonians, are spreading far and wide.

Now this report, circulated from mouth to mouth, contains two main topics, the second of which is again divided into two subordinate news-items, as follows:

A. "Paul, Silas, and Timothy entered in among the Thessalonians in such and such a manner." (As a result, through the operation of the Spirit)

B. "The Thessalonians turned to God from *the* idols" (meaning: from those idols of theirs):

1 "to serve a God living and real

         and

2 "to await his Son out of the heavens, whom he raised from the dead, Jesus, who rescues us from the wrath to come."

Various corroborative details are undoubtedly added: there is amplification and clarification.

Naturally, Paul in writing *to the Thessalonians* changes the direct to the indirect form of discourse: in the present instance the pronoun "they" becomes "we," "the Thessalonians" (or something similar) becomes "y o u," and there is undoubtedly abbreviation. Hence, we read:

A. ". . . *how* we entered in among y o u, and

B. *"how* y o u turned to God from the idols:

1 "to serve a God living and real
   and
2 "to await his Son from heaven, whom he raised from the dead, Jesus,
who rescues us from the wrath to come."

The "entering in" (εἴσοδος also 2:1; cf. Acts 13:24; Heb. 10:19; II Peter
1:11) of which Paul speaks must not be viewed as a mere "introduction,"
as is done by some ("how we were introduced to y o u"). It has reference
to whatever pertained to the coming of the missionaries to Thessalonica
and to their work in and outside of the synagogue. The commentary is
supplied by Paul himself in I Thess. 1:5 and 2:1-12; see on these verses.
What Paul means, therefore, is this: "The charges that are being leveled
against us by base opponents are vain. Our way of operating when we
came to y o u and worked among y o u has become a matter of public
knowledge. Y o u yourselves remember it, and others far and wide have
heard about it."

And how y o u turned. A very significant verb is used (ἐπεστρέψατε from
ἐπιστρέφω): *to turn,* often *to return,* but here obviously not the latter but the
former. The readers (many of whom must have been Gentiles, for they
had been worshipping idols) had experienced a real, inner change which
had become outwardly manifest: their whole active life was now moving in
the opposite direction: *away from* (ἀπό) idols, *to* (πρός; see N.T.C. on John
1:1) God.[39]

When God *converts* a man, he changes the entire person, not only *the
emotions,* sothat one *regrets* his former manner of life (cf. the idea which
predominates in the verb μεταμέλομαι), but also *the mind and will,* with
respect to which he experiences a complete change-over (cf. the thought
that is placed in the foreground by μετάνοια [40]), and all of this becomes
apparent in his *outward conduct* (this being the main import of the verb
used here in I Thess. 1:9).

It was from *the*[41] *idols* (both the images themselves and the deities

[39] For the various terms used in Scripture to indicate *conversion,* and a discussion
of their meaning, see L. Berkhof, *Systematic Theology,* Grand Rapids, Mich., 1949,
pp. 480-492; R. C. Trench, *Synonyms of the New Testament,* Grand Rapids, Mich.,
1948 (reprint), par. lxix. On the synonym μετάνοια see especially W. D. Chamber-
lain, *The Meaning of Repentance,* Philadelphia, 1943.
[40] Though mind and will are in the foreground when μετάνοια is used, the emotions
are not excluded: complete "transformation" or "conversion" is meant. The word
looks forward as well as backward; hence, "repentance," a term which merely looks
backward, is not the proper translation, and, of course, "penance" is even worse.
An excellent study-passage in this connection is II Cor. 7:8-10, in the original.
[41] Generic use of the article. This comprehends the class as a single whole, definitely present to the mind of the writer (and, of course, to the mind of the reader),
especially from the point of view of this or that characteristic: the idols in all their
helplessness! In such a case the article should not be omitted in the translation
(hence not: "from idols"), for if this is done one loses the flavor of the original. I
would suggest that in translating such a generic article, one either simply retain it

whom they represented) that the Thessalonians had turned away. The apostle and his companions had observed this idol-worship, and knew all about it. These idols were merely "vain things" (see the parallel passage, Acts 14:15). They were dead; hence, totally unable to render any assistance to anyone in time of need.

Now it must have been a momentous change, this turning away from the idols. It is not easy to reject and eject gods which one has worshipped from the days of childhood, and which by one's ancestors, from hoary antiquity, have always been considered very real, sothat their names and individual peculiarities have become household-words. It amounts to nothing less than a religious revolution. The enemies were right when they said that the missionaries were men who "turned the world upside down." Idol-worship affected life in all its phases. And we can well imagine that especially to the Thessalonians these deities had seemed very real, for it must be borne in mind that Mt. Olympus, whose celebrated summit was considered the home of the gods, was close by, only about fifty miles to the S.W. And according to tradition, when Zeus shook his ambrosial curls, that mighty mountain trembled!

Nevertheless, as a result of the operation of God's grace whereby the message was applied to the hearts, the eyes of the Thessalonians had been opened, sothat they saw that their idols were vanities. They had turned from them to *a God living and real*. Here the true God is not so much pointed out as described. All the emphasis is on his character, which is the very opposite of the idols. *They* are dead, *he* is living. *They* are unreal, *he* is real, genuine. *They* are unable to help, he is almighty and eager to help. To this God the Thessalonians have turned *to serve* him continually, submitting themselves to him as completely as does a slave to his master, nay *far more completely* and *far more willingly*.[42]

Now, turning to a God living and real implies turning to his only-begotten Son and salvation through him; hence, there follows:

10. and to await his Son out of the heavens. It seems that it was especially the teaching with reference to Christ's return upon the clouds of

---

in English (hence, "the idols") or else — in order to bring out its force even more clearly — choose as its English equivalent the demonstrative (hence *"those idols* which y o u used to serve," or simply "those idols of y o u r s"). Cf. a similar use of the article in Matt. 8:20 ("the foxes"), and with a noun in the sing. Luke 10:7 ("the laborer"); I Tim. 3:2 ("the overseer or bishop"). In the use of the generic article (as well as the article with abstract nouns) German and Dutch usage more nearly approaches the Greek than does English usage. Here in I Thess. 1:9 the German "von den Abgöttern" and the Dutch "van de afgoden" is very normal.
[42] For that reason I do not favor the translation *to be slaves of*. Although that rendering does bring out the idea of complete submission, it clashes with the voluntary and joyful character of the worship that is rendered to God. See also N.T.C. on John 15:15.

heaven that had captivated the minds and hearts of the readers. *As they saw it — and rightly so — a man is not truly converted (or "turned," verse 9) unless he glories in this doctrine and shows its force in his life.* For them true conversion implied (at least) these two things: a. turning away from the idols, and b. turning to God and to his Son who is coming *out of the heavens* (cf. Eph. 4:10 for the plural; and for the idea of the descent see 4:16; II Thess. 1:7; then also Dan. 7:1; Matt. 24:30; 25:31-46; 26:64; Acts 3:21; and Rev. 1:7).

From the heaven of heavens (where in a special sense dwells God surrounded by the redeemed and the angels), and the starry heaven, and the heaven of the clouds, Jesus will descend to take into his embrace his people. This coming they are *awaiting*. The force of the verb *to await* must not be lost sight of. It means *to look forward to with patience and confidence*. This *awaiting* means far more than merely *saying*, "I believe in Jesus Christ, who ascended into heaven, and from thence he shall come to judge the living and the dead." It implies (both in Greek and in English) *being ready* for his return. When you *await* a visitor, you have prepared everything for his coming. You have arranged the guest-room, the program of activities, your time and your other duties, and all this in such a manner that the visitor will feel perfectly at home. So also, awaiting the very *Son of God* (see N.T.C. on John 1:14) who is coming out of the heavens implies the sanctified heart and life.

This Son of God who is coming out of the heavens is none other than the "historical" Jesus (see on 1:1), the very One whom God actually and physically raised from the dead (cf. Rom. 4:24, 25; 8:11; I Cor. 15:15; Gal. 1:1; Eph. 1:20; Col. 2:12; II Tim. 2:8; and cf. N.T.C. on John 20:1-10).

The thought of his coming does not spell terror for the believer. Rather, "the lord is at hand . . . in nothing be anxious!" (Phil. 4:5, 6), for it is this Jesus **who rescues** (is rescuing) **us from the wrath to come** (the coming wrath). Jesus, *the Savior* (see on 1:1) is ever true to his name: he *saves, rescues*. He does not rescue everybody but *us* (Paul, Silas, Timothy, believers at Thessalonica, all the elect).

From *the settled indignation* (ὀργή) which by nature rests on the sinner (Eph. 2:3), and which by his idolatry and immorality and especially (in the case of those who have heard the good news) by his rejection of the gospel he daily increases, and which will be revealed most fully in the coming day of judgment, Jesus delivers all those who embrace him by living faith. For the concept *wrath* see also N.T.C. on John 3:36. In II Thess. 1:5-12 (see on that passage) Paul amplifies the thought of 1:10.

The Synthesis is found at the end of chapter 2.

CHAPTER II

2 1 Indeed, y o u yourselves know, brothers, our entering in among y o u, that it was not empty-handed. 2 On the contrary, though we had previously suffered and had been shamefully treated at Philippi as y o u know, still by the help of our God we summoned courage to tell y o u the good news [43] of God with profound solicitude.[44] 3 For our appeal (does) not (spring) from delusion or from impurity nor (does it come) with deceit. 4 On the contrary, as we have been approved by God to be entrusted with the good news, so we are accustomed to tell it, as pleasing not men but God who tests our hearts. 5 Indeed, we never came with flattering speech, as y o u (well) know, or with a pretext for greed—God is witness! — 6 or seeking honor from men, whether from yourselves or from others, although we were in a position to make ourselves formidable as apostles of Christ. 7 But we were gentle in the midst of y o u, as when a nurse cherishes her own children: 8 so, being affectionately desirous of y o u, we gladly shared with y o u not only the gospel of God but also our own souls, because y o u had become very dear to us. 9 For y o u remember, brothers, our toil and hardship: by night and by day (we were) working at a trade, in order not to be a burden to any of y o u while we proclaimed to y o u the gospel of God. 10 Y o u (are) witness and (so is) God, how piously [45] and righteously and blamelessly we conducted ourselves in the estimation of y o u, believers; 11 just as y o u know how, like a father (dealing) with his own children (so we were) admonishing each and all of y o u, and encouraging and testifying 12 that y o u should live lives worthy of God, who calls y o u into his own kingdom and glory.

2:1-12

2:1. Indeed, y o u yourselves know, brothers, our entering in among y o u, that it was not empty-handed.

A careful study of Paul's Defence shows that the slander by means of which his enemies were trying to undermine the influence of his message amounted to this: "Paul and his associates are deluded individuals who for selfish reasons and with trickery are trying to exploit the people." For

---

[43] We generally speak of "proclaiming (or preaching) the gospel" and of "telling good news." As the verb which is used here in the original is *telling* rather than *proclaiming*, I have here given as the English equivalent: to tell y o u the good news.
[44] Or "with deep anxiety (concern)" or "with strenuous exertion." Not, however, "in spite of heavy opposition."
[45] Or *holily*

the sake of the gospel this charge had to be answered, in order that suspicion might be swept aside. The opponents knew very well what they were doing. They reasoned thus: "If we succeed in awakening distrust with respect to *the messengers, the message* will die a natural death." Accordingly, Paul had no choice: love for the gospel necessitated self-defence.

For the meaning of the expression "our entering in" see on 1:9. It is the apostle's contention that this entering in had not been *empty* (κενή). The question is, "Just what is meant by *empty?*" Does Paul mean, "Our entering in has not been *futile;* there were results"? Thus the term is explained by some. However, no one denied this. Every one knew that the work of the missionaries had borne fruit. Besides, if that should be the meaning here, it is very difficult to establish any connection between this verse and those which immediately follow. But the word used in the original may also mean *empty-handed;* e.g., "And they took him and beat him and sent him away empty-handed" (Mark 12:3; cf. Luke 1:53; 20:10, 11). According to this meaning of the word, what Paul is saying is this: "Far from aiming to take something away from y o u, we *brought* y o u something. When we came to y o u, our hands were not empty." We adopt this interpretation for the following reasons:

(1) It harmonizes beautifully with the preceding context; see 1:5: "our gospel did not come to y o u in words only but also in power and in the Holy Spirit and with full assurance." The message had not been empty: it was filled with divine meaning, being the good news which came from God. It was accompanied by power and the Holy Spirit, and it was presented with firm conviction.

(2) It also matches the following context, in which Paul stresses the fact that he (and his associates) had come to Thessalonica with the good news from God, with courage, and with real, deep-seated concern for the people. Truly, the hands of the missionaries had not been empty! They had something to bring, something to give away.

(3) It is in keeping with the general trend of Paul's defence against the malicious insinuations coming from the camp of the evil one. Throughout the apostle represents himself as one who did *not* come *to take* but *to give* (see especially 2:5, 8, 9). And what was true with respect to himself was true also with respect to Silas and Timothy.

Once this interpretation of verse 1 is adopted, what follows is not difficult:

2. On the contrary, though we had previously suffered and had been shamefully treated at Philippi as y o u know, still by the help of God we summoned courage to tell y o u the good news of God with profound solicitude.

For the treatment which the missionaries (especially Paul and Silas) had received at Philippi read Acts 16:11-40; also see on 1:6, 7. We do not share the view of those who think that when Paul spoke of having been *shamefully treated* (insulted, abused), he was referring only to the fact that he and Silas, uncondemned men, *had been beaten publicly though they were Roman citizens.* That was *part* of the shameful treatment but not all of it: the men — Roman citizens, yes; apostles of Jesus Christ besides! — had been arrested, dragged into the market-place before the rulers, slandered, robbed of their clothing, thrown into a prison with their feet made fast in the stocks, etc. The verb employed in the original (study its use in Acts 14:5; then Matt. 22:6 and Luke 18:32) is comprehensive enough in meaning to include *all* this insolent treatment to which the missionaries had been exposed and which had caused them much suffering.

Nevertheless (i.e., in spite of this suffering and shameful treatment), *by virtue of their union with God* (ἐν τῷ θεῷ), hence, by his help, they had summoned courage [46] to continue the work. They had done what Jesus had enjoined, "When they persecute y o u in this city, flee into the next" (Matt. 10:23). Thus a journey of a hundred miles had brought them to Thessalonica. Their interest in this city did not spring from any selfish motive. They desired most eagerly to téll, in plain language and in a forthright manner, the good news of God, uttering (note the verb λαλῆσαι) the message which God himself had given them, and doing this with profound solicitude (deep anxiety) for the people involved. The phrase ἐν πολλῷ ἀγῶνι has been interpreted variously, as follows:

a. "in spite of heavy opposition" (cf. A.V. "with much contention"; A.R.V. "in much conflict," which may also be linked with b.)

b. "in great anguish"

c. "with strenuous exertion"

d. "with profound solicitude (deep concern or anxiety)"

The term (ἀγών) refers first to a gathering, especially for games or contests; then the contest itself, and finally the *agony* (cf. the Greek word), anguish, or anxiety that is connected with it, or also any kind of agony, anguish, or anxiety, concern or solicitude. Hence, viewed by itself (apart from the context) it could have any of the four meanings listed above. The context, however, seems to favor c. and d. (there is not much difference between these two). The *affectionate desire* or *yearning* of the missionaries for the people of Thessalonica is mentioned also in verse 8 (and see verse 11). Paul and his companions had exerted themselves to the utmost, as an athlete who is aiming for the prize, in order that they might do the will of God (2:4) and might win these people for whom they yearned so earnestly.

Now this profound solicitude or affectionate desire was, of course, the

---

[46] In this context the ingressive or inceptive aorist seems the most natural.

very opposite of the base selfishness of which their enemies accused them. Hence, Paul continues:

3. For our appeal (does) not (spring) from delusion or from impurity nor (does it come) with deceit.

The noun and the verb *appeal* (παράκλησις, παρακαλέω related to παράκλητος; see N.T.C. on John 14:16), basically a calling to one's side, can have various meanings: appeal or entreat(y), exhort(ation), encourage-(ment), comfort. The exact meaning depends on the context in each in-stance. Here *appeal* or *entreaty* (cf. the use of the verb in II Cor. 5:20), fits as well as any. It was the message by means of which the missionaries, clothed with authority from God and with yearning sympathy, had pleaded with the hearers to forsake their wicked ways and to turn to God in Christ.

Now in connection with this appeal, the slur from the side of the op-ponents probably amounted to this:

a. "Their appeal springs from error. They are self-deluded imposters."

b. "Their motives are not pure."

Did these opponents ascribe sexual uncleanliness to Paul, Silas, and Timothy? — Pagan religions were characterized by immorality — . Did they perhaps insinuate that it was strange that so many *women* were to be found among the converts? Cf. Acts 17:4. The context, however, does not point in that direction. Desire for *money* and a hankering after *honor,* rather than sexual abberation, seem to have been the vices of which they accused the missionaries.

c. "They use trickery (guile, deceit) to capture their audience." The world of that day was full of roaming "philosophers," jugglers, sorcerers, fakers, swindlers. In order to impress their audiences many tricks were used. See on II Thess. 2:9; then also Matt. 24:24; Rev. 13:14.

Now here in verse 3 Paul denies all three charges. Then he places the truth over against the lie. It is characteristic of Paul to employ this method of argumentation: direct refutation of the charge, followed by a positive assertion (see 1:5; 2:3, 4; 2:5 ff.).

Paul is his own best commentator. Notice:

"Our appeal does not spring from delusion (or *error*)." Commentary: "We have been approved by God to be entrusted with the good news" (verse 4).

". . . or from impurity" (impure motives). Commentary: "We never came with flattery . . . a disguise for greed . . . seeking honor from men" (verses 5, 6). The very opposite is the truth. Our motives were wholly unselfish: "being affectionately desirous of y o u, we gladly shared with y o u not only the gospel of God but also our own selves" (verse 8).

"nor (does it come) with deceit." Commentary: "Y o u (are) witnesses and (so is) God, how piously and righteously and blamelessly we conducted ourselves" (verse 10).

4. On the contrary, as we have been approved by God to be entrusted with the good news, so we are accustomed to tell it, as pleasing not men but God who tests our hearts.

Not error but truth, the good news that comes from God, had been the objective source of Paul's appeal to the Thessalonians. These three official ambassadors *had been approved* by God and therefore *stand approved* (the perfect of abiding result of a verb which in the present tense means *to test;* perfect tense, *to have been tested*, here: with favorable results; hence, *approved;* cf. II Macc. 4:3). For the divine approbation entrusting Paul, Silas, and Timothy with the gospel of salvation, the following passages come into consideration: Acts 9:15; 13:1-4; 15:40; 16:1, 2; I Tim. 1:2, 12, 18; 6:12, 20; II Tim. 1:5, 13, 14.

Now it was in strict accordance with God's directive, that these missionaries were always telling (note present continuative) the good news. Hence, their message was not an error, but truth springing from the highest source. And the motive in bringing it was not selfish — for instance, pleasing men in order to gain favor; cf. Gal. 1:10 — but most commendable: pleasing God (cf. 4:1; II Thess. 2:4), the One before whom nothing is hid, and who tests our hearts (see Jer. 17:10; then 11:20; Ps. 7:9; ·Ps. 139). The human eye cannot discern the inner motive of his fellowman, whether good or bad; hence, Paul, as it were, appeals to God's omniscience.

5, 6. Indeed, we never came with flattering speech, as y o u (well) know, or with a pretext for greed — God is witness! — or seeking honor from men, whether from yourselves or from others, although we were in a position to make ourselves formidable as apostles of Christ.

Not any impure but the purest possible motive had been the subjective source of the entreaty. To prove this, Paul permits the facts to speak for themselves. By saying, "as y o u (well) know," he appeals to the readers' memory of these facts. Had the motive been impure and selfish (see verse 3), the missionaries would have copied the charlatans who roamed the country. Like these quacks they too would have made use of flattery. And their message would have amounted to nothing more than *a pretext to cover up their greed.*[47] But with an appeal to God the writer of this

---

[47] It makes little difference whether "of greed" is viewed as objective genitive: *a pretext for greed* (to cover up greed) or as subjective genitive: *a pretext of greed* (produced by greed, used by greed as a cover-up). The resultant idea is about the same. The rendering *a cloke (cloak) of covetousness* (A.V.; A.R.V.; R.S.V.: *a cloak for greed*) is also excellent, though *pretext* (something that is woven *in front*) or *pretense* (something that is spread *in front*) — hence, *a disguise* — brings out more precisely the meaning of the prefix in the Greek word. Note also that while

epistle solemnly affirms that they have never made use of either flattery or disguise. Their aim, moreover, had never been to seek human fame (see N.T.C. on John 5:41), whether from the Thessalonians or from anybody else; and this in spite of the fact that they were in a position to make *weighty* claims with respect to themselves, being Christ's apostles (used in the broader sense) commissioned to represent him, and therefore invested with authority over life and doctrine. For *apostle* see N.T.C. on John 13:16; 20:21-23.

7. But we were gentle in the midst of y o u.

Over against *formidable* stands *gentle*.[48] The Thessalonians had discovered that these missionaries were affable, easy to speak to. They were mild, kind in their dealings. Paul's own commentary on this word *gentle* is found in verses 8, 9, 11, as well as in the remainder of verse 7: **as when a nurse cherishes her own children.** The sense, in all probability, is not "as when a nurse takes care of the children of her mistress," namely, the children that had been entrusted to the care of this nurse; but "as when a mother-nurse warms, fondles, cherishes the children that are *her very own* (because she gave birth to them)." This interpretation is in line with the more usual sense of the original for *her own*, with Paul's language elsewhere (Gal. 4:19), and with the immediate context (verse 11): the missionaries, far from trying to promote their own interests, had become both father and mother to the Thessalonians! Their love had reached a glorious climax of tenderheartedness, as is clear from the words which follow:

8. so, being affectionately desirous of y o u, we gladly shared with y o u not only the gospel of God but also our own souls.

What a powerful combination: here is the true gospel combined with the most affectionate presentation! And all this in the service of the Holy Spirit! How then can it cause surprise that these missionaries had been so successful?

It is probably impossible (except for the spacing of the letters of the pronoun) to improve on the rendering "being affectionately desirous of you" (thus A.V., taken over by A.R.V., and retained even by R.S.V.). Wy-

---

the older Dutch rendering is *bedeksel* (i.e., cloak or cover), the new translation, Amsterdam, 1951, has *voorwendsel* (pretext).

[48] This is the correct word, not *infants*, though that has considerable textual support. But the change from *gentle* to *infants* (the difference is just one letter in the original: ἤπιοι to νήπιοι) may have arisen from the fact that *gentle* is rare (used in the New Testament only here and in II Tim. 2:24. See also M.M., p. 281). This is better than to say (with those who favor the reading *infants*) that the first letter of νήπιοι was omitted by scribal error because the same letter ends the preceding word. After all, the context very definitely argues for *gentle: gentle* stands over against "in weight" (*formidable, weighty*); it also matches the description which immediately follows: "as when a nurse cherishes her own children."

clif translates: "desirynge you with greet loue." Others: "yearning for (or yearning after) you." The word used in the original occurs only here in the New Testament. Cf. its use in Job 3:21: the bitter in soul "long for" death. In a sepulchral inscription the sorrowing parents are described as "greatly desiring their son." [49]

It is very well possible that there is a bit of irony in this expression, as if Paul wanted to say, "Those who slander us are saying that we were out to get y o u; well, they are right, we were indeed yearning for y o u, but the purpose was not to take something from y o u but to share something with y o u." And that something consisted of nothing less than these two treasures: *the gospel of God and our very souls* (or perhaps *selves* as in John 10:11; see N.T.C. on that passage), our talents, time, energies; see on the next verse; and all this **because y o u had become very dear to us.** Paul, Silas, and Timothy have a vivid recollection of their work in Thessalonica. All those scenes of joyful acceptance of the good news, and this in spite of bitter persecution, pass in review once more. They recall how close had been the fellowship and how the bond between themselves and these people had become more and more strong and enduring. These believers who were God's beloved had also become very dear to God's special envoys. An appeal is made to their own memory:

9. For y o u remember, brothers, our toil and hardship: by night and by day (we were) working at a trade (or "working for a living"), in order not to be a burden to any of y o u while we proclaimed to y o u the gospel of God.

The trend of the connection between this passage and what precedes is: "What we have just now affirmed with respect to the fact that we were not trying to receive anything from y o u (see verse 5 above) but rather to impart something to y o u, who had become very dear to us (see verse 8), is true, *for* our toil and hardship in order not to burden any of y o u while we were with y o u proves it."

The word of endearment *brothers* is very fitting especially in the present connection: Paul, Silas, and Timothy had placed themselves on one level with the laborers of Thessalonica: they all worked for a living! See also on I Thess. 1:4. Yet, *more* is implied: the bond is spiritual! They are brothers *in Christ!* The expression *toil and hardship* — or "toil and moil" (the words used in the original rhyme: κόπος — μόχθος) — refers not so much to the labor and weariness connected with tent-making as to the entire thought expressed in the sentence, namely, that the missionaries had been working by night and by day [50] (part of the night, part of the day; note the geni-

---

[49] See ὁμείρομαι in M.M., p. 447. Cf. the use of the word in Symm. Ps. 62:2.
[50] Night and day (instead of day and night) is the order also in 3:10; II Thess. 3:8; I Tim. 5:5; II Tim. 1:3; cf. Jer. 14:17; contrast 16:13.

tive), and had been preaching besides! It must have been very hard, indeed, to find time for all this, and not to break down under the load. Yet, for the sake of the gospel of God and out of love for the Thessalonians, most of whom were ordinary laborers, the burden had been gladly borne. Note: "the gospel *of God.*" Had it been *from men,* for example from traveling "philosophers," the Thessalonians would not have been treated with such consideration.

Paul and his companions must have reflected very carefully on the question, "Shall we accept financial remuneration for the work of bringing the gospel; particularly, shall we accept it from the converts themselves?" Paul's stand may be summarized in the following ten propositions:

(1) Titus 1:11: He definitely does not want to give any occasion for being placed in a class with "vain talkers" who are interested in "filthy lucre."

(2) I Cor. 9:6-15: He, nevertheless, emphatically asserts *the right* to receive remuneration from the church for performing spiritual work, and to receive it even from the converts themselves (see especially verse 11).

Nevertheless, as far as the latter group is concerned (the converts), *he has decided not to make use of that right* (see verse 15).

(3) Acts 20:33: He will now be able to say, "I coveted no man's silver, gold, or apparel."

(4) II Cor. 11:8: He does at times "take wages" from already established churches, while he is working in a new field.

(5) Phil. 4:10-20: He accepts gifts from an already established church (Philippi).

(6) Acts 20:34, 35; I Thess. 2:9 and II Thess. 3:8: Most of all, he provides for his own needs (and even for the needs of others) by laboring with his own hands.

(7) Acts 18:3: He is tent-maker by trade.

(8) I Cor. 6:12; 8:9, 13; 9:12; 10:23: The principle on which he insists again and again (applying it to various questions) is this: All things are lawful, but not all things are helpful: there are a good many things which I have a right to do, but that does not mean that I should therefore do them! The real question is always: "What course of action will be most useful in promoting the work of the kingdom and the glory of God?"

(9) II Cor. 11:7: Even so, in spite of this carefully worked out plan with respect to work and wages, he does not escape criticism. If he takes money, or if his enemies suspect that he does, they are ready to charge him with selfishness, greed; if he does not, they accuse him of making a show of his humility.

(10) I Cor. 4:12; Eph. 4:28; I Thess. 2:9; II Thess. 3:8, 10: He (and the Holy Spirit through him!) dignifies labor, and proclaims the great principle: "If any man will not work neither let him eat." Now in his day

and age, laboring with the hands is not always and everywhere being held in honor. Cicero (Roman orator and writer, 106-43 B. C.) states that the "general opinion" was as follows:

"The callings of hired laborers, and of all that are paid for their mere work and not for their skill, are unworthy of a free man and vulgar; for their wages are given for menial service. . . . All mechanics are engaged in vulgar business; for a workshop can have nothing respectable about it. . . . Commerce, if on a small scale, is to be regarded as vulgar; but if large and rich . . . it is not so very discreditable" (*De Officiis* I. xlii).

In sharp contrast with all this stands the gospel of God, the teaching of Paul and his companions!

10. Y o u (are) witnesses and (so is) God, how piously and righteously and blamelessly we conducted ourselves in the estimation of y o u, believers.

The writers appeal to *the believers* to bear witness that in the latter's own estimation — had some of them openly expressed it on occasion? — Paul and Silas and Timothy had *carried on their work* (ἐργαζόμενοι) among them with devotion to God (*piously, holily,* as men separated unto God and his service), ever striving to do what is *right* according to his law; hence, in an *irreproachable* manner. But inasmuch as man's judgment is, after all, fallible, — for, "Man looks on the outward appearance, but Jehovah looks on the heart" — the statement, "*Y o u* are witnesses," is immediately followed by: "and (so is) *God.*"

The idea here begun is amplified in verses 11, 12:

11, 12. just as y o u know how, like a father (dealing) with his own children, (so we were) admonishing each and all of y o u, and encouraging and testifying that y o u should live lives worthy of God, who calls y o u into his own kingdom and glory.[51]

---

[51] The attempts at constructing this difficult sentence are legion. The one which looks the best to us is as follows:

(1) Literal translation: "just as y o u know how each one of y o u as a father his own children admonishing y o u and encouraging and testifying for y o u to walk worthy of God, the One calling y o u into his own kingdom and glory."

(2) The statement beginning with "just as y o u know" runs parallel with the one beginning with "y o u are witness and (so is) God" (verse 10); hence, "how each one of y o u" is co-ordinate in thought with "how piously," etc. The thought with reference to the holy, righteous, and blameless manner in which these three had carried on their work (verse 10) is elaborated in the statement that they had dealt with the Thessalonians as does a father with his children, admonishing them, encouraging and testifying that they should live lives worthy of God, etc.

(3) The participles *admonishing, encouraging, and testifying* should be combined with the imperfect of the verb *to be* (understood), forming the imperfect periphrastic. The use of the periphrastic has the effect of making the sentence more vivid, as if to say, "We *were doing* so and so; don't y o u remember?" The omission

Paul, Silas, and Timothy, while in Thessalonica, had loved these people like a mother loves and cherishes her own children (verse 7), and had admonished them as does a father. As Bengal points out, they had *admonished* them so that they would act *freely, encouraged* them, sothat they would act *gladly,* and *testified,* sothat they would act *reverently* (with a proper sense of respect for the will of God as expressed in his Word; hence, with fear). They had dealt with *each one of them,* having done individual pastoral work among them. (The stay in Thessalonica must have lasted more than three weeks.) They had also dealt with *all* of them as a group, addressing them collectively, teaching them, explaining the Word of God to them, and exhorting them to accept it by faith and to live in accordance with it.[52] They had figured with the immaturity of these people, and had loved them dearly. Both of these ideas (immaturity, love) are implied in the term *children.*

Now the object of all this fatherly exhortation was that the readers would *walk* (pass their lives) in a manner *worthy of* (in harmony with) their relation to God, who, by means of preaching and pastoral care, was calling them into that *future realm* (cf. II Thess. 1:5; I Cor. 6:9, 10; Gal. 5:21; Eph. 5:5; II Tim. 4:1, 18) where his kingship is fully recognized and his *glory* (radiant splendor; cf. N.T.C. on John 1:14) is reflected in the hearts and lives of all his subjects.

---

of the copula in such cases is not at all unusual (cf. II Cor. 7:5) and may be due to Aramaic influence.

(4) The words "his own children" are to be considered the object of the main idea in the participles. Had the sentence been more fully expressed, the participles would have been repeated.

(5) The pronoun *y o u* after *admonishing* (see literal translation above, under 1) is resumptive, resuming the idea expressed in *each one of y o u.* This repetition of the pronoun may also be due, in part, to Aramaic influence. However, in Koine Greek (as well as in other languages, even today) such "redundance" is not rare. It should not be viewed as superfluous repetition: the missionaries, while in Thessalonica, had administered to each person *individually,* and had also dealt with the people *collectively.*

(6) More fully expressed, the sentence, accordingly, would run somewhat as follows: (after verse 10: "Y o u are witnesses and so is God, how piously," etc., verse 11 continues) "just as y o u know how, like a father admonishing his own children, and encouraging and testifying, so we were admonishing each and all of y o u, and encouraging and testifying that y o u should live lives worthy of God, who calls y o u into his own kingdom and glory." In slightly abbreviated form this is the rendering which we have adopted in the text.

[52] As Calvin says so strikingly (Commentarius In Epistolam Pauli Ad Thessalonicenses I, *Corpus Reformatorum,* vol. LXXX, Brunsvigae, 1895, p. 150): Et certe nemo unquam bonus erit pastor, nisi qui patrem se ecclesiae sibi creditae praestabit. Nec vero se universo modo corpori talem fuisse asserit, sed etiam singulis. Neque enim satis est, si pastor omnes pro suggestu in commune doceat, nisi particularem quoque adiungat doctrinam, prout vel necessitas postulat, vel occasio se offert.

13 And for this reason we also thank God constantly, that when y o u had received from us the word which y o u heard, namely, God's word, y o u accepted it not as a word of men but as it really is, a word of God, which is also at work in y o u who believe. 14 For y o u, brothers, became imitators of the churches of God in Christ Jesus which are in Judea; for y o u suffered the same things from y o u r own countrymen as they did from the Jews, 15 who killed both the Lord, namely, Jesus, and the prophets, and drove us out, and please not God, and we are contrary to all men 16 in that they try to prevent us from speaking to the Gentiles in order that they may be saved, so as always to fill up the measure of their sins. But upon them the wrath has come to the uttermost! 53

2:13-16

2:13. And for this reason we also thank God constantly, that when y o u had received from us the word which y o u heard, namely, God's word, y o u accepted it not as a word of men but as it really is, a word of God, which is also at work in y o u who believe.

That in this section the Defence continues will become clear, the main point being, "The enemy is trying to undermine y o u r faith, but y o u r willingness to suffer persecution for the sake of Christ proves that y o u r faith is genuine, and that the foe will not succeed."

In order to bring home this idea Paul states that not only the Thessalonians are grateful for the spiritual blessings which they have received, but so are the missionaries (hence, "we also," that is, "we as well as y o u"). Without ceasing they thank God for the manner in which the Thessalonians have accepted the message and for the influence which this word of God has exerted upon their lives. In other words, we have here a further elucidation and amplification of 1:6, just as 2:1-12 is an expatiation of the thought begun in 1:5. For that very reason we do not agree with those who would interpret the present passage as if it meant: "We thank God that when y o u received our message, y o u actually obtained the Word of God, and not merely the word of men." The sense is: when y o u *received* (external reception) from us "the word of hearing" (meaning: the word which y o u heard), which was nothing less than God's own word, y o u *accepted* (inward welcoming) it *as such,* that is, as a word of God and not as a word of men. The genuine character of this acceptance was proved by the fact that this divine word was actually bearing fruit in the lives of the people, as the passage 1:6-10 has already shown (they had turned away from idols toward God and toward the coming of his Son, and even amid much affliction they were joyfully proclaiming the new faith); and as verse 14 is going to show. The word, accordingly, was operating; it was "at work," 54 effective in the lives of believers. And the reason why the

---

53 Or *at last;* or *to the end.*
54 Paul is fond of this verb *is at work* (ἐνεργέω). He uses it again and again (Rom.

word was at work, and this in a favorable sense, was that it was the word
of God: by means of that word, God himself was working (cf. Phil. 2:13).
To substantiate this fact, namely, that the word was really at work, and that
it was *God's* word, Paul continues:

14. For y o u, brothers, became imitators of the churches of God in
Christ Jesus which are in Judea; for y o u suffered the same things from
y o u r own countrymen as they did from the Jews.

Willingness to suffer for Christ is proof of discipleship. It shows that
the word of God is at work in the heart. It unites believers, sothat they
constitute a true brotherhood (note: "for y o u, *brothers";* see on 1:4), to
which no one belongs who is not willing thus to suffer.

Now the Thessalonians were not only willing to suffer but had actually
experienced persecution. Hence, they had become imitators of other believers. The story is ever the same. It is repeated in every age and in
every clime (see on II Tim. 3:12 and N.T.C. on John 15:20; 16:33). For
a true believer not to suffer persecution in some form is impossible. The
readers had become imitators of the missionaries and of Christ himself (see
on 1:6). Now another thought is added, namely, that they had also become
imitators of the Judean believers. Now in Judea there were various *assemblies* (see on 1:1), by no means all of them Christian. To indicate
clearly that the assemblies here meant are *Christian* assemblies or *churches*
(*assembly* or *church* is the same word in the original: ἐκκλησία) there is
added: "of God in Christ Jesus" (literally, "imitators of the assemblies
of God that are in Judea *in* — in spiritual union with — Christ Jesus," cf.
Gal. 1:22). These Judean churches had suffered *from the Jews.* Paul knew
all about it, for he himself, while still unconverted, had taken part in it
(Gal. 1:13; cf. Acts 9:1, 13) at the behest of the Jewish authorities. Moreover, think of Stephen, of James (the brother of the apostle John), and of
Peter (Acts 6 and 7; 12:1-19; note especially 12:3, "it pleased *the Jews").*
Again and again persecution from the side of the Jews had flared up in
Judea (Acts 8:1; 11:19). And it was going to flare up again, as Paul himself
was going to discover (Acts 21:27-36; 23:12; 24:1-9).

Believers in Thessalonica had been similarly persecuted. However, the
persecution which Paul has immediately in mind here in verse 14 is not
(at least not primarily) the one recorded in Acts 17:5-8 but the one which
just now had been reported by Timothy. This later persecution had

---

7:5; I Cor. 12:6, 11; II Cor. 1:6; 4:12; Gal. 2:8 twice; 3:5; 5:6; Eph. 1:11, 20;
2:2; 3:20; Phil. 2:13 twice; Col. 1:29; I Thess. 2:7). Of the twenty-
one instances in which this verb occurs in the N.T., no less than eighteen are to be
found in Paul. In addition to this he alone employs the corresponding nouns
(ἐνέργεια, ἐνέργημα; cf. our *energy*). In Paul's way of thinking principles are never
dead; they are always doing something; though not always something good (Rom.
7:5; II Cor. 4:12; II Thess. 2:7).

taken place after the departure of the missionaries. That the Gentiles had taken a prominent part in it is clear. On any different inter-pretation the comparison: "You suffered the same things from your fellow-countrymen as they did from the Jews" would make no sense. Is it not altogether probable that the husbands of those many women who had become Christians (Acts 17:4) — these husbands being themselves lead-ing men — were making life hard for their wives? And is it not logical that these men and their friends would also subject other believers (both men and women) to scorn, ridicule, physical suffering, and even death?

Two important lessons are clearly implied:

(1) Whether the persecution comes from the Jews or from the Gentiles, it is ever *the same* in character, because at bottom it is the age-old warfare of the devil against "the Christ, the woman, and the rest of her seed." See my book *More Than Conquerors* (Interpretation of the book of Revelation), Grand Rapids, Mich., seventh edition, 1954, pp. 162-188. This conflict goes back to Gen. 3:15.

(2) Willingness to suffer such persecution reflects honor on the one who experiences it. It is as if Paul and his companions are saying, "The church in Jerusalem is generally thought of as an example for others. Now you, Thessalonians, by your willingness to suffer as the mother-church suf-fered, have shown that you are equal to her in honor."

When Paul mentions the Jews and the havoc which they had wrought in *Judea,* he realizes, of course, that they, too, as well as the Gentiles, had tried and were trying to destroy the faith of the *Thessalonian* believers. It was as a result of *their* instigation that the missionaries had been forced to leave the city (Acts 17:5-9). In the beginning the Jews had aroused the Gentiles, including the magistrates, to take a stand against the Gospel and its messengers. There is no good reason to believe that their hostile attitude had ceased since that time (see, e.g., Acts 17:13). It is for this reason that the apostle, having made specific mention of the persecution carried on by the Jews in Judea, and mindful of their sinister plotting in Thessalonica and elsewhere, continues:

15. who killed both the Lord, namely, Jesus, and the prophets,
> **and drove us out,**
> **and please not God,**
> **and are contrary to all men.**

In the original the words *Lord* and *Jesus* are separated (the order of the words being: "who the Lord killing Jesus"), thus stressing the fact that it was no one less than the exalted Lord whom the Jews had killed, the one who as to his earthly manifestation was Jesus, the Savior. For both names see on 1:1. All attempts (also modern attempts) to mitigate the guilt of the Jews in killing Jesus (by saying that not they but the Gentiles — particularly

71

Pilate — committed this crime) are crushed by this passage: I Thess. 2:15. Just as at Thessalonica the Jews had aroused the Gentile rabble, so also before this in Jerusalem the Jews had used Pilate as their tool in bringing about the crucifixion of the Lord (see N.T.C. on the Gospel of John, chapters 18 and 19). Note how Paul, having mentioned Jesus, reaches back in time to the Old Testament *prophets* and then forward to the New Testament *apostles,* particularly to himself, Silas, and Timothy. Thus it becomes apparent that at bottom the hostility is ever directed against the central figure, namely, the Lord, even Jesus (see on 2:14).

As will be indicated in connection with verse 16, it is probable that the apostle was thinking of the actual words of Jesus with respect to the Jews, for example, such words as those which are recorded in Matt. 23:37-39 (for similar passages see under verse 16). If this is correct, it also becomes evident that "the prophets" are not those of the New Testament but those of the Old (see Matt. 23:34, 35).

For the meaning of "and drove us out" see Acts 17:5-9 (cf. Acts 17:10-15; then 9:29, 30). The clause "and please not God" is, of course, a typical understatement. To glorify God and *to please* him is the purpose of man's existence (see on 4:1; cf. Rom. 8:8; I Cor. 7:32; 10:31). These Jews not only displease *God* but are also "contrary to all *men,*" and this not only in the sense that they are filled with "terrible hatred against all others" (Tacitus, *History* V. v), but in the sense indicated in verse 16:

16. in that they try to prevent us from speaking to the Gentiles in order that they may be saved, . . .

The Jews are constantly interfering, *hindering,* though they cannot *actually prevent* the progress of the Gospel. They are obstructionists, and their constant opposition marks them as the enemies of all men, for the more the Gospel spreads, the more are all men benefited. Right here in Corinth, the place where this epistle was being written, the work of the missionaries was being impeded, as is indicated very vividly in Acts 18:6. And this in spite of the fact that Paul, Silas, and Timothy were trying to be the means in God's hand for bestowing upon the Corinthians the greatest gift of all, namely, salvation full and free.

With respect to the Jews, the old story was being repeated: the story of rebellion against God. Again and again in times past this spirit of obstinacy had revealed itself: e.g., in the wilderness-journey from Egypt to Canaan, during the period of the judges, during the reigns of several kings, just before the Babylonian Captivity. In the ministry of Christ (especially on Golgotha) and in the period immediately following this it had risen to a climax. Hence, Paul is able to write **so as always to fill up the measure of their sins.** Note that adverb *always.* However, God's wrath had overtaken the mass of the Jews. We read: **but upon them the wrath has come.**

We immediately understand that *the* wrath is God's wrath. (It is not necessary nor even advisable to adopt the weakly attested reading which would add these words: "of God").

The explanation offered by several commentators, to the effect that when Paul wrote these words he was in a bad mood because his work at Corinth was being hampered by the Jews, is without any foundation. The theory which finds in events unfavorable to the Jews which had happened during the reign of Caligula and that of Claudius (who at first was kindly disposed to them) a complete commentary of Paul's statement about the arrival of God's wrath, is equally objectionable. Worst of all is the position of those who hold that I Thess. 2:16 must refer to the fall of Jerusalem in the year A. D. 70, and that, accordingly, Paul cannot have written this epistle or at least that he cannot have written this passage, it being an interpolation.

The true explanation is simple: Paul was well acquainted with the words which Jesus had spoken while still on earth. In very emphatic language the Lord had revealed that, as a punishment for the sin of rejecting him, God's displeasure (his *vengeance*) was now resting upon the Jewish people, and that this wrath would manifest itself in woes to be visited upon them (which woes, in turn, would foreshadow those immediately preceding the end of the world). Anyone can see this for himself by reading such passages as the following: Matt. 21:43; 23:38; 24:15-28; 27:25; Mark 11:14, 20 (in its context); Luke 21:5-24; 23:27-31. In this connection it must not be overlooked that the apostle does not say that God's wrath has even now been fully poured out, or that it has become outwardly manifest in punishments. All he says is that *the wrath itself has come!* The woes will follow.

This wrath, moreover, has come **to the uttermost**. While *previously,* whenever Israel sinned grievously it had been *punished, this time* it is not only punished but *rejected*. This time God himself hardens Israel with a hardening which lasts "until the fulness of the Gentiles be come in" (Rom. 11:25). Hence, this time God's wrath has come upon them *to the uttermost*.[55]

What Paul teaches is in full harmony with Rom. 9-11. (See also p. 19.) However, in Romans there is additional revelation. He there shows that though this wrath to the uttermost has reached the Jewish *masses,* there is, nevertheless, in every period of history, "a remnant according to the election of grace." These remnants of all the ages, taken together, constitute

[55] Though "to the uttermost" (so also A.V., A.R.V., Lenski, footnote R.S.V., etc., and see N.T.C. on John 13:1) would seem to be the meaning that best suits the context, it is not certain. The phrase εἰς τέλος can also mean *at last* (cf. Luke 18:5; here in I Thess. 2:16 it is so rendered by R.S.V., Berkeley Version, Williams, Robertson, Frame); or *to the end* (study Dan. 9:27; see the use of the phrase in Matt. 10:22; 24:13; Mark 13:13; here in I Thess. 2:16 it is so rendered by the New Dutch Version, by Van Leeuwen in *Korte Verklaring,* etc.).

"all Israel" which "shall be saved" (Rom. 11:26 a).[56] Hence, no one has a right to say, "God is through with the Jews." Anti-Semitism, moreover, is very definitely anti-scriptural! In the present passage (I Thess. 2:16), however, all the emphasis is on the curse which the Jews have called down upon themselves by rejecting the Christ and his ambassadors.

---

17 Now we, brothers, having been torn away from y o u for a short time — out of sight but not out of heart [57] — endeavored all the more eagerly to see y o u r face with intense longing; 18 for we did wish to come to y o u, I, Paul, myself once and again, but Satan stopped us. 19 For who is our hope or joy or glory-wreath — or are not also y o u — in the presence of our Lord Jesus Christ at his coming? 20 Indeed, it is y o u who are our glory and (our) joy!

2:17-20

2:17. Now we, brothers, having been torn away from y o u for a short time — out of sight but not out of heart — endeavored all the more eagerly to see y o u r face with intense longing.

The Defence continues. Not inaptly what precedes verse 17 has been called Paul's *apologia pro vita sua;* while 2:17-3:5 (see also on 3:1) has been called *apologia pro absentia sua.* Not only was it true that during their stay in Thessalonica the missionaries had conducted themselves in a most unselfish manner, as has now been shown, but also after the enforced departure from that city their loving concern for the *brothers* (note that word in verse 17; and see on 1:4) whom they had left behind had asserted itself. At this point Paul's style becomes intensely emotional. The very words seem to tremble. The reason for the depth of feeling which comes to expression here is probably that the enemies of the faith were insinuating that the sudden departure of the missionaries proved lack of genuine concern for the people whom they had misled. Over against that charge Paul stresses the fact that by the missionaries the separation which had taken place was felt as being nothing less than a being *torn away from* those whom they loved so dearly. The verb (ἀπορφανισθέντες) occurs only here in the New Testament (see, however, Aeschylus, *Choephori* 249; cf. for the form without prefix Theocritus, *Epigrammata* V. vi). Literally, the meaning is, first, *to be orphaned;* then, *to be bereaved.* However, the meaning of the prefix (ἀπό, *from, away from*) of the composite verb is brought out better in the rendering which we favor, namely, *to be torn away from.*[58]

---

[56] See my booklet *And So All Israel Shall be Saved,* Grand Rapids, Mich. (Baker Book House), 1945.
[57] Literally *in face not in heart.*
[58] For this translation of the verb as used here in I Thess. 2:17 we are indebted to H. G. Liddell and R. Scott, *A Greek-English Lexicon,* Oxford, 1940, Vol. I, p. 216. Words, in the course of their history, often acquire a slightly modified mean-

The clause "having been torn away from y o u a short time," *may* (but does not necessarily) convey the idea that Paul was convinced that he would soon revisit the Thessalonians. In all probability he actually revisited them on the third missionary journey (Acts 20:1, 2). However, the meaning might also be, "When (or *though*) we had been torn away from y o u for a short time only, we already endeavored all the more eagerly to return to y o u." According to this second view the *short time* [59] is wholly antecedant to the action of the main verb. The attempt to revisit those left behind was given an added impetus by the enforced character of the separation. It is as if Paul were saying, "The more Satan tried to effect a separation the harder we tried to effect a reunion." (For this sense of περισσοτέρως see Phil. 1:14.) With this interpretation agrees the final phrase: *with intense longing* (or *desire*).

The parenthetical "in face not in heart" [60] (cf. II Cor. 5:12; Col. 2:5) must probably also be viewed as a refutation of the slander that the missionaries did not really care for those whom they had "duped"; that they would know better than to try to return to them; in short, that for Paul and company "out of sight" meant "out of heart." Thus interpreted, we can also understand what immediately follows, namely,

18. for we did wish [61] to come to y o u, I, Paul, myself once and again, but Satan stopped us.

"We endeavored" (verse 17), "for we wished" (verse 18): this sequence is logical. Far from being glad that we had an excuse to get away from Thessalonica, we — Paul, Silas, and Timothy — having been. driven out, longed to come back. In view of the fact that the sinister attack of the enemy was directed against Paul more than against anyone else, the apostle adds, "I, Paul, *once and again*" (cf. Phil. 4:16), that is, *repeatedly.*

Satan, however, had prevented the missionaries from carrying out their ardent wish to return to Thessalonica. Just how did Satan do this? By influencing the minds of the politarchs at Thessalonica, sothat they would have caused Jason to forfeit his bond (Acts 17:9) in case the missionaries had returned? By bringing about a sufficient amount of trouble elsewhere sothat neither Paul alone nor all three were able to return? We just do

---

ing. Thus the word *orphan* in John 14:18 tends in the direction of *friendless.* Even in English the adjective *orphan* may have the wider meaning *bereaved.* So also here in 2:17 the basic element of the verb has attained a somewhat modified meaning.
[59] The expression πρὸς καιρὸν ὥρας combines πρὸς καιρόν (Luke 8:13; I Cor. 7:5) and πρὸς ὥραν (II Cor. 7:8; Gal. 2:5).
[60] *We* say "out of sight out of *mind*", but the Greek has *heart;* cf. the Dutch: *uit het oog, uit het hart.*
[61] Those who favor the rendering, "We made deliberate plans," fail to show a solid reason why the verb θέλω rather than βούλομαι was used. The enemy denied that Paul and his companions (but *especially* Paul) ever even *wished* to return to Thessalonica!

not know. Moreover, it does not matter. The fact as such that Satan exerts a powerful influence over the affairs of men, especially when they endeavor to promote the interests of the kingdom of God, is sufficiently clear from other passages (Job 1:6-12; Zech. 3:1; cf. Daniel, chapter 10). Nevertheless, God ever reigns supreme, over-ruling evil for good (II Cor. 12:7-9; the book of Job). Even when the devil tries to *chop up* the road that lies ahead, thus apparently blocking our advance, God's hidden plan is never wrecked. Satan may *cut in on* us, preventing us from doing what, for the moment, seems best *to us,* God's ways are always better than ours.

The reason why Paul and his companions were so eager to revisit the Thessalonians is now stated:

19, 20. For who is our hope or joy or glory-wreath — or are not also y o u — in the presence of our Lord Jesus Christ at his coming? Indeed, it is y o u who are our glory and (our) joy!

Paul and his companions love these Thessalonians, and "are proud" of them. It must be borne in mind that amid severe persecution these people had turned away from their idols and had turned to God, the living and true One, and that they are now waiting for the glorious coming of the Lord.

At this *coming* of *the Lord Jesus Christ* (for this full title see on 1:1) for the purpose of blessing his people with his abiding *presence* the missionaries will see the ultimate realization of their *hope,* and will experience supreme *joy* when they behold the fruits of their missionary efforts standing there, with gladness, thanksgiving, and praise, at Christ's right hand. For these missionaries this will be the *glory-wreath,* the prided victor's chaplet.[62]

The term *coming* (in *at his coming*) is Parousia (παρουσία). This word is sometimes used in the non-technical sense of a. *presence;* for the use of the term in that sense the following passages come in for consideration: I Cor. 16:17; II Cor. 10:10; Phil. 1:26 (?); 2:12; or of b. *a coming, advent,* or *arrival:* II Cor. 7:6, 7; Phil. 1:26(?); II Thess. 2:9. In other passages — and I Thess. 2:19 is one of them — it definitely refers to the *Return* or *Advent of the Lord,* his "coming" *in order to bless his people with his presence.* See Zech. 9:9. In addition to I Thess. 2:19 to illustrate this meaning, the following should be studied: I Thess. 3:13; 4:15; 5:23; II Thess. 2:1, 8; Matt. 24:3, 27, 37, 39; I Cor. 15:23; Jas. 5:7, 8; II Peter 1:16; 3:4, 12;

---

[62] We take the genitive καυχήσεως to be adjectival in nature. This is in harmony with similar expressions in other passages: Prov. 16:31; Is. 28:5; Jer. 13:8; Ezek. 16:12; 23:42. Besides, the New Testament has many genitives of this kind, the frequency of their occurrence being due, perhaps, to Aramaic influence (see also on 1:3). Hence, the main concept here is not *boasting* (or glorifying) but *wreath.* The new Dutch translation has *erekrans;* cf. *roemkrans.* That is correct.

and I John 2:28. This meaning may be viewed as a modification of the sense: "the arrival" or "the visit" of the king or emperor.[63]

Paul and his companions, stirred by the slanders of those who insinuate that the missionaries are people who do not care a whit about their converts, express the deepest conviction of their hearts in the form of a question, but that question requires an affirmative answer. It may be paraphrased as follows: "For who is our hope or joy or glory-wreath? Others only? Or are not also y o u (along with others; see, e.g., Phil. 4:1) in the presence of our Lord Jesus Christ at his coming?" And that there may be no doubt about it, Paul himself supplies the answer: "Indeed (this is the meaning of γάρ here) it is y o u (note the emphatic position of ὑμεῖς) who are our *glory* (that is, our reason for glorying in the Lord) and (our) joy!"

Synthesis of Chapters 1 and 2

See p. 36. *Defence. Paul writes to the Thessalonians, reminding them how the Gospel had come to Thessalonica, as a genuine work of God and not as a product of human deception.*

chapter 1 This chapter contains the names of the senders (Paul and his companions Silvanus and Timothy) and of the addressee (the church of the Thessalonians), the salutation, and the thanksgiving together with its grounds.

The reasons why Silvanus (or Silas) and Timothy are mentioned in one breath with Paul as authors and senders is that they have been associated with the great apostle in bringing the gospel to Thessalonica and are with him now in Corinth where this letter is written.

Upon the readers the missionaries pronounce *grace* (God's unmerited favor in operation) and its result, *peace* (the conviction of reconciliation through the blood of the cross, spiritual prosperity).

They inform the Thessalonians that they never allow a day to go by without giving thanks for them, in view of their "work resulting from faith, exertion prompted by love, and endurance inspired by hope in our Lord Jesus Christ." The ultimate reason for this thanksgiving is the conviction that the readers have been chosen from eternity unto salvation. The writers base this conviction on two facts:

a. the message which the readers had received and the messengers who had brought it are trustworthy.

b. the manner in which the readers had responded is proof positive of the operation of the Spirit of God in their hearts. They had welcomed God's word with Spirit-imparted joy even in the midst of great tribulation.

---

[63] See A. Deissmann, *Light From The Ancient East,* fourth edition, New York, 1922, p. 368; G. Milligan, *St. Paul's Epistles to the Thessalonians,* London, 1908, p. 145 ff.

They had cast away their idols, "to serve God, the living and real One, and to await his Son out of the heavens." From *imitators* they had become *examples*. Their faith was being broadcast and was having its blessed effect everywhere.

Paul (i.e., "Paul, Silvanus and Timothy," but Paul is chiefly responsible) gives evidence of deep concern for his readers. Probably as an answer to malicious slander he declares, "Y o u well know what kind of men we became among y o u for y o u r sake." Thus, even in the first chapter there is an undertone of *defence*. This gains strength in the next chapter.

chapter 2 The apologetic tone continues and becomes predominant. First, the missionaries defend their *manner of life* while still at Thessalonica (verses 1-16); then, their *departure and continued absence* from Thessalonica (2:17-20, or even 2:17-3:5). As the charges were hurled especially against *Paul*, this may be considered *his* defence even more than *theirs*. Accordingly, we have:

Apologia pro vita sua

The key-passage is verse 3, "For our appeal does not spring from delusion or from impurity nor does it come with deceit." It may probably be inferred from this that the slanderers had directed their attack against Paul's *m* essage, *m* otive, and *m* ethod.

Accordingly, in this section Paul points out that his *message* was the good news which had come directly from God; that the *motive* in presenting it was most unselfish, even the motive of self-sacrificing love, the attitude of a father or of a mother toward his (her) own children; and that the *method* was above reproach ("Y o u are witnesses and so is God, how piously and righteously and blamelessly we conducted ourselves in the estimation of y o u, believers"). Paul shows that the willingness of the readers to suffer persecution for the sake of Christ proves that the word is "at work" in them, and that they are equal in honor with the mother-church in Judea. In a passage filled with deep emotion he reveals that upon the Jewish instigators of persecution God's wrath has come to the uttermost.

Apologia pro absentia sua

The enemy seems also to have insinuated that Paul's departure from Thessalonica and his failure to return had not been entirely unplanned, or that, while he complained about "tribulation," he had not been entirely unhappy about finding an excuse to get away. The apostle definitely and with much feeling denies this, ardently and unequivocally avowing his love for the readers, whom he calls "our hope or joy or glory-wreath in the presence of our Lord Jesus Christ at his coming." He states that he and his companions had been "torn away" from the readers, and had repeatedly "endeavored all the more eagerly" to see their face "with intense longing," but had been stopped by Satan.

Summary of I Thessalonians 3 (or 3:6-13)

Paul Writes to the Thessalonians

Informing Them How He Rejoices over Timothy's Report of Their Continued Spiritual Progress Even in the Midst of Persecution.

This section comprises *the Apostle's Expression of Joy over Timothy's Report.*

It may be divided as follows:

3:1-5   What moved Paul to send Timothy

3:6-10 · What reason for rejoicing Timothy's report had brought

3:11-13 A fervent wish

CHAPTER III

3 1 Therefore when we could not stand it any longer, we thought it best to be left behind in Athens alone; 2 and we sent Timothy, our brother and God's minister in the gospel of Christ, in order to strengthen y o u and to encourage (y o u) with respect to your faith; 3 to prevent any one of y o u from being deceived in the midst of these afflictions. For y o u yourselves know that we are appointed for this; 4 for when we were with y o u, we kept telling y o u in advance that we were about to be afflicted, just as y o u know that it (actually) happened. 5 For this reason I, too, when I could stand it no longer, sent to learn about y o u r faith, (fearing) lest by any means the tempter might have tempted y o u, and our toil might turn out to have been useless.

6 But now that Timothy has just come to us from y o u, and has brought us the glad tidings of y o u r faith and love, and that y o u cherish an affectionate recollection of us at all times, longing to see us, just as we also (long to see) y o u, 7 for this reason, brothers, in all our distress and affliction, we were comforted about y o u, through y o u r faith; 8 for now we (really) live if y o u stand fast in the Lord. 9 For what thanksgiving can we offer to God concerning y o u in return for all the joy by means of which we rejoice on account of y o u in the presence of our God, 10 by night and by day praying with intense earnestness that we may see y o u r faces and may supply the deficiencies of y o u r faith?

11 Now may he, our God and Father and our Lord Jesus, direct our way to y o u; 12 and as for y o u, may the Lord cause y o u to abound and overflow in love toward one another and toward all, just as also we (do) toward y o u, 13 in order that he may strengthen y o u r hearts so that they may be blameless in holiness in the presence of our God and Father at the coming of our Lord Jesus with all his saints!

3:1-13

The transition between Defence and Expression of joy is very gradual. In fact, the information which Paul supplies with respect to the decision to send Timothy is, in a sense, a part of the Defence, for it shows that far from being indifferent to the needs of the Thessalonians (as the enemies charged), the apostle was willing to make a real sacrifice in their interest. Hence, there can be no great objection to extending the first main division sothat it ends at 3:5 (see also on 2:17). The reason why, nevertheless, *this entire chapter* may be considered *as a unit* is that even the first five verses, as well as the rest, concern *Timothy:* what moved Paul (or Paul after con-

81

sultation with the others) to send him (verses 1-5), and what comfort his report had brought (verses 6-10, closing with a fervent wish which almost amounts to a prayer, verses 11-13).

3:1. Therefore when we could not stand it any longer, we thought it best to be left behind in Athens alone.

The sense of verse 1 is: in view of the fact that our immediate attempt to return to y o u was frustrated by Satan, and that, nevertheless, we could not *stand* or *endure* (cf. I Cor. 9:12; 13:7) the separation any longer, we *decided* (*thought it good;* cf. the noun εὐδοκία, *good pleasure,* Lk. 2:14; Eph. 1:5, 9; Phil. 1:15; 2:13; see on II Thess. 1:11) to deprive ourselves of the valued presence of one of our number, even though that meant that we would be left alone in the very worldly and idolatrous city of Athens.[64]

The position of the clause "to be left behind at Athens alone" shows that the emphasis falls on this decision, which disclosed so beautifully Paul's love for the Thessalonians.

The problem which arises at this point is, "Just what is meant by *alone* (the plural μόνοι is used, but that, demanded by concord, does not decide the issue either way); does this have reference to Paul only or to Paul *and Silas?*" Commentators are sharply divided, as follows:

a. Some conveniently skip the problem, or treat it as if it did not exist;

b. some, while expressing a preference, leave room for the possibility that the truth might be on the other side;

c. some are certain that what Paul meant was that *he* had decided to remain *all alone* at Athens; and finally,

d. some are of the opinion that Paul, Silas, and Timothy had consulted together, sothat the "we" is not a *literary* (or *editorial* or *author's*) plural,[65] but a *real* plural. To this it is sometimes added that while the departure of Timothy left Paul *and Silas* behind in Athens, Silas too must have departed very soon (see Acts 18:5), sothat for a while, at least, Paul must have been *all alone* in Athens.

The information which can be gleaned from the book of Acts and from I Thessalonians does not *definitely* settle the question, so as to leave no inkling of doubt. Surely, if Silas (for any length of time) was with Paul in Athens, the *we* here in I Thess. 3:1 could include him. But *was* he actually with Paul in Athens? A probable view is that *Timothy* had left Berea

---

[64] As we see it, the idea of Lenski, *op. cit.,* p. 281 that Timothy was chosen because he had not been driven out of Thessalonica, finds no support in the text. See also above, p. 5.

[65] See Gram.N.T., p. 407 for a discussion of the *literary* plural. Those who believe that Paul at times makes use of this plural refer to such passages as the following: I Thess. 2:18 (see, however, our explanation); then also Rom. 1:5; I Cor. 9:11, 12, 15; II Cor. 2:14; 10:1-11:6; Col. 4:3. Very interesting is also the article by W. R. Hutton, "Who Are We?" in *BTr,* Vol. 4, Number 2 (April, 1953) 86-90.

and had found Paul while the latter was still in Athens; that Paul, anxious about the affairs of the church at Thessalonica, sent him back to that congregation in order to establish and comfort it, and that *sometime later* both Silas and Timothy rejoined the apostle at Corinth (see I Thess. 3:1, 2, 6; Acts 18:5). However, this still leaves open the question, "Did Silas rejoin Paul *twice*, not only subsequently at Corinth, when also Timothy rejoined the group, but even before this (though for only a very short time), when Paul was still in Athens?" As far as the book of Acts is concerned, the only hint in the direction of a possible answer is found in Acts 17:15, 16 according to which Paul, arriving in Athens, tells the brothers, who had accompanied him to this city and are now departing, that they must tell Silas and Timothy to "come to him with all speed." Paul, accordingly, waited for *them* at Athens, that is, *for both of them.*

As to I Thessalonians, the idea that there was a joint consultation and that here in 3:1 the phrase *at Athens alone* refers to both Paul and Silas would seem to have at least this in its favor, that the reader, perhaps half consciously, has been including Silas and Timothy in all the "we" sections so far. Thus, not only Paul, but Paul, Silvanus, and Timothy pronounce the salutation (1:1). Not only Paul but also Silvanus and Timothy give thanks (1:2). Not only Paul but also Silvanus and (very probably) Timothy had been involved in the "entering in" of which 2:1 speaks. Also, we know that not only Paul had suffered and had been shamefully treated at Philippi (2:2). Not only Paul but also the others had been entrusted with the gospel (2:4). And not only Paul but also Silvanus and Timothy had been torn away from the brothers at Thessalonica (2:17). On that basis when now once more the reader meets a "we" (namely, here in 3:1) he is hardly prepared to think only of Paul. "We . . . alone" accordingly, in the light of the context, *probably* means: Silvanus and I *without the brothers who had accompanied us to Athens and without the valued presence of Timothy.* That this was a sacrifice of love follows not only from the fact that by and by Silvanus too would be sent to Macedonia, but also from the high esteem in which Paul held his young companion Timothy, as is clear from the next verse:

2. and we sent Timothy, our brother and God's minister in the gospel of Christ, in order to strengthen y o u and to encourage (y o u) with respect to y o u r faith.

Timothy is called a *brother* (cf. II Cor. 1:1; Col. 1:1), that is, a fellow-believer (see on 1:4), one who by sovereign grace belongs to the family of God in Christ. He is *our* brother, the word *our* being probably inclusive: brother of the Thessalonian believers as well as of the missionaries. But while he is *our* brother, he is at the same time *God's* minister.[66] The term

---

[66] The external evidence in favor of the reading *God's co-worker* is not any stronger

minister (διάκονος) indicates a servant, attendant (see N.T.C. on John, vol. I, p. 119). It is the same term as our *deacon,* and is at times employed in that technical sense (Phil. 1:1; I Tim. 3:8, 12). On Timothy see N.T.C. on the Pastoral Epistles. The particular sphere in which Timothy ministers is *the gospel of Christ,* the glad tidings (good news) of salvation through him.

The purpose for which Timothy was sent was *in order to strengthen* (by Paul used also in 3:13; II Thess. 2:17; 3:3; further, in Rom. 1:11; 16:25) and *to encourage* (see on 2:11; then also on 2:3). An additional purpose is stated in verse 5, namely, "to know y o u r faith." In view of fierce persecution and a sinister slander-campaign from without and also in view of the immature intellectual, moral, and spiritual development of the Thessalonian believers, the mission of Timothy was altogether proper, though it meant a real sacrifice for those who were left behind at Athens. Timothy, then, must tell these recent converts to the Christian faith, "Y o u're doing fine. Continue to do so. But do so more and more." That this *encouragement* was proper is shown by the following passages: 1:3, 4, 6-10; 2:13-14; 3:6-8; 4:1, 9, 10; 5:11. That *strengthening* was likewise needed follows from 3:5, 10; 4:1, 3, 4-8, 10; 5:23. It is true, of course, that the two terms overlap: when one is encouraged, he is also strengthened!

3, 4. The hoped for result of Timothy's mission of encouragement and strengthening is now stated: **to prevent anyone of y o u from being deceived in the midst of these afflictions.**

The enemy of the faith does not always come *only* with the sword. Sometimes he appears "with horns like a lamb" (Rev. 13:11), with soft words and flattery, like a dog *wagging his tail* (which is the primary meaning of the verb "deceived" used in the original). The danger was very real that those who were already being *oppressed* (note "in the midst of these afflictions") might be beguiled (either for the time being, if their faith was genuine, or permanently if it was merely historical or temporal) by language such as this:

"We can fully understand how it was that y o u were led astray by these enthusiastic foreigners who came from Philippi. Y o u were led to believe that they had y o u r interest at heart. But their sudden departure and failure to return clearly proves that they are not concerned about y o u at all. Moreover, the things that have happened to y o u since their coming shows that the gods are not pleased with y o u. Why exchange that which is tried and tested for something novel? Rejoin our ranks, the ranks of

---

than that in favor of the reading *God's minister.* The assumed scribal substitution of *minister* for *co-worker,* a substitution supposed to have been made because of the *bold* character of the latter designation, is answered by I Cor. 3:9. Frame is among those who favor *God's co-worker, op. cit.,* pp. 126, 127.

those who have always admired and respected y o u, and we'll promise y o u that we'll never mention the subject again." [67]

To prevent such fawning amid the stress of persecution from being successful, Timothy was sent.

For y o u yourselves know that we (inclusive: the missionaries and the believers at Thessalonica; in a sense, all believers) **are appointed for this.** Some of the reasons why believers are "set" for this (tribulation) and/or why they should rejoice in it may be found in passages such as the following: John 16:33; Acts 14:22; Rom. 5:3; 8:35-39; 12:12; II Cor. 1:4; 7:4; II Tim. 3:12. The Thessalonians are reminded of the fact that these afflictions should not take them by surprise. After all, they have been warned: **for when we were with y o u, we kept telling y o u in advance that we were about to be afflicted, just as y o u know that it (actually) happened.** How these words resemble those of the Master himself, spoken on the eve of his most bitter suffering! See N.T.C. on John 16:1, 4. Afflictions that have been *predicted,* and that take place in accordance with this prediction, serve to strengthen faith.

5. For this reason I, too, when I could stand it no longer, sent to learn about y o u r faith. For this reason, then, that is, in view of the fact that Paul had been frustrated once and again by Satan in his ardent desire to return to the believers at Thessalonica (who were his hope, joy, and glory-wreath), in view of the fact that his love for them was genuine, and also in view of the fact that on the basis of what he himself had seen and experienced in the past (Acts 17:5-9, 13) he was convinced that they must be suffering severe persecution and was wondering how they were faring under it, in view therefore of all that is stated and implied in 2:17-3:4, the apostle, no longer able to stand the suspense, sent *to learn* (or *to get to know*) about their faith. It is clear that verse 5 resumes the thought of verses 1, 2, with these differences: a. that another reason is now added to the two stated previously, and b. that the apostle stresses the fact that he himself no less than the others (hence, "also I") was responsible for the sending of Timothy. Since the slander of maligners must have been directed especially against Paul, this additional statement was altogether proper.

The purpose of the mission as now expressed was in order that Paul might get to know their faith, (fearing) **lest by any means the tempter might have tempted y o u, and our toil would turn out to have been useless.**[68]

---

[67] We cannot agree here with those commentators (for example, Van Leeuwen) who are of the opinion that here in 3:3, 4 Paul is thinking only of the tribulations suffered by the missionaries themselves. Passages such as 1:6 and 2:14 (cf. Acts 17:5-10) clearly indicate that the reference is to the afflictions borne alike by Paul, Silas, Timothy, the Thessalonian believers, and, in a sense, by all true believers.

[68] The past (aorist) indicative (ἐπείρασεν after μή πως) is best explained as that

Such fear on the part of Paul was altogether reasonable, and does not contradict 1:4 ("knowing y o u r election") in any way. The sequence was as follows:

a. Paul and his companions carry on their evangelistic activity in Thessalonica but are soon forced to leave. While still there, the Thessalonians (that is, many of them) appear to accept the gospel with enthusiasm. But was this a merely emotional reaction or was it genuine faith?

b. In their absence, the missionaries wonder about this. Meanwhile persecution continues. Will the genuine character of the faith of the Thessalonians be proved by their willingness to endure tribulation for the sake of Christ? Will they understand that this tribulation is not contrary to God's plan but in accordance with it?

c. So Timothy is sent in order to learn about this. He returns with a glowing report, praising the Thessalonians for their work, exertion, and endurance under persecution.

d. Being now thoroughly convinced that the conversion of the Thessalonians had been genuine (that their acceptance of the Gospel "with joy" had been a work of the Spirit) and not merely outward, Paul sits down at once to write I Thessalonians. He now writes about their work *resulting from faith,* their exertion *prompted by love,* and their endurance *inspired by hope,* and he derives all this from their *election* by God.

If we view the order of events in this light, justice is done both to the *fear* expressed here in 3:5 and the *conviction* expressed in 1:3-6. In no sense whatever is it true that 3:5 teaches that God's truly chosen ones can, after all, perish everlastingly.

Here, in close connection with verse 3, the prince of evil is called *the tempter.* His meanness consists especially in this, that he first tempts a man into sin and then accuses him of it! Moreover, he will even continue to accuse the man after the latter's sin has been forgiven. He is, accordingly, the *devil* or *slanderer* (Eph. 4:27; 6:11; II Tim. 2:26); he is *Satan,* the wicked *adversary* (I Cor. 5:5; II Cor. 2:11; II Thess. 2:9). He is, moreover, *the god of this world* (II Cor. 4:3), *the prince of the powers of the air* (Eph. 2:2) and of *the world-rulers of this darkness, spiritual hosts of wickedness in the heavenlies, seducing spirits and demons* (I Tim. 4:1). Indeed, for Paul the devil was real, an actually existing, very powerful and very terrible opponent! Those who deny the real and personal existence of Satan should be honest enough to admit that they do not believe in the Bible!

---

which expresses unfulfilled purpose: the tempter actually failed in his endeavor to lead the Thessalonians astray. Cf. Gal. 2:2: actually Paul had not run in vain. The use of the past indicative in such clauses may be compared to its use in contrary-to-fact conditional sentences. — The subjunctive (γένηται "and in vain would get to be our toil," that is, "and our toil would turn out to have been useless") is regular in such clauses of negative purpose or fear (cf. I Cor. 9:27; II Cor. 9:3; and see Gram.N.T., pp. 987, 988).

The fears of the missionaries were banished by Timothy's return and gladdening report:

6, 7. But now that Timothy has just come to us from y o u, and has brought us the glad tidings of y o u r faith and love, and that y o u cherish an affectionate recollection of us at all times, longing to see us, just as we also (long to see) y o u, for this reason, brothers, in all our distress and affliction, we were comforted about y o u, through y o u r faith; . . .

Here at least (if not even before; see on 3:1) the emphasis shifts from Defence to Expression of Joy, though consciousness of opposition in Thessalonica is never completely absent. The expression "Timothy has come to us from y o u" is much more cordial and intimate than the formal "Timothy returned" would have been. It is as if Paul were writing, "Timothy was our representative to y o u. Now he has become y o u r representative to us, revealing to us y o u r very heart." As disclosed in verses 6 and 7, the report which Timothy brought was twofold. It was somewhat as follows:

"a. The faith and the love of the Thessalonians endure even in the midst of persecution; hence, they are genuine; and

"b. the yearning to see one another is mutual. On the side of the Thessalonians it is an evidence of the loving remembrance in which they constantly retain y o u (Paul and Silas)."

Note the expression ". . . has *just* come to us." Hence, Paul must have replied immediately. A hint for all those who tend to postpone answering important letters! For the term of endearment *brothers* see on 1:4 and on 2:17. From the side of Paul and Silas (more precisely: and *probably* Silas; see on 3:1) it was not only *absence* but also *distress and affliction* (cf. Job 15:24; Zeph. 1:15) which had made the heart grow fonder. For *affliction* or *tribulation* see on 1:6. The original term which is correctly rendered *distress* (thus A.V., A.R.V.) is related to our *anguish* (see also I Cor. 7:26; II Cor. 6:4; 12:10).

The expression *"all* our affliction and distress" shows that the difficulties which Paul and Silas had been (and, to a certain extent, were still) experiencing were considerable. We can hardly agree that opposition from the side of the Jews here in Corinth — where I Thessalonians was being written — was not included. It is true, of course, that the particular (and probably most vehement) flare-up recorded in Acts 18:5-17 *followed* the return of Silas and Timothy, but it would be strange if the underlying hostile attitude had been wholly dormant before that time. Among other afflictions and distresses which Paul may have had in mind are, perhaps, all or some of the following (and maybe others besides): doubt with respect to the effectiveness of the work in Thessalonica, concern about the safety of Timothy (these distresses were now removed), bad news from Galatia, and the physical strain due to the double load: on the one hand, carrying on an important and time-consuming gospel-ministry here at Corinth, and on the other hand, making good tents! And see also II Cor. 11:28.

But amid all these afflictions and distresses Paul and Silas were immeasurably *comforted* (see on 2:3; 2:11; also N.T.C. on John 14:16) by the report which Timothy brought. It is not at all surprising that Paul, in reply, comments on the *love* and on the *faith* of the Thessalonians (both mentioned by Timothy, *faith,* as the most basic, being repeated and viewed here as the agency that produced comfort), that is, on the work resulting from faith, and the exertion prompted by love, and the endurance inspired by hope (see on 1:3).

8. Paul continues: **for now we (really) live if y o u stand fast in the Lord.** This is the utterance of profound and overpowering emotion. Paul's heart is on fire for the Lord (see on 1:1), and at the same time is filled with tender affection for the believers at Thessalonica who have made possible Timothy's favorable report. The thoughts crowd each other, sothat verse 8 is actually a combination of two ideas:

a. We live if y o u stand fast in the Lord

and

b. Now we live seeing that y o u are standing fast in the Lord.

Paul is saying, therefore, that whenever the Thessalonians *stand fast* (keep on taking a firm position; cf. II Thess. 2:15; also I Cor. 16:13; Gal. 5:1; Phil. 1:27) *in* (*metaphorical* use of this preposition, derived from the local sense) the Lord, rooted in him, trusting in him, loving him, hoping in him, those who brought them the gospel really live, being filled with joy and gratitude (cf. the use of the word *live* in Deut. 8:3 and Is. 38:16); and that such a climax of blessedness has now arrived. That such *living* does, indeed, include thanksgiving is indicated in the next two verses:

9, 10. **For what thanksgiving can we offer to God concerning y o u in return for all the joy by means of which we rejoice on account of y o u in the presence of our God, by night and by day praying with intense earnestness that we may see y o u r faces and may supply the deficiencies of y o u r faith?**

This is a rhetorical question. Paul's soul is flooded with gratitude to God, and this to such an extent that the consciousness of his own inability to make *an adequate return* to God grieves him. What has been received by the Thessalonians has also been received, in a different form, and *on account of them,* by him and his companions. The report of Timothy has given Paul and Silas a new lease on life. It has caused them to revive. They are deeply convinced of the fact that anything they can bring to God *in return for* [69] "all the joy by means of which they rejoice" is as nothing. See N.T.C. on John 3:29: the cup of joy is running over; cf. Is. 66:10.

But even though Paul is still struggling with the problem how to make an adequate return for blessings already received, this does not deter him from asking for still more! In fact, the very manner in which previous petitions have been answered makes him all the more earnest (note *over-abundantly* or *with intense earnestness*) in praying for something in addition to what has already been received. Hence, thanksgiving ("rejoicing before our God") is accompanied by prayer. Note how Paul, though working at a trade *by night and by day* (see on 2:9), still finds time to pray, and this also *by night and by day!*

The content of the prayer or petition is stated in *two* infinitive-clauses, but the two really express *one* idea, namely, that God's providence may permit the missionaries to return sothat they may once more see the face(s) of (that is, be present among, and rejoice in the fellowship of) the Thessalonian believers in order to supply *the deficiencies* (see also I Cor. 16:17; Phil. 2:30; Col. 1:24; then II Cor. 8:13, 14; 9:12; 11:9) of their faith. The verb *to supply* has the primary meaning *to knit together, to unite* (I Cor. 1:10). The idea of knitting together (think of the work of an *artisan*, which is related to the Greek verb), by an easy transition, has become *to make whole, to round out* (cf. Gal. 6:1 *to re-instate* or *restore*) or, as here, *to supply* what is still lacking.

Deficiencies have to be supplied or made up. Although the nature of these deficiencies is not pointed out in the present passage, the epistle contains the following hints:

a. The Thessalonians are somewhat confused with respect to the doctrine of Christ's return. Hence, by speaking about deficiencies Paul is already preparing for what he is going to say in 4:13-5:3.

b. Though these recent converts have been blessed with many a spiritual grace, there is room for improvement. The virtues already present must begin to abound *more and more* (4:1, 10).

c. Some of the members of the congregation are disorderly, some faint-hearted, some weak (5:14).

If this exposition of the term *deficiencies* be correct, it is clear that the

---

[69] The verb ἀνταποδίδωμι occurs in a favorable sense in Luke 14:14; Rom. 11:35; I Thess. 3:9; in an unfavorable sense in Rom. 12:19; II Thess. 1:6; and Heb. 10:30. In Luke 14:12-14 it is used in connection with ἀντικαλέω. In that same passage we also find ἀνταπόδομα, which occurs there in the favorable sense; in Rom. 11:9, unfavorable. Note also the slightly different form of the noun in Col. 3:24. The fact that the prefix ἀντί in all these cases must mean *in return* is immediately clear from the vivid passage Luke 14:12-14. No other meaning would give a comprehensible sense to the entire passage. See W. Hendriksen, *The Meaning of the Preposition ἀντί in the New Testament*, doctoral dissertation submitted to the Faculty of Princeton Seminary, 1948, Princeton Seminary Library, pp. 78, 79.

word *faith* ("the deficiencies of y o u r faith") is used in a sense which includes both *the subjective* exercise of trust in the Lord and *the objective* revelation of God with respect to the work of redemption.

Having informed the readers about the constant prayer which both Paul and Silas are constantly uttering — a prayer that "we may see y o u r faces" — , the ardent wish is now expressed that this petition may be granted (verse 11), and that additional spiritual blessings may be bestowed upon the Thessalonians (verses 12 and 13):

11. Now may he, our God and Father and our Lord Jesus, direct our way to y o u.

Although with respect to its solemn tone this statement approaches a prayer, we cannot agree with those commentators who call it a prayer. In a prayer God is addressed, and the second person is *generally* used; here the exalted names or titles are *entirely* in the third person (note the pronoun *he*). This, then, is not quite a prayer but rather the devout utterance of a wish that the petition of verse 10 may be fulfilled. For the names of the exalted persons mentioned here see on 1:1. Nevertheless, there are a few points of difference between the titles of 1:1 and those here in 3:11. Note *our* here in 3:11 (cf. 1:3). Also the official name *Christ* is here omitted. The intensive pronoun *he* precedes. Moreover, the essential unity (hence, unity of work and purpose) of the Father and the Son is stressed, the pronoun *he* referring to the combination, and the singular verb (third person singular aorist optative) being employed. We consider the pronoun αὐτός intensive (hence, *he*), not reflexive (*himself*), as if the thought had ever occurred either to Paul or to Silas that *they* might wish to direct their own way. The context here is very clear: note verse 9: thanksgiving was offered *to God,* the rejoicing was in *his* presence; and verse 10: the accompanying prayer was, of course, also uttered *to God.* Hence, very logically, there follows in verse 11, "Now may *he,* our God and Father and our Lord Jesus," etc. It is comforting to know that the Father and the Son are, indeed *one.* We never need to be afraid that the Father is less loving than the Son or that the two work at cross-purposes.

The wish, so touchingly expressed here, is that *our* (inclusive sense) God and Father and *our* (again inclusive, of course) Lord Jesus *may direct* (*make straight;* then *direct, prosper*) our way to y o u. It is obvious that the verb is used here in a more literal sense than in II Thess. 3:5 or in Luke 1:79.

The question may be asked, "Did God really grant this petition?" If we bear in mind that the prayer had been offered in complete submission to the divine will, the answer is, "Yes." See N.T.C. on John 14:13; 15:7; 15:16; and 16:23. Besides, there is Acts 20:1, 2, which indicates that Paul, on his third Missionary Journey, "gave much encouragement" to those in Macedonia. See also Acts 20:3, 4. The possibility of a still later visit (between the first and the second Roman imprisonment) must not be excluded (see on I Tim. 1:3). Of course, the time and the manner in which God answers prayer is not determined by us but by him.

12. Paul, however, also realizes that the spiritual progress of the Thessalonians can be considered even apart from any visit which he (or he and his companions) might make. Hence, there follows: **and as for y o u, may the Lord cause y o u to abound and overflow in love toward one another and toward all, just as also we (do) toward y o u.**

"*As for ourselves,* we ardently hope that God may direct our way to y o u; and (or *but*) *as for y o u ,* whether or not God permits us to revisit y o u, may *the Lord* (that is, *the Lord Jesus* in closest possible connection with *our God and Father;* see on verse 11) cause y o u to abound and overflow in love." That expresses the sense of the passage in the light of its preceding context. Note the emphatic position of "as for y o u" at the very beginning of the sentence. The verbs *to abound* and *(to)overflow* are close synonyms. Together they express *one* idea, namely, that the Thessalonian believers may not merely *increase* in that most eminent virtue, namely, love — as the outward evidence of their living faith —, but may actually *abound* (also used by Paul in II Thess. 1:3; then Rom. 5:20; 6:1; II Cor. 4:15; 8:15; Phil. 4:17); yes, that they may *abound* in such a manner that this ocean of love, being full, reaches to the top edge of its borders *round about* (περισσεύσαι, a very descriptive verb of which Paul is fond, using it also in 4:1, 10, and frequently elsewhere), and even *over*flows (for the sense of περισσεύω is probably not far removed from that of ὑπερπερισσεύω, as in Rom. 5:20; II Cor. 7:4), so that it reaches not only fellow-Christians, in fulfilment of Christ's "new commandment" (see N.T.C. on John 13:34), but even outsiders (5:15; cf. Gal. 6:10; cf. Matt. 5:43-48), being a love "toward one another *and toward all.*"

For the meaning of the noun *love* and of the verb *to love* see N.T.C. on John 13:35 and 21:15-17. The addition "just as we also (do) toward y o u" (that is, "just as we also abound and overflow in love toward y o u") finds its commentary in preceding passages (see on 2:7-12; 2:17-3:1; 3:7-11; see also on 1:6).

13. The *purpose* (cf. 3:2) of this abounding and overflowing in love is expressed as follows: **in order that he may strengthen** [70] **y o u r hearts, so that they may be blameless in holiness in the presence of our God and Father.**

The Lord by means of love *strengthens* (see on 3:2) the inner purposes and desires. Hearts thus strengthened will be less prone to crave the

---

[70] As to form, the verb can be either aorist infinitive active or third person singular aorist optative active, but in harmony with the verbs which precede, the latter is probably intended.

unseparated life, the life of the world. Rather, they will tend in the direction of the wholly *separated* life, sothat, trusting entirely in Christ and in his redemption and having experienced the transforming influences of his Spirit, they will be *blameless* (cf. I Thess. 2:10), in a state and condition of *holiness* (separation from sin, consecration to God), and this in the very presence of *our God and Father,* that is, before his judgment-seat (Rom. 14:10).

This immediately introduces the thought of Christ's second coming unto judgment, as is evident both from the parallel passage (5:23) and from the immediately following phrase **at the coming of our Lord Jesus with all his saints.**

With respect to this compound phrase there is wide disagreement among commentators. There is first of all a difference of opinion with respect to the term *coming* or *Parousia,* which we have defined as being "the return of the Lord in order to bless his people with his presence" (see on 2:19).[71] But the main point of controversy has to do with the modifier *with all his saints.* And here again there are two problems that require solution:

a. What does this phrase modify?
b. What is the meaning of the word *saints?*

As to the first question, many commentators (for example, Van Leeuwen and Lenski) make this phrase dependent upon "in order that he may strengthen," or connect it loosely with the entire first part of verse 13. The sense then would be somewhat on this order (starting with verse 12): "And as for y o u, may the Lord cause y o u to abound and to overflow in love . . . in order that he may strengthen y o u r hearts sothat they *with all his saints* may be blameless in holiness in the presence of our God and Father at the coming of our Lord Jesus."

We doubt, however, whether any reader (either of the Greek original or of the English translation) will mentally so construe the phrase. The translations (A.V., A.R.V., R.S.V., Weymouth, etc., etc.), in strict accordance with the original, place the words *with all his saints* immediately after *at the coming of our Lord Jesus.* In fact, though Lenski says that these two phrases should be separated by a comma, even in his own rendering he does not so separate them! (See R. C. H. Lenski, *op. cit.,* p. 301, then p. 296.) Other versions indicate the right connection by translating: "when our Lord Jesus appears (or *comes back*) with all his people (or *with all his consecrated ones*)." Thus, for example, Goodspeed and Williams.

The reason we agree with the translators and not with some commentators (Van Leeuwen, Lenski) is that we regard the construction favored by the latter to be unnatural (so does also Frame, *op. cit.,* p. 140). Surely, un-

---

[71] We disagree with the view of Lenski, according to which the Parousia is the Lord's presence *and not his coming out of heaven; op. cit.,* p. 301.

less there is a sound reason for an exception, we should not depart from the rule that a phrase should be construed with the words nearest (or at least *near*) to it.

One sometimes wonders whether the difficulty of conceiving the saints as coming *with* the Lord has led to the unnatural construction. Whether or not one happens to belong to the camp of the Premillennialists, in all fairness to them one must admit that when they link *with all his saints* with the immediately preceding words, sothat we get, "at the coming of our Lord Jesus with all his saints," they are entirely correct!

As we see it, they (as well as others who do not share their millennial views) are also correct in interpreting the term *saints* (ἅγιοι) as referring to the redeemed, and not to the angels. This introduces problem b. mentioned above. On this point we are in complete agreement with those commentators (like Van Leeuwen and Lenski) whose view with respect to the construction of the sentence we have just criticized. And, on the other hand, we are in complete disagreement here with Frame, who boldly translates "with all his angels" (*op. cit.*, p. 136). Reasons for our position:

(1) Paul loves this word *saints,* using it again and again in his epistles. Not once does he employ it to indicate the angels, always the redeemed. Why then introduce an exception here in I Thess. 3:13?

(2) Paul in this same passage mentions the terms *holiness* (ἁγιωσύνη) and *saints* (ἅγιοι). In the original the two words are from the same root, just as are our words *consecration* and *consecrated ones.* Hence, those who at Christ's coming will be blameless in holiness most likely resemble the redeemed saints.

(3) In the parallel passage (4:14), these saints are defined as *those who have fallen asleep in Jesus.* See on that verse.

It is certainly true that the angels will accompany Christ at his return (see on II Thess. 1:7; Matt. 25:31), but that is not taught here in I Thess. 3:13. Here the thought is that when the Lord Jesus (see on 1:1) returns, God will *bring with him* (exactly as is stated in 4:14) those who, throughout the ages, have lived the life of Christian separation from the world and of devotion to God. By God they had been "set apart" to his worship and service sothat, through the sanctifying power of the Holy Spirit, they had become saints "in experience as well as position" (to use a phrase employed by K. S. Wuest, *Golden Nuggets,* p. 72), and at death had entered the kingdom above. Not a single one of them will be left behind in heaven: *all* those who at death went to heaven — and therefore are now with him in heaven — will leave their celestial abodes at the very moment when the Lord begins his descent. Very quickly they will reunite with their bodies, which now become *gloriously resurrected* bodies, and will then immediately (together with those children of God who still survive on earth, and who will be changed "in a moment, in the twinkling of an eye") ascend in order to meet the Lord.

This interpretation brings 3:13 into complete harmony with 4:13-18; see on that passage. It also shows that there is no need nor good reason to accept the theory, held by *many* (but not by all of our brothers in Christ, the) Premillennialists, according to which Christ comes first *for* his saints, and seven years later *with* his saints. The coming is *one;* but it is a coming both *with* and *for* his saints.

Synthesis of Chapter 3

See p. 80. *Expression of Joy. Paul writes to the Thessalonians, informing them how he rejoices over Timothy's report with respect to their continued spiritual progress even in the midst of persecution.*

Verses 1-5. What moved Paul (or Paul after consultation with the others) to send Timothy

Paul informs the Thessalonians that the continued separation had at length become unbearable. Hence the decision had been reached to be left behind in Athens *alone* (which may mean either *all alone* or, perhaps preferably, *alone with Silas*), and to send Timothy to them, with this three-fold purpose:

a. in order to strengthen the Thessalonians

b. in order to encourage them

c. in order to learn (and bring back information) about their faith.

In view of the fact that Thessalonica counted among its members some that were disorderly, some that were faint-hearted, and some that were weak (perhaps, prone to fall back into the immorality of heathendom), *strengthening* was necessary. In view of oppression and the valiant resolution to stand up under it *encouragement* was in order. In view of the constant and sinister attempt of the tempter to "lure away" God's children from the faith, by striving to entice them with words of flattery, *information* about the state of their faith was desired.

In connection with this last point, one of the older commentators points out that the devil is often more dangerous when he fawns than when he roars: David won the victory over Satan in the field of battle (I Sam. 17:49), but in the cool of the evening on the housetop Satan won the victory over David.

Paul reminds the Thessalonians that, while the missionaries were still with them, the tribulation under which they were now suffering had been predicted again and again. "Forewarned is fore-armed." Persecution that has been planned by God in his love and that happens "according to plan" should strengthen faith.

Verses 6-10. *What comfort (or reason for rejoicing) Timothy's report had brought*

Timothy had returned and had brought tidings concerning the readers' faith and love, their deficiencies, and their yearning to see Paul and Silas. *On the whole* (but note "the deficiencies") the report had been very encouraging. It had given Paul and Silas a new lease on life. The great apostle gives expression to his feeling of inadequacy in attempting to bring a proper thank-offering to God. He informs the readers of his constant, intense, and earnest prayer for the privilege of returning to them in order to see them face to face and to supply the deficiencies of their faith.

Verses 11-13. *The fervent wish*

He expresses the fervent wish that his prayer may be heard and that, whether or not it be granted, the Lord may fill them with such an overflowing measure of love that their hearts may be strengthened, sothat there may be fruit for the day of judgment, when Jesus comes with all his saints.

Summary of I Thessalonians 4:1-12

Paul Writes to the Thessalonians

Exhorting Them How They Should Conduct Themselves
This Section Comprises *the Apostle's Exhortation:*

4:1-8 with respect to sex and marriage
sex in general: immorality condemned, sanctification urged
in particular, the taking of a wife "in sanctification and honor"
and
the duty with respect to the brother, namely, not to defraud him
"in this matter"

4:9-12 with respect to love of the brotherhood and diligence in daily
conduct
commendation of love toward the brotherhood
commendation of diligence in daily conduct: fanatics, busybodies
and loafers are reprimanded

CHAPTER IV

4 1 For the rest, brothers, we request y o u and urge y o u in the Lord Jesus, that as y o u received from us (instructions) as to how y o u ought to conduct yourselves [72] and to please God — as in fact y o u are conducting yourselves — that y o u abound the more. 2 For y o u know what instructions we gave y o u through the Lord Jesus. 3 For this is God's will, y o u r sanctification, that y o u abstain from immorality, 4 that each one of y o u know how to take a wife [73] for himself in sanctification and honor, 5 not in the passion of lust like also the heathen who do not know God; 6 that no one go beyond what is proper and defraud his brother in this matter, because an Avenger is the Lord in all these things, as previously we told y o u and solemnly testified. 7 For God did not call us for uncleanness but in sanctification. 8 Therefore, he who rejects (this instruction), rejects not man but God who even gives his Holy Spirit to y o u.

9 Now concerning love to the brothers y o u have no need to (have anyone) write to y o u, for y o u yourselves have been taught by God to love each other; 10 and in fact y o u are also doing this to all the brothers in the whole of Macedonia. But we urge y o u, brothers, to abound the more, 11 and to be ambitious about living calmly, and to be engaged in y o u r own affairs, and to work with y o u r hands, just as we charged y o u, 12 in order that y o u may conduct yourselves properly with respect to outsiders and be dependent on nobody.

4:1-12

4:1. For the rest, brothers, we request y o u and urge y o u in the Lord Jesus, that as y o u received from us (instructions) as to how y o u ought to conduct yourselves and to please God — as in fact y o u are conducting yourselves —, that y o u abound the more.

Both the phrase of introduction ("for the rest") and the subject-matter makes it clear that a new section begins here. This is neither Defence nor Expression of Joy but Exhortation to live sanctified lives with respect to all classes and at all times.

This Exhortation extends from verse 1 through verse 12 of the fourth chapter, and is resumed in chapter 5. The first 11 verses of that chapter form a transition, and may be classified either as Exhortation (see espe-

---

[72] Or: *how y o u ought to live* (literally *walk*); so also in verse 12; cf. 2:12.
[73] Literally *vessel*.

97

cially verses 6, 8, 11) or (together with 4:13-18) as Instruction with respect to the return of Christ. From 5:12 on the Exhortation has been fully resumed, as is clear from all the "instructions" found in that section.

It is evident then that the section with reference to Christ's return is wedged in between two Exhortation-paragraphs dealing with the affairs of daily life and conduct. This is significant. It indicates that Paul was neither an ascetic nor an ecstatic or dreamer. He wanted his readers to have a healthy outlook upon life, sothat in meditating upon events "on the other side" (of death) they would not forget about their duties "on this side."

Nevertheless, he did not want them to separate these two. On the contrary, he desired that "on this side" they would arrange everything sothat they would be ready for "the other side." Or, stating it differently, *he wanted them to set their house in order with a view to the earnestly awaited coming of the glorious Visitor from "the other side," even the Lord Jesus.* They must ever be ready to receive him.

In a sense there is a difference between the present section (4:1-12) and the resumption of admonitions (5:12-28). The present section emphasizes the duty of living sanctified lives and of giving evidence of this both to fellow-Christians (by loving them, particularly by not trespassing the bounds of propriety in matters pertaining to sex) and to outsiders (by proper conduct). The section at the close of the epistle is far more specific. It contains a good many detailed directions with respect to various matters (see especially 5:12-22, 24-27).

In another sense, however, there is a close resemblance between the two sections, as the following comparison will show:

4:1-12	**5:12-28**
verses 1, 2, 3, 4, 7: y o u r *sanctification*	verse 23: "Now may he, the God of peace, *sanctify* y o u completely."
verse 3: ". . . that y o u abstain from immorality."	verse 22: "Abstain from every form of evil."
verse 6: "An Avenger is the Lord."	verse 15: "Take care that none of y o u repays evil for evil."
verse 8: ". . . who even gives his Holy Spirit to y o u."	verse 19: "Quench not the Spirit."
verse 9: ". . . love each other."	verse 14: "Admonish the disorderly, encourage the fainthearted, help the weak, have patience with all."
verse 11: ". . . be ambitious about living calmly."	verse 13: "Be at peace among yourselves."

verse 12: ". . . conduct yourselves properly with respect to outsiders."

verse 15: "Always aim at doing good to each other *and to all.*"

Note how here in 4:1 (and also in what follows) Paul is dealing with the Thessalonian believers "as a nurse cherishes (and as a father admonishes) her (his) own children" (2:7, 11). For the meaning of *brothers* see on 1:4. The apostle (supported by his companions, of course) *requests* (the asking is friendly and polite, yet is no begging; see N.T.C. on John 11:22; 14:16) and *admonishes* or *urges* (see on 2:11; 3:2, 7) *"in* the Lord Jesus" (see on 1:1) — that is, by virtue of union with the Lord whom he represents and whose spirit inspires him — that they will *overflow* or *excel* or *abound* (περισσεύω see on 3:12) more and more in the business of conducting themselves properly, thus pleasing God. It is evident that what he desires so ardently is that the Thessalonians, in keeping God's law, shall be prompted by gratitude for their deliverance. With wonderful tact he injects the parenthetical clause: "as in fact y o u are conducting yourselves." What the apostle really desires, therefore, is that the branches that bear fruit shall bear *more* fruit (see N.T.C. on John 15:2). That was necessary not only in view of the immaturity of these recent converts from paganism and of "the deficiencies of faith" which had to be supplied in their particular case (3:10), but also in view of the more general consideration, namely, that the believer never attains to complete spiritual perfection in this life. For the concept *pleasing God* see on 2:15.

2. For y o u know what instructions we gave y o u through the Lord Jesus.

In order to preclude the charge of being guilty of issuing arbitrary orders, hence, in order to add weight to his exhortation, the apostle stresses two matters:

a. That those *instructions* or *directives* (a military term occurring also in Acts 5:28; 16:24; I Tim. 1:5, 18) are *not new.* They are orders given previously, while Paul was with them.

b. That they are given *through* the Lord Jesus; that is, at his command; hence, with his authority. Though commentators differ with respect to the interpretation of the preposition *through* as here used, the explanation which we have just given has the context in its favor (see below on verse 8). The readers must be made aware of the fact that whoever rejects the instructions here given rejects not man but God.

When this interpretation is adopted, the logic of the statement which immediately follows is clear at once. Note the connection: "through the Lord Jesus Christ. For this is God's will." It is not merely *Paul* writing but *God* directing.

3-8. Because of the exegetical problem involved in verses 3-8, and in order to show the relationship of the several parts to each other and to the whole, it was necessary to print these six verses together as one unit, and to print them in such a manner that these relationships are at once apparent.

For this is God's will, y o u r sanctification,

(a) that y o u abstain from immorality,

(b) that each one of y o u know how to take a wife for himself in sanctification and honor, not in the passion of lust like also the heathen who do not know God;

(c) that (no one) go beyond what is proper and defraud his brother in this matter,

because an Avenger is the Lord in all these things, as previously we told y o u, and solemnly testified. For God did not call us for uncleanness but in sanctification. Therefore, he who rejects (this instruction), rejects not man but God who even gives his Holy Spirit to y o u.

Thus, it becomes apparent at once that, according to the most simple construction (also the most logical, it seems to us), the words *This . . . God's will . . . y o u r sanctification* are in apposition. The three co-ordinate clauses (a, b, and c) are added for further elucidation (in other words, they are *epexegetical*) of the concept y o u r *sanctification*. (See also on verse 9.) They are in apposition with it and give it a somewhat restricted application. Also (b) sheds light on (a), (a) on (b), (c) on (b), and (b) on (c). Though (b) and (c) are parallel to each other and in a sense also to (a), yet they may be viewed as presenting a specific exemplification of (a).

The clause "because an Avenger is the Lord in all these things . . ." modifies (a), (b), and (c), as the very words *all these things* indicate. The sense of that clause is: God avenges immorality, and in particular the taking of a wife in the passion of lust, and the evil of going beyond what is proper and defrauding the brother in the matter of marital relationships. God punishes the man who refuses to tread the path of sanctification. This is true, "*for* God did not call us for uncleanness but in sanctification." The final sentence — "Therefore, he who rejects (this instruction) rejects not man but God who even gives his Holy Spirit to y o u" — shows that because it was God himself who called in connection with sanctification, the man who disregards this admonition squarely opposes *him* (see N.T.C. on John 13:20; cf. I Sam. 8:7; Luke 10:16), and that this is all the more reprehensible because the Author of sanctification is God's great *gift* to the Church.

From the preceding it is clear that Paul is discussing *one* matter, not *two*. He is discussing *sanctification,* and here in verses 3-8 in particular the duty of everyone to abstain from *immorality,* such as is practiced, for example, by those who, instead of taking a wife and doing this in a manner that is in keeping with the requirement of sanctification, are motivated by lust; or, disregarding the bounds of decency, enter into illicit, clandestine relationships with their brother's wife or daughter. Though the brother, who has thus been outwitted and defrauded, may never discover the wrong that was done against him, there is, nevertheless, an Avenger, even God (cf. Lev. 25:14, 17; Ps. 94:1), just as Paul had solemnly declared while he was still with them. Let the believers in Thessalonica, so recently converted from a world in which such sinful practices prevail, bear in mind that they have been called out of this world, and this not for the purpose of committing uncleanness, but in connection with the great work of *sanctification* [74] which the Holy Spirit, God's gift to the Church, is performing in their hearts. For the name, character, coming, and work of the Holy Spirit see N.T.C. on John 14:16, 17, 26; 15:26; 16:7, 8, 13-15.

That, in brief, seems to be the plain import of the entire passage (verses 3-8). There are, however, certain translators and commentators who adhere to a view which, in one important respect, differs radically from ours. Their view amounts to this, that Paul in this brief paragraph is condemning *two* heathen vices, namely, *sexual immorality* and *dishonest business practices*. Verse 6 is then translated as follows (or on this order): "that no one go too far and cheat his brother *in business.*" We believe, however, that those translators are correct who have: "that no one go beyond what is proper and defraud his brother *in this matter.*" [75]

Our reasons for adopting the rendering, "that no one go beyond what is proper and defraud his brother *in this matter*" are as follows:

---

[74] The active verbal noun ἁγιασμός is here used, also in I Thess. 4:7; II Thess. 2:13; then Rom. 6:19, 22; I Cor. 1:30; Heb. 12:14; I Peter 1:2. The verbal idea is probably not entirely absent either in I Thess. 4:4 (in choosing a wife the principle of sanctification should make itself manifest) or in I Tim. 2:15. The resultant state or quality is expressed by the term ἁγιωσύνη as the ending suggests.

[75] In favor of the rendering "in this matter" (or something similar) and of interpreting the admonition as a warning against "sins of the flesh," especially the sin of illicit sexual relationships (for example, of a man with his fellow believer's wife or daughter) are the following: A.R.V., R.S.V., Goodspeed, Weymouth, Williams, the new Dutch rendering, the French (Version d'Ostervald); also: Alford, Bengel, Denney (in *The Expositor's Bible*), Ellicott, Erdman, Frame, Fausset (in Jamieson, Fausset, Brown *Commentary*), George Milligan, Moffatt (in *Expositor's Greek Testament*), and Robertson (in *Word Pictures*), these in addition to many other commentators among whom there are some whose works are probably less well known or less easily accessible.

In favor of the rendering "in business" (or something similar) are the following: Wyclif ("in chaffaringe"), Tyndale ("in bargayninge"), Cranmer, Rheims, the Berkeley Version (by Verkuyl), the older German versions, Frisian, South African; also: Auberlen-Riggenbach (in Lange's Commentary), Calvin, Grotius, Lenski, Veldkamp, and several others.

Barnes is among those who accept the position that the injunction is against defrauding in any sense, shape, or manner, whether in business or otherwise. Cf. "in *any* matter" of the Geneva Version and of the A.V.

(1) When a subject is introduced with so much feeling, an abrupt change to something quite different (like "in business") is not to be expected. Paul is speaking about sanctification, and in that connection, about abstaining from immorality and uncleanness. *Sanctification, immorality, uncleanness,* are the key-words of the entire paragraph (verses 3-8).

(2) The injunction, "that each one of y o u know how *to take* (χτᾶσθαι *present* infinitive; hence, not *to possess,* for which we would rather expect the *perfect* tense) a wife (literally *vessel,* a term used also by the rabbis for *wife*) for himself in sanctification and honor" certainly supports the idea that the πρᾶγμα about which Paul is speaking in verse 6 is that of purity in sex and marital relationships. One should choose a wife for himself, and in this choice the sanctifying power of God, which causes one to hold his wife in honor, should come to expression. The evil of shamefully defrauding a brother (by practicing immorality with his wife or daughter) instead of honorably taking a wife is here condemned.

(3) Our interpretation is also supported by what Paul says in a somewhat parallel passage: I Cor. 7:2, and cf. verse 39: in order not to fall into the temptation of committing immorality a man should have *a wife of his own.* Marriage, moreover, must ever be *in the Lord.*

(4) The verbs a. *go beyond* or *step over* or *over-reach* (ὑπερβαίνω-ειν, occurring only here in the New Testament), whether used intransitively (*to go beyond what is proper*) or transitively (*to over-reach or outwit the brother*), and b. *have more than, take advantage of, defraud* (πλεονέκτω-ειν), are very fitting in connection with immoral practices in sex-relationships. (It is not true that they can apply only to business-transactions.) Such sins are often practised *in secret:* the father or the husband does not know what is going on and his rights are being denied; he is being *defrauded.* But God knows, and he will prove to be the Avenger!

(5) In the New Testament the word πρᾶγμα nowhere else means *business,* but always means *thing, matter* (sometimes *deed, practice*). See footnote 76. Objections to this explanation are answered in the same footnote.[76]

---

[76] The main objections are as follows:
a. *The majority of commentators favor the translation "in business."*
   Answer: When so many scholars of high rank are to be found on each side of a question, this argument (which is never strong) has very little value.
b. *The clause, "An Avenger is the Lord in all these things" indicates that at least two different sins must have been mentioned in the preceding.*
   Answer: Strictly speaking, even *two* is not enough to account fully for the expression *all these things.* But on our own explanation the three co-ordinate clauses, mentioning the sin of immorality, the taking of a wife in the passion of lust, and the going beyond what is proper and defrauding the brother, are all that is needed, especially if it be borne in mind that this is not a little problem in addition, and that similar sins, though not actually mentioned, are *implied.*
c. *The omission of a subject in connection with "go beyond what is proper and defraud his brother in this matter" shows that a new sin, not yet thought of before, is mentioned here.*

9. A new admonition is now added. Nevertheless, it is not entirely new. Love to the brothers is another illustration of *sanctification,* mentioned in verse 3. Moreover, in verse 6 *defrauding the brother* was prohibited. Hence, it is not surprising that something is now said with reference to *loving the brother(s):*

Now concerning love to the brothers y o u have no need to (have any-one) write to y o u, for y o u yourselves have been taught by God to love each other.

The question whether Paul is here reflecting on a letter from the Thessalonians has been discussed in footnote 4. No such letter is required to explain the present passage. As has already been indicated, the transition from verses 3-8 to verse 9 is not abrupt. And the expression "Y o u have no need to (have anyone) write to y o u," does not necessarily indicate reluctance on Paul's part. Rather, it is accounted for as follows:

(1) Paul has just said that the Holy Spirit had been given to the Church (in this case specifically to the brothers at Thessalonica); see verse 8. In this very connection he now adds that this indwelling Spirit (in connection with the message from the missionaries) has already taught them to love each other. Hence, writing about this at length is not now considered necessary. The mere mention ought to suffice.

(2) The Thessalonians — see the next verse (10) — are actually showing

---

Answer: The omission of the subject, so that it has to be supplied (perhaps from the preceding clause; hence, "that each one of y o u . . . not" or "that no one . . .") does not in and by itself settle the question in either direction. In arriving at a conclusion it is the predicate, far more than the subject, that is of importance.

d. *The articular infinitive in verse 6* (τὸ μὴ ὑπερβαίνειν), *by its very contrast with the anarthrous infinitives in the two preceding clauses* (ἀπέχεσθαι *and* εἰδέναι) *proves that a new sin is introduced here, namely, that of dishonesty in business.* Answer: The use of the article with the infinitive in verse 6 (so that τὸ μὴ ὑπερβαίνειν results) may be explained as an attempt to indicate that this μή is not parallel to the μή at the beginning (and again toward the end) of verse 5, but introduces a new clause. (There are other explanations.) It is not true that the article proves that a new sin is introduced here.

e. Πρᾶγμα *is a regular commercial term, meaning* "business." *Hence, that must be the meaning here in I Thess. 4:6.* Answer: The simple fact is that nowhere else in the entire New Testament does the word have that meaning.

Matt. 18:19: "as touching any *thing*"
Luke 1:1: "a narrative concerning those *matters.*"
Acts 5:4: ". . . this *thing* (perhaps *deed*) in thy heart"
Rom. 16:2: "assist her in whatever *matter*"
I Cor. 6:1: ". . . having a *matter* (or *grievance* or *law-suit*) against his neighbor
II Cor. 7:11: ". . . to be pure in the *matter*"
Heb. 6:18: "by two immutable *things*"
Heb. 10:1: "not the very image of the *things*"
Heb. 11:1: "a conviction of *things* not seen"
Jas. 3:16: "and every vile *deed* (or *practice*)"

this love, and this on a very wide scale (cf. 1:3). Why then should Paul write about it at length?

(3) Paul was probably the most tactful missionary who ever walked the earth. He wishes to avoid giving offence, and he desires to give credit where credit is due. By stating that, broadly speaking, it is not even necessary to write about love to the brothers, inasmuch as the readers have been taught by God and are showing the effects of this teaching in their lives, he is the better prepared to point out certain deficiencies. Let it be borne in mind that the man who is writing is the one who told others that their speech should ever be gracious, seasoned with salt (Col. 4:6). He never flatters (see on I Thess. 2:5), but he is gentle as when a nurse cherishes (or as when a father deals with) her (his) own children (see on 2:7, 11).

The term *philadelphia* (φιλαδελφία) or *love to the brother*(s), which in classical Greek means love to the brother *by birth,* in the New Testament always denotes love to the brother *in Christ* (thus also in Rom. 12:10; Heb. 13:1; I Peter 1:22; II Peter 1:7). The Thessalonians had been *taught by God* thus to love one another. The passive verbal adjective θεοδίδακτοι occurs only here in the New Testament, but cf. Is. 54:13; 60:2, 3; Jer. 31:33, 34; Joel 2:28; Mic. 5:2; Zeph. 3:9; Mal. 1:11; and see N.T.C. on John 6:45. For loving one another see N.T.C. on John 13:34; 15:12. On the verb *to love* see N.T.C. on John 21:15-17.

10. The effectiveness of this divine teaching is now indicated:
And in fact y o u are also doing this to all the brothers in the whole of Macedonia.

To the industrial, political, and social connections between the people of the large city of Thessalonica and those of other places in Macedonia (for example, Philippi, Berea) the faith-in-Christ relationship had now been added. To all the brothers in Christ with whom the Thessalonians came into contact, throughout the whole of Macedonia, genuine "brotherly love" was being revealed. Cf. 1:7, 8. Hence, Paul can only add: **But we urge** (see on 2:11) **y o u, brothers, to abound the more.** See on 4:1. Perfection had not yet been reached. This admonition is always timely, for in this life no Christian ever reaches the ideal of ethical perfection. Besides, in *this* case there were special reasons why the admonition was necessary, as is clearly intimated in such passages as 3:10; 4:3-8, 11; 5:13-15.

11. A few brief admonitions are added. Also with respect to the matters here mentioned the work of sanctification (see verse 3) must become evident:
    a. **and to be ambitious about living calmly**
    b. **and to be engaged in y o u r own affairs**
    c. **and to work with y o u r hands, just as we charged y o u,**

Fanatics, busybodies, and *loafers,* nearly every church has them! Often one and the same person is all three. Hence, the three admonitions do not concern three separate classes of people, but in a sense the entire congregation, for the seed of every sin is embedded in every heart.

The attempt to find in the second and the third admonition a reference to two distinct groups — businessmen and laborers — must be rejected. Certain commentators favor this idea, probably in order to add a touch of realism to the "businessmen" whom they have introduced in verse 6 ("in business"?). The admonitions concern the membership in general, though naturally they concern some far more than others. Also, the first admonition was particularly adapted to one person, the second to another, etc.

Although there is nothing here that proves a connection between conditions in the church and excitement about Christ's expected return, such a connection is, nevertheless, probable. See on II Thess. 2:1, 2. Note also that here in I Thess. 4 the three admonitions are immediately followed by instruction with reference to the second coming.

Some people had become restless. Paul now urges that this restlessness be turned into the proper channel. With that admirable ability to express himself paradoxically which again and again becomes evident in his epistles, Paul admonishes the Thessalonians to become all stirred up about being quiet (living calmly)! Let the restless one *be ambitious* about attaining this goal. The original has here the verb φιλοτιμεῖσθαι. The primary meaning is *to love honor,* then *to be ambitious, to aspire, to strive* (perhaps *to take pride in;* see also Rom. 5:20; II Cor. 5:9).[77]

Glorying in the doctrine of Christ's Return is proper. Awaiting this blessed coming is natural for the genuine believer. But being so excited about it that one becomes arrogant, thinking that he — he alone! — has discovered "the light," sothat as a result one begins to meddle in the affairs of other people, particularly with the affairs of the leaders of the church, is all wrong. Hence, to the first admonition a second is added: ". . . to be engaged in y o u r own affairs (τὰ ἴδια)." It seems that the busybodies did not take this admonition to heart. Their meddling grew worse instead of better (see on II Thess. 3:11).

The tendency of such people to leave their workshop or other form of manual labor evoked the third admonition: ". . . to work with y o u r own hands, just as we charged y o u." See on 2:9. Manual labor was even more common in those days than it is now. There were slaves, hired laborers, independent artisans (cf. Acts 19:24) each having his own workshop, farmers or helpers on farms. Of course, a harbor-city like Thessalonica also had its ship-owners and its leaders in commercial enterprises. And there were the men who owned or worked in bazaars. It is certainly within the realm

[77] See the article by J. S. M. Hooper "Translation of Biblical Terms: An Illustration," in *BTr,* Vol. 4, Number 3 (July, 1953), 126-129.

of possibility that some of the men in control of business, whether big or small, belonged to the church. In many cases, no doubt, manual labor was combined with business on a small scale. But in the present passage, at any rate, the emphasis is not on doing business but on working with the hands. The bulk of the membership must have consisted of manual laborers, skilled or unskilled. See also p. 11. Paul knew what this meant. Perhaps he himself, just before writing this letter, had been working on a tent! The intent then of the present admonition is that the members of the recently established congregation, instead of seeking to be supported by the church and of interfering with the leaders if they did not get their way, should continue at their daily occupation, earning their own living. The gospel of salvation is intensely practical. It dignifies labor. All these things had been made perfectly plain to the Thessalonians when the missionaries first visited them. Definite orders had been given. Hence, fanatics, busybodies, and loafers could not offer any reasonable excuse for their misconduct.

12. The purpose of these admonitions is stated in the following words: **in order that** [78] **y o u may conduct yourselves properly with respect to outsiders and be dependent on nobody.**[79]

To *walk* (same verb as in 2:12; 4:1) or behave "according to good fashion" or "in good form" (εὐσχημόνως from εὖ and σχῆμα; cf. I Cor. 14:40; then Rom. 13:13), becomingly, with respect to *outsiders*, that is, non-Christians (cf. I Cor. 5:12; Col. 4:5), sothat the Gospel would not be brought into discredit; and *to be dependent on* (literally *to have need of*) nobody, is a worthy aim. Thus, one is able even to help support those worthy persons who are really in need (cf. Acts 20:34, 35).

Synthesis of 4:1-12

See p. 96. *Exhortation. Paul writes to the Thessalonians exhorting them how they should conduct themselves*

verses 1-8 *with respect to sex and marriage*

Very tactfully the apostle points out that he is not issuing new commands, that his precepts are given through the Lord Jesus Christ (in harmony with Christ's will and by his authority), and that to a certain extent the readers are already pleasing God by their conduct in harmony with his will. They should, however, abound the more.

---

[78] The change from infinitives to ἵνα would seem to imply purpose here (perhaps result: *so that;* the difference being very trivial in this case), not an object-clause after "We urge y o u." It is entirely true, of course, that ἵνα frequently introduces an object-clause, but for the reason stated that is not probable here.

[79] Of course, μηδενός can also mean *on nothing,* but in view of the immediately preceding πρὸς τοὺς ἔξω, the translation *on nobody* is probably better.

Now, the will of God is their *sanctification*.

Applying this to the sphere of sex and marriage, Paul insists that each man, far from clinging to or falling back into heathen vice, for example, defrauding a brother by means of dishonorable conduct with that brother's wife or daughter, should take a wife for himself in sanctification and honor, not in the passion of lust. He points out, moreover:

a. that God is an Avenger,

b. that the readers must bear in mind that they have been called not for uncleanness but in sanctification,

c. that anyone who rejects this instruction rejects not man but God, and

d. that this God, in order to help them in their struggle against sin, even gives his Holy Spirit to them.

verses 9-12 *with respect to love of the brotherhood and diligence in daily conduct*

With respect to love toward brothers in Christ, Paul can be brief, for God's indwelling Spirit has taught the brothers to love each other; besides, they are already doing this on a wide scale. Let them *abound* in this virtue, however.

With respect to diligence, *fanatics* — afflicted probably with Parousia hysteria (cf. II Thess. 2:1, 2) — should become "ambitious to be calm"; *busybodies* (Paul uses the actual term in II Thess. 3:11, but *the idea* is implied here in I Thess. 4:11) should begin to mind their own affairs; and *loafers* should start working with their hands. (In all probability the same persons were all three: fanatics, busybodies, and loafers.) No offence should be given to outsiders. Besides, by working diligently a person develops the art of being "dependent on nobody."

Summary of I Thessalonians 4:13 — 5:11

Paul Writes to the Thessalonians

Instructing Them How Christ Will Come Again
This Section Comprises *the Apostle's Instruction,* showing that the Lord's Return will be

4:13-18 *with impartiality* toward all believers, sothat survivors will have no advantage over those who have fallen asleep

5:1-11 *with suddenness,* taking people by surprise, though believers will be (and ever should exert themselves to be) fully prepared

13 Now we do not wish y o u to be in ignorance, brothers, concerning those who fall asleep, in order that y o u do not grieve as do the rest, who have no hope. 14 For if we believe that Jesus died and rose again, so also those who fell asleep through Jesus God will bring with him. [80] 15 For this we say to y o u by the word of the Lord that we, those who remain alive, who are left until the coming of the Lord, shall have no advantage at all over those who fell asleep. 16 For with a shouted command, with a voice of an archangel and with a trumpet of God the Lord himself will descend from heaven, and the dead in Christ will rise first; 17 then we who are alive, who are left, shall be caught up together with them in clouds to meet the Lord in the air. 18 And so we shall always be with the Lord. Therefore encourage one another with these words.

4:13-18

A new section begins here. This is neither Defence nor Expression of Joy nor Exhortation but Instruction, though these four are never entirely separated. Note, for example, the exhortation in verse 18.

This section shows how Christ will come again. It has two subdivisions, showing first, that he will come with impartiality toward all believers, sothat survivors will have no advantage over those who have fallen asleep (4:13-18), and secondly, that his arrival will be sudden, taking people by surprise (5:1-11).

4:13. Now we do not wish y o u to be in ignorance, brothers, concerning those who are falling asleep.

The introductory clause, *Now we do not wish y o u to be in ignorance,* has its analogies in many letters that have come down to us from the ancient world. Paul often uses this formula (Rom. 1:13; 11:25; I Cor. 10:1; 12:1; II Cor. 1:8; cf. Phil. 1:12; Col. 2:1). But in Paul's epistles words are never mere empty forms. They are divinely inspired. There is a special reason for them. So also in the present case. Ignorance concerning spiritual realities is always bad for the believer. It leads to lack of comfort. That was particularly true in this case. The *brothers* (note affectionate form of address; see on 1:4) are worrying about those who *fall* (an inferior reading has *had fallen) asleep.*

The death of believers is often compared to sleep (Matt. 27:52; John 11:11-13; Acts 7:60; I Cor. 7:39; 15:6, 18; cf. "rest from their labors," Rev. 14:13). The expression is based on Old Testament terminology with reference to death (Gen. 47:30; II Sam. 7:12). The comparison of death to sleep is particularly appropriate in implying not only rest from labor but also the glorious awakening which believers expect on the other side. This falling asleep does not indicate an intermediate state of unconscious re-

---

[80] We have tried to retain in the translation the amphibolous position of the phrase διὰ τοῦ Ἰησοῦ. See on verse 14.

pose (soul-sleep). Though the soul is asleep to the world which it has left (Job 7:9, 10; Is. 63:16; Eccl. 9:6), it is awake with respect to its own world (Luke 16:19-31; 23:43; II Cor. 5:8; Phil. 1:21-23; Rev. 7:15-17; 20:4). For other beautiful and comforting words and phrases describing the death of believers see N.T.C. on John 11:11-13.

A fair inference from the present passage is that during the short period which had elapsed since the Thessalonians first heard the Gospel some believers had passed from this earthly scene. It was with reference to them that friends and relatives were deeply disturbed. In fact, they were so alarmed that Paul adds: **in order that y o u do not grieve as do the rest, who have no hope.**

The reason for this perturbation is not stated in so many words, though a safe but very general inference can be drawn from the following verses. That these friends and relatives actually thought that the departed ones "were lost" [81] does not necessarily follow from anything in the present paragraph. It is possible, especially in view of the immediately following context, that they had given up all hope for the future glory of *the bodies* of the deceased. See on verse 15. However, verse 13 does not even state in so many words that believers were *actually* grieving "as the rest who have no hope." It may simply mean that there was that definite danger, that tendency. If so, then in order to prevent wrong beliefs and wrong reasons for sadness from deteriorating into *pagan* grief Paul writes as he does.

The Greek and Roman world of Paul's day was, indeed, a *hopeless* world (Eph. 2:12). According to the Greek (and afterward also the Roman) conception, there was no future for *the body*, which came to be regarded as the soul's "prison-house." As for *the soul* of man, it reluctantly departs from the body with the dying breath or by means of open wounds. This soul, in its separate existence, is not entirely immaterial. Its texture, however, is very thin. It retains many of the characteristics of its former body and is therefore immediately recognized when it appears in the other world. It enters Hades, a very dismal realm of "shades." Compared to its former life on the sunny earth, sunless Hades where the dead bemoan their existence, failed to inspire any comfort. The modification of this pagan myth of the Hereafter, sothat Elysian fields were introduced as the special abode for a few favorites of the gods, the creation of Tartarus (for the condemned) and of Erebus (for the unsentenced), all this did not furnish any reliable ground for confidence. The pagan world was without real hope. The Iliad ends with funeral-rites! Philosophers, at least by implication, rejected the highly colored descriptions transmitted from generation to generation by illustrious poets, and began to interpret them

---

[81] As Lenski seems to think, *op. cit.,* p. 325.

allegorically. They taught the immaterial nature of *the soul* and based arguments upon it in favor of its indestructibility and immortality. For *the body* they held out no hope whatsoever. In public plays the fancies accepted by the more unsophisticated were at times subjected to open ridicule. The Stoics expressed grave doubts with respect to man's future state. Conditional survival was the best they could offer, but even this was temporary. At length the soul is swallowed up in the fiery substance which is identical with deity. The Epicurians adopted a position which amounted to this: "The punishments of Tartarus are not to be feared, for *the soul,* being material, will share the fate of *the body.* As long as we are alive, *death* does not exist for us, and when death appears, *we* no longer exist." The Mystery religions (even assuming that our main sources are trustworthy and not too late), with their weird stories of resurrections which are hardly deserving of the name — hair that begins to grow, a little finger that begins to move, sections of a dead body that are reunited and become alive — , and with, at best, a promise to make one *happy* but not to make one *holy,* could not give lasting satisfaction.

Indeed, apart from Christianity there was no solid basis for hope in connection with the after-life. In the second century A. D. a certain Irene, an Egyptian, writes a letter to a family in mourning. She writes that she is sorry and that she weeps over her friend's departed one just as she had previously wept over the loss of her own dear one. She concludes her letter by saying:

> "But, nevertheless, against such things one can do nothing.
> Therefore, comfort one another. Farewell."

It is clear that such an expression "Comfort one another," when every ground for comfort was lacking, is, to put it mildly, very insufficient! [82]

14. For (i.e., such ignorance and hopelessness is inexcusable, *for*) **if we believe that Jesus died and rose again, so also those who fell asleep through Jesus God will bring with him.**

Over against pagan hopelessness Paul now proceeds to lay a solid foundation for Christian hope with reference to believers who have departed from this life.

Verse 14 has been interpreted in various ways. It is necessary to say

---

[82] For thoughts regarding the after-life in Greek and Roman literature see The Loeb Classical Library, especially such Latin-English volumes as Vergil (Aeneid, the sixth book), *The Letters* of Pliny the Younger, Lucretius, Horace; also: Greek-English: Homer (*Iliad* and *Odyssey*), Aeschylus, Diogenes Laertius, Epictetus, Euripedes, and Plato (Apology, Crito, Cheaedo). W. R. Alger, *A Critical History of the Doctrine of a Future Life,* New York, 1866, contains much worthwhile material. For the letter of "Irene" see A. Deissmann, *Light from the Ancient East,* English translation, New York, 1927, pp. 176-178.

something with reference to its grammatical structure, its logic, and its meaning.

With respect to a. *grammatical structure,* the main question for controversy is, "Just where does the phrase *through Jesus* belong?" Should we place a comma before or after this phrase? Either is possible, and *the difference is really rather unimportant.* Those who maintain that the sense is, "For if we believe that Jesus died and rose again, so also *through Jesus God will bring with him* those who are fallen asleep" [83] are willing to admit that it is also through the mediation of Christ that believers are able *to fall asleep* in him. In other words, they (with few exceptions) have no real objection to the expression "those who fall asleep through Jesus," but they do not believe that in the text as we have it Paul says this. They often assert that if the apostle had meant to write anything of the kind, he would have written "those who fall asleep *in* Jesus" (cf. I Cor. 15:18), not *"through* Jesus."

On the other hand, those who favor the rendering ". . . even so *them also which sleep in Jesus* (or: *who fell asleep through Jesus*) will God bring with him" [84] — gladly confess that not only the falling asleep is *in* (or *through*) Jesus, but so is also the act whereby God brings with Jesus those believers who have already departed from this life. Cf. I Cor. 15:21. In favor of reading "fell asleep through Jesus" are the following arguments: (1) thus we get a logical and sharply expressed grouping: on the one hand, *Jesus;* on the other, those who fell asleep through *Jesus;* cf. I Cor. 15:23: *Christ,* the firstfruits, then they that are *Christ's;* and (2) the expression "God will bring" already has a modifier, namely, *with him* (that is, with Jesus). It is doubtful whether in such a case it must be loaded down with still another modifier, especially with one which also makes excellent sense if construed with "fell asleep." But either construction is possible and makes good sense.

With respect to b. *logic,* it is immediately evident that something must be mentally inserted if the statement is to be made intelligible. As it stands, the conclusion does not fit the condition. The implied words, however, are readily supplied. Were the thought fully expressed, the sentence would read somewhat as follows:

"For if we believe that Jesus died and rose again, *we should also believe that* God will bring with him those who fell asleep through Jesus" (or: ". . . that through Jesus God will bring with him those who are fallen asleep"). If we are right in believing *this,* we must also believe *that.*

---

[83] So, for example, the following: A.R.V. (margin), R.S.V., Dutch (the new version), Bavinck, Denney, De Wette, Goodspeed, Lenski, Lünemann, Moffatt, Van Leeuwen, and Williams.
[84] So, for example, the following: A.V., A.R.V. (text), Auberlen-Riggenback, Barnes, Bengel, Berkeley (Verkuyl), Calvin, Chrysostom, Frame, Grotius, Hilgenfeld, Luther, and Robertson (though he leaves room for either construction).

Finally, with respect to c. *meaning*, the main question which divides commentators is, "Just what is meant by the clause *God will bring with him?*" Some maintain that the meaning is sufficiently clear from verses 15-17, and that the logic of the entire passage is as follows:

"For if we believe that Jesus died and rose again, we should also believe that the same God who raised Jesus will raise believers who have fallen asleep, and will cause them, together with such believers as are still left on earth, to be caught up in the clouds, to meet the Lord in the air, and to remain always with him." This *raising, catching up* in the clouds *to meet the Lord* in the air, *and remaining ever with him,* is what Paul meant by saying, "God *will bring* them with Jesus." As proof for this position they usually state that the conjunction *for,* at the beginning of verse 15, shows that *all* that which is stated in verses 15-17 is simply the expanded form of the clause, "God will bring them with Jesus."

Others, however, while by no means denying that there is a considerable element of truth in the above representation, have felt that it is not entirely adequate:

(1) The clause "God will bring with him" (verse 14) refers directly only to the departed ones; but the passage 15-17 refers clearly to two groups: the already departed and the survivors. Hence, it will not do to carry *all* that is said in these verses into the final clause of verse 14.

(2) This interpretation hardly does full justice to the meaning of the expression *bring with.* It will hardly do to say that the clause "God *will bring them with* Jesus" means simply this: by raising their bodies and causing them to ascend, God will *bring them up to Jesus,* so that they meet him in the air.

It is for this reason that several commentators, without in any way doing injustice to the very clear connection between verse 14 and the following verses, have felt, nevertheless, that the expression "God will bring them with him (Jesus)" has a meaning which in a sense is more restricted and in another sense broader than what is stated in verses 15-17. It is more restricted, for it refers only to those who have already departed, not to the others. It is broader, for it refers to these departed ones not only *after* but even *before* they have been raised.

To Paul and his companions (as well as to the readers, of course) the departed ones are very real. *They are persons!* They are definitely alive and active! They are persons, moreover, whom Jesus will bring with him from heaven at his coming. However, Paul does not say that *Jesus* will bring them (though this is implied in the phrase *with him*), but that *God* will bring them. The characteristically Pauline (cf. Rom. 8:11) reasoning seems to be this: "The same *God* who raised Jesus from the dead will also raise from the dead those who belong to Jesus." He will cause them to come along with Jesus, from heaven, that is, *he will bring their souls along from heaven, sothat these may be reunited quickly (in a flash) with their bodies, in which they go forth to meet the Lord in the air, to remain with him forever.* The *bringing with him,* then, includes everything that happens to these departed ones, from the moment of their departure from heaven until in their raised and glorified bodies they meet the Lord in the air, nevermore to be separated from him in any sense whatever.[85] It is in that full sense that 3:13 mentions "the coming of our Lord Jesus *with all his saints.*" See also on that passage.

15. Verse 14 has made clear that Christ, at his coming, will think of the departed ones, and not only of the survivors. Verse 15 carries this thought a little farther, and shows that in no sense whatever will those who are still on earth at the return have any advantage over those who have fallen asleep in Jesus. The inspired writer expresses it this way: **For this we say to y o u by the word of the Lord that we, those who remain alive, who are left until the coming of the Lord, shall have no advantage at all over those who fell asleep.**

This passage comes closer than any other in suggesting the nature of the difficulty in Thessalonica regarding the doctrine of the second coming. But even this states the problem only in a general way. So much is clear, namely, that the readers wondered whether, in some way or other, at the Parousia, the believers who had departed from this life would be at a disadvantage in comparison with those still living on earth. Did they believe that for those that had been previously translated to heaven there would be no rapture in any sense? Did they suppose (at least, were they in danger of supposing) that though *the souls* of these departed ones would be in glory, yet their *bodies* would remain buried, and is that why Paul in verse 13 compares their attitude (or their fear) to that of the heathen (who also had no hope with respect to the body)? Did they suppose that while both as to soul and body *all* believers (departed and survivors) would share in the glory of Christ's Return, yet in the rapture the already departed saints would receive a lesser degree of glory or would have to follow the others in going forth to meet the Lord in the air? Or were they thinking of some other disadvantage for those who had fallen asleep? Scripture does not reveal the answer.

It is enough to know that Paul, *by a word of the Lord* (whether directly to Paul or through oral tradition, but not by means of any passage recorded in the Gospels), assures the readers that they can dismiss their fears. At

---

[85] This interpretation is in line with a remark by A. Kuyper, *Dictaten Dogmatiek,* second edition, Grand Rapids, Mich., 1910, Locus de Consummatione, p. 244 ("alle zielen moeten naar de aarde terug") and also meets an objection which he raises. See also B. B. Warfield, *Biblical and Theological Studies,* Philadelphia, 1952, p. 467: "The rising of Christ's dead is secured before he reaches the earth." That is correct.

Christ's coming the most absolute impartiality will be shown. One group of believers will have no advantage over another. This thought receives further elaboration in verses 16, 17.

16, 17. For [86] **with a shouted command, with a voice of an archangel and with a trumpet of God, the Lord himself [87] will descend from heaven, and the dead in Christ will rise first; then we who are alive, who are left, shall be caught up together with them in clouds to meet the Lord in the air.**

By separating these two verses — 16 and 17 — many readers have failed to see the true meaning. By printing and reading them together we see at once that here are the same two groups of believers whom we met in verse 15.[88] One might present this graphically as follows:

Verse 15	Verses 16, 17
"we, those who remain alive, who are left until the coming of the Lord"	"we who are alive, who are left"
"those who fell asleep"	"the dead in Christ"

It is clear also that both groups — the survivors and the dead (or those fallen asleep) — are *believers.* Anyone can see at once that the apostle is not drawing a contrast between believers and unbelievers, as if, for example, believers would rise first, and unbelievers a thousand years later. He states:

"And *the dead* in Christ will rise first; then *we who are alive, who are left* shall be caught up together with them in clouds . . ."

Both groups ascend to meet the Lord. *Both* consist of nothing but believers.

The various elements in this vivid description of Christ's descent and the rapture of the saints are as follows:

a. *With a shouted command.*

This is the first of *three* phrases showing the *two* circumstances that will attend the Lord's glorious return. He returns as Conqueror.[89] The *shouted*

---

86 Not *that.* Had this been the meaning ὅτι would have been replaced or preceded by καί.

87 Or *he, the Lord.*

88 Note, however, that verse 15 is negation, verses 16 and 17 affirmation. This too is characteristically Pauline. Also, note the chiastic order: verse 15: survivors, sleepers; verses 16, 17: sleepers, survivors (the latter, however, *together with* the former).

89 The idea of the Conquering Christ is as a thread running through the book of Revelation. Christ has conquered, is conquering, is going to return as Conqueror. See my *More Than Conquerors* (Interpretation of the book of Revelation), Grand Rapids, Mich., seventh edition, 1954, p. 116. Paul's presentation is in complete harmony with this.

command (χέλευσμα, in the New Testament occurring only here, but see Prov. 30:27 in the LXX) is originally the order which an officer shouts to his troops, a hunter to his dogs, a charioteer to his horses, or a ship-master to his rowers. In the present connection it is clearly the command of the Lord, as he leaves heaven, for the dead to arise. Note the context: those who have fallen asleep shall not be at a disadvantage (verse 15), *for* with a *shout* . . . the Lord himself will descend from heaven, *and the dead in Christ will rise* . . . (verse 16). Just as even here and now the voice of the Son of God is life-giving, causing those who are spiritually dead to be quickened (see N.T.C. on John 5:25), so also when he comes back "all who are in the tombs will hear his voice and will come out" (see N.T.C. on John 5:28). The command, therefore, is definitely *his own,* proceeding from *his* lips. It is not a command issued *to* him, but an order given *by* him. Leaving heaven in his human nature, he utters his voice, and immediately the souls of the redeemed also leave, and are quickly reunited with their bodies, which, thus restored to life, arise gloriously.

b. *With a voice of an archangel and with a trumpet of God.*

These two phrases, united by the conjunction *and,* probably belong together, sothat the archangel is represented as sounding God's trumpet. The term *archangel* or chief angel occurs only here and in Jude 9. In the latter passage Michael is the archangel. On Michael see also Rev. 12:7; then Dan. 10:13, 21; 12:1. He is represented as leader of good angels and as defender of God's people.[90] With respect to the question whether Michael is the only archangel Dr. A. Kuyper expressed himself as follows:

"This question cannot be answered, because Scripture says nothing about it. It is possible that Michael is *the* archangel, that is, the *only* archangel, but it is also possible that he is *one of* the archangels (one of the seven angels that stand before God's throne), as in Daniel 10:13 he is called *one of the chief princes,* sothat Gabriel as well as Michael might be an archangel." [91] With that opinion we are in hearty agreement. The fact that the article *(the)* is not used here — sothat we have translated *"an* archangel" — does not definitely decide the matter. It may indicate that he is one of several, but it is also possible that the term *archangel* was felt to be definite (a proper name, as it were) even without a preceding article. However that may be, one fact at least is well-nigh certain: "a shouted command" and "an archangel's voice" are two different things. The former proceeds from the Christ, the latter from his archangel. Nevertheless, the two sounds have this in common, that they are the signal for the dead to be raised (I Cor. 15:52). (Note that also in Josh. 6:5 and Judg. 7:21, 22 the shout and the trumpet-blast go together.) At the sound of the trumpet the surviving be-

---

[90] See *More Than Conquerors,* p. 170.
[91] A. Kuyper, *De Engelen Gods,* Kampen, 1923, p. 189.

lievers are changed, in a moment, in the twinkling of an eye (again I Cor. 15:52).

The trumpet-blast, in this connection, is certainly very fitting. In the old dispensation, when God "came down," as it were, to meet with his people, this meeting was announced by a trumpet-blast (e.g., Ex. 19:16, 17: "and the sound of a trumpet exceeding loud . . . and Moses brought the people out of the camp to meet God"; cf. Ex. 19:19). Hence, when the marriage of the Lamb with his bride reaches its culmination (cf. Rev. 19:7), this trumpet-blast is most appropriate. Also, the trumpet was used as a signal of Jehovah's coming to rescue his people from hostile oppression (Zeph. 1:16; Zech. 9:14). It was the signal for their deliverance. So also this final trumpet-blast, the signal for the dead to arise, for the living to be changed, and for all the elect to be gathered from the four winds (Matt. 24:31) to meet the Lord, may well be interpreted as being also the fulfilment of the trumpet-ordinance found in Lev. 25, and, accordingly, as proclaiming liberty throughout the universe for all the children of God, their everlasting jubilee!

From all this it becomes abundantly clear that the Lord's coming will be open, public, not only visible but also audible. There are, indeed, interpreters, who, in view of the fact that the Bible at times employs figurative language, take the position that we can know nothing about these eschatological events. To them these precious paragraphs in which the Holy Spirit reveals the future convey no meaning at all. But this is absurd. Scripture was written to be understood, and when it tells us that the Lord will descend from heaven with a shout, with a voice of an archangel and a trumpet of God, it certainly must mean at least this: that in addition to the shouted command of our Lord (which might be compared with John 11:43; see N.T.C. on that passage), a reverberating sound will actually pervade the universe.[92] What forces of nature will be employed to produce this sound has not been revealed. One fact has now become evident: for believers this sound will be full of cheer. This is *God's* trumpet! It is *his* signal, for the archangel is *his* angel. It is sounded to proclaim *his* deliverance for *his* people. Cf. Rev. 15:2 ("harps *of God*"). It announces the coming of *his* Son (as "Lord of lords and King of kings," Rev. 19:16) for the deliverance of *his* people!

c. *The Lord himself* (or *he, the Lord*) *will descend from heaven.*

This descent is visible (Rev. 1:7), audible (as has just been shown), majestic (see on II Thess. 1:7), unto judgment and deliverance (Matt. 25:31-46). If the words, "He shall so come in like manner as y o u beheld him going into heaven" may be interpreted somewhat broadly, it would seem

---

[92] Cf. J. J. Knap, *The Resurrection and Life Eternal*, Grand Rapids, Mich., 1928, p. 48. Also my *Lectures on the Last Things*, Grand Rapids, 1951, p. 34.

that the actual *descent* (as distinguished now from the suddenness and un-expectedness of Christ's appearance, and from the suddenness and finality that characterizes the entire return) will be characterized by a kind of majestic leisureliness. Note the description of the ascension in Acts 1:9, 10. At any rate, it will not be an *instantaneous* change of location from heaven to earth. There will be time (Rev. 10:6, correctly interpreted, is not in conflict with this [93]) for the souls of those who had fallen asleep to leave their heavenly abodes, to be reunited with their bodies, and then in these gloriously raised bodies to ascend to meet the Lord in the air!

d. *And the dead in Christ will rise first.*

See what has been said about this in the preceding. The meaning here is very clearly that those who departed from this life in Christ, and are here viewed as having remained in Christ, shall not be at a disadvantage. They will rise before the believers who survive on earth will ascend to meet the Lord. The survivors will have to wait a moment, as it were.

e. *Then we who are alive, who are left, shall be caught up together with them in clouds to meet the Lord in the air.*

In addition to what has already been said, note the following: the fact that Paul says *we* does not necessarily mean that he expected to be among those who would still be living at Christ's return. He says *we* because right now he, Silas, Timothy, the readers, are among those believers still living on earth. He immediately modifies this by interpreting it to mean: "those who are left (when the Lord comes)," in order to indicate that only God knows who they may be. Paul knows that the second coming will not take place immediately (see on II Thess. 2:2); and while he was in Thessalonica, this element in his teaching regarding the last things was not neglected (II Thess. 2:5). Moreover, the saying of Jesus recorded in Matt. 24:36 was certainly not unknown to Paul (see also on I Thess. 5:1). Of course, it is also true that Paul never taught that the Lord would definitely not come during this apostle's life-time. He probably hoped that he might live to see it. He wanted everyone to conduct himself in such a manner as to be always ready. But he does not set any date.

Note: *we, together with them.* There is complete impartiality: survivors have no advantage. The predicate is *shall be caught up* (cf. for the verb also Acts 8:39 — Philip the evangelist was caught away by the Spirit of the Lord; II Cor. 12:2-4 — a man in Christ was caught up to the third heaven; and Rev. 12:5 — the Christ-child is caught up, snatched away, from the power of the dragon).

The suddenness, the swiftness, and the divine character of the power which is operative in this *being snatched up* are here emphasized. The survivors have been changed "in a moment, in the twinkling of an eye"

[93] See *More Than Conquerors*, p. 150.

(I Cor. 15:52). The heavens and the earth, in their present form, are *put to flight* (Rev. 20:11; cf. 6:14). Now while figurative language abounds in this vivid description, one fact remains: the dramatic suddenness and swiftness of the series of events is stressed. Once the Lord appears upon the clouds of heaven and begins to descend, there will be no opportunity for conversion. His coming is absolutely decisive. He comes not to convert but to judge. See also on II Thess. 2:8; cf. Matt. 25:31 ff; II Cor. 6:2; and II Peter 3:9. *Now* is the acceptable time; *now* is the day of salvation.

The raised and the changed are caught up together *in clouds to meet the Lord in the air.* Although these clouds may well be taken literally, nevertheless, they also have a symbolical meaning. They are associated with the coming of the Lord in majesty, for the punishment of the enemies of his saints, hence for the salvation of his people (cf. Dan. 7:13; then Matt. 26:64; finally, Ex. 19:16, 20; Ps. 97:2; Nah. 1:3).

According to M.M. (p. 53) the expression *to meet* (εἰς ἀπάντησιν) was used in connection with an official welcome accorded to a newly arrived dignitary. No doubt the *welcoming* idea is also included in the expression as used here in I Thess. 4:17. That all believers, the raised as well as (and together with) the changed, shall ascend to meet the Lord *in the air* is clearly taught here. Whether such passages as Job 19:25; Acts 1:11 actually teach that *the judgment* is going to take place *on earth* is debatable. At any rate, nothing with respect to this is taught in the present passage. However, the main thrust of I Thess. 4:17 is not that we shall meet the Lord *in the air,* but that all believers together shall *meet the Lord, never to be separated from him:*

18. And so shall we always be with the Lord. Therefore encourage one another with these words. In these words is stated the conclusion of the entire paragraph. Since it has become clear that those who fell asleep in Christ are not at a disadvantage as compared with those who survive, there is solid ground for encouragement. For the verb here used (*encourage*) see on 2:11. See also on 5:14. Naturally such encouragement is meant not only for the close relatives of bereaved ones, but for all. It must be borne in mind that the members of this very young church were closely united by the bond of love. Hence, when *one* sorrowed, *all* sorrowed; when *one* rejoiced, *all* rejoiced. The encouragement, then, is for all. The members must encourage *one another.*

The Synthesis is found after the explanation of 5:11.

CHAPTER V

5 1 Now concerning the duration-periods and the appropriate seasons, brothers, y o u have no need that anything be written to y o u. 2 For y o u yourselves know very well that the day of the Lord comes like a thief in the night. 3 When they are saying, "Peace and Safety," then a sudden (thing) comes upon them, namely, destruction,[94] like a birth-pang upon the pregnant woman, and by no means will they escape.

4 But y o u, brothers, are not in darkness, so that that day should seize y o u as a thief. 5 For y o u are all sons of light and sons of day. We belong neither to night nor to darkness. 6 Accordingly, let us not sleep as do the rest, but let us remain watchful and sober. 7 For it is at night that sleepers sleep, and at night that drunkards are drunk. 8 But since we belong to the day, let us be sober, putting on a breastplate of faith and love, and for a helmet (the) hope of salvation; 9 for God did not appoint us for wrath but for the obtaining of salvation through our Lord Jesus Christ, 10 who died for us, in order that [95] whether we wake or whether we sleep we may live in fellowship with him. 11 Therefore encourage one another, and build up one the other, as in fact y o u are doing.

5:1-11

5:1. Now concerning the duration-periods and the appropriate seasons,[96] brothers, y o u have no need that anything be written to y o u.

The relation of this paragraph to the rest has been shown (see on 4:13). The question whether Paul is here replying to a *written* question has been discussed (see footnote 4 above).

It would seem that in addition to worry with respect to a possible disadvantage which departed believers might suffer at Christ's return (4:13-18), there was also curiosity with respect to the exact time when this great event would take place. "How long" do the readers still have to wait? "Just when" is the Lord going to arrive? It was for them a question of *times* or *duration-periods* (χρόνοι) and *appropriate seasons* (καιροί). See also N.T.C. on John 7:6, and see on Titus 1:2, 3.

---

[94] Or "then suddenly there comes upon them destruction." That is the correct rendering if the adjective *sudden* is here used for the adverb *suddenly*.
[95] Or *so that*.
[96] A trifle less exact but, perhaps, more understandable would be the rendering, "Now concerning the *How long?* and the *When?* . . ."

With an obvious reference to:

a. a saying of the Lord spoken when he was about to ascend to heaven ("It is not for y o u to know duration-periods and appropriate seasons," Acts 1:7);

b. the truth, also clearly revealed by the Lord, that no man knows the day and the hour of the coming of the Son of man (Matt. 24:36), which, accordingly, will be as a thief in the night (cf. Matt. 24:43); and

c. the fact that these facts had previously been made clear to the readers, Paul informs them — affectionately addressing them as "brothers" (see on 1:4) —

"Y o u have no need that anything be written to y o u." Cf. 4:9.

2. For, says Paul, y o u yourselves know very well that the day of the Lord comes [97] like a thief in the night.

The thief takes the owner of the house by surprise. He does not send a warning letter to this effect, "Tomorrow, at such and such a time, I'll pay you a visit. Be sure to hide all your valuables." He comes *suddenly* and *unexpectedly*. So also will be the coming of the day of the Lord (that is, the day of his arrival unto judgment). Hence, it is foolish to inquire about the *how long* and the *when*.

However, the comparison holds also in another, closely related, respect: the thief generally finds people *unprepared*. But here the comparison is true only with respect to unbelievers, not with respect to believers (see on verse 4). Several passages immediately occur to the mind: Matt. 24:43 (= Luke 12:39); II Peter 3:10; Rev. 3:3; 16:15.

These matters had been so clearly presented to the Thessalonians while the missionaries were still with them that, if they will only reflect on them, they will realize that the things about which they are wondering are really *very well* (ἀκριβῶς accurately, cf. Luke 1:3) known to them. Sometimes men wonder about facts which, deep down in their hearts, they really know accurately!

3. Turning now to the second application with respect to the figure of the thief at night (namely, that he not only arrives suddenly, but that his victim is totally unprepared), Paul continues:

When they are saying *Peace and Safety,* then a sudden (thing) comes upon them, namely, destruction, like a birth-pang upon the pregnant woman, and by no means will they escape.

Note the combination of *suddenness* and *unpreparedness*. Note also the striking sentence-order, retained in our translation, making both the adjective *sudden* and the noun *destruction* very emphatic. The world in

---

[97] Gnomic — not prophetic — present. Yet the reference is here to the coming day, as the context shows.

general will be eating and drinking, buying and selling, building and planting, marrying and giving into marriage, when Jesus comes again. Of course, in themselves not any of these things is wicked. What could be wrong with receiving physical nourishment, carrying on commerce and industry, being engaged in agriculture, or planning a wedding? By means of these things God can even be glorified (I Cor. 10:31). But when the soul becomes entirely wrapped up in them, sothat they become ends in themselves, and sothat the higher, spiritual needs are neglected, they are a curse and no longer a blessing. "All for the body and its enjoyments, nothing for the soul," was the slogan of the wicked contemporaries of Noah and of Lot; and that too will be the outstanding characteristic of the human race in the evil days to come. Cf. Ezek. 13:10; Amos 6:1; Matt. 24:37-44; Luke 17:26-30. Meanwhile, like the artist on top of the ocean-rock, painting the beauty of the village upon the shore, and so completely absorbed in his painting that he sees no danger and pays no attention to the returning tide, though the waves lash higher and higher against the pedestal of his very temporary throne, so also these foolish and wicked people, fascinated with earthly charms, will not realize that judgment is creeping in upon them, coming closer and closer, until very suddenly it overtakes them, catching them wholly *unprepared*. They will be saying "Peace and Safety." Some will even ridicule the very idea of Christ's return (cf. II Peter 3:1-10). However, they will by no means escape, no more than the pregnant woman who is seized by a very sharp and sudden birth-pang while she is helpless. Cf. Ex. 15:14; Is. 13:8; Jer. 4:31; 6:24; 13:21; 22:23; 49:24; 50:43; Hos. 13:13; Mic. 4:9, 10; see also Matt. 24:8; Mark 13:8. (The figure and the third of comparison is, however, not always exactly the same. Sometimes the point of resemblance is entirely different; cf. N.T.C. on John 16:21, 22.) The desperate attempt of the wicked to escape is also vividly portrayed in Rev. 6:12-17. No one escapes.

4. A contrast is now drawn: But y o u, brothers, are not in darkness, sothat that day should seize y o u as a thief.

What Paul desires is that the readers, instead of being filled with vain curiosity or getting all excited, shall be *prepared*. He again uses the term of affectionate address, *brothers* (see on 1:4). These brothers form a sharp antithesis with the people of the world. The latter are *in darkness*, surrounded by it and embedded in it. The darkness has penetrated their hearts and minds, their whole being. This is the darkness of sin and unbelief. It is on account of this darkness that unbelievers are not sober and watchful (hence, not prepared). It is because of this that they lack faith, love, and hope. As has been stated repeatedly in the present series of Commentaries, *in order to grasp the meaning of a word one must read on and on.* In the present instance the meaning of *darkness* becomes plain by reading verses 5-8. See also N.T.C. on John 1:5 for the concepts *darkness* (which in that passage is personal) and *seize* (καταλαμβάνω).

The day is, of course, the day of Christ's return unto judgment, as is clear from the entire preceding context, beginning at 4:13. That day, here personified, will *seize* unbelievers, catching them *unprepared,* just as a thief *seizes* [98] the owner of the house. Believers, however, are not in darkness. They are not seized, for they are *prepared.*

5. For y o u are all sons of light and sons of day. We belong neither to night nor to darkness. By means of this truly striking Hebraism, Paul stresses the fact that *all* the brothers at Thessalonica (for "y o u . . . all" refers back to "brothers" in the preceding verse), that is, all those who by sovereign grace have been adopted into the family of Jesus Christ, are *lights.* See N.T.C. on John 12:36. Cf. Rom. 13:11, 12. The idea is *one:* the light of day has already arisen in their hearts, and they are destined for the realm of everlasting light. They belong to it, for it has taken possession of them. They have faith, love, hope, etc. They are "light in the Lord" (Eph. 5:9). And because *he* is the light of the world (see N.T.C. on John 8:12), *they too* are the light of the world (Matt. 5:14). As "sons of light and of day" (lights shining in the day) they form a sharp contrast with the "sons of this age" (Luke 16:8). They belong neither to night nor to darkness, that is, sin no longer has dominion over them. Wrath is not in store for them. A great change has taken place. Cf. Eph. 5:8; 2:1-10.

Note the tactful transition from *y o u* to *we:* "*Y o u* are all sons of light . . . *we* (the readers, Paul, Silas, Timothy, all other believers) belong neither to night nor to darkness." The reason for this transition is that Paul is about to convey a solemn warning. By including himself (hence, not *y o u* but *we*) he makes the following exhortation more palatable and effective:

6-8a. Accordingly, let us not sleep as do the rest, but let us remain watchful and sober. For it is at night that sleepers sleep, and at night that drunkards (or that those who get drunk) are drunk. But since we belong to the day, let us be sober.

In view of the fact, then, that the writers and the readers (together with all Christians everywhere) are sons of light and not of darkness, belonging to the day and not to the night (see on verse 5), they are exhorted not to sleep but to remain watchful and sober.

---

[98] We disagree here with Frame, *op. cit.,* p. 179. The illustration of *the thief in the night,* both here and elsewhere, is that the thief surprises (or at least tries to surprise) the owner of the house, not that the thief is himself taken by surprise. The meaning is not: "so that the day should seize (or *surprise*) y o u as a thief (or *as thieves*) is (*are*) seized (or *surprised*)," but "so that the day should seize y o u as a thief seizes" the owner of the house, in order to rob him of his goods. Cf. Matt. 12:29.

It is clear that the terms *to sleep, to be watchful,* and *to be sober* are used metaphorically here. *Thus used,* their meaning is as follows:

To sleep (cf. Mark 13:36; Eph. 5:14) means to live as if there will never be a judgment-day. Spiritual and moral laxity is indicated. Luke 12:45 pictures this condition vividly. So does the description of the foolish virgins, who had taken no oil in their vessels with their lamps (Matt. 25:3, 8). It means *not* to be *prepared.*

To be watchful means to live a sanctified life, in the consciousness of the coming judgment-day. Spiritual and moral alertness is indicated. The watchful individual has his lamps burning and his loins "girded," and it is in that condition that he looks forward to the return of the Bridegroom. On this read Luke 12:35-40. The watchful person is *prepared.*

A study of this verb *to be watchful* (γρηγορέω, whence the proper name *Gregory*), as used elsewhere, is rewarding. In addition to I Thess. 5:6 the passages in which the verb indisputably has a figurative sense are the following: Matt. 24:42; 25:13; Mark 13:35, 37; Acts 20:31; I Cor. 16:13; Col. 4:2; I Peter 5:8; Rev. 3:2, 3; 16:15.[99]

These passages lead to the following conclusions:

a. The uncertainty (on our part) of the day and the hour of Christ's return is a reason for watchfulness (Matt. 24:42; 25:13; Mark 13:35, 37).

b. Another reason for constant vigilance is the presence of enemies, seen and unseen, who threaten the flock (Acts 20:31; I Peter 5:8).

c. To be watchful means to be spiritually awake (Rev. 3:2, 3; 16:15).

d. It implies the habit of regular prayer, including thanksgiving (Col. 4:2).

e. What is probably the fullest description of watchfulness is given in I Cor. 16:13, 14: "Be watchful, stand fast in the faith, acquit yourselves like men, be strong. Let all that y o u do be done in love."

To be sober means to be filled with spiritual and moral earnestness, being neither overly excited on the one hand, nor indifferent on the other, but calm, steady, and sane (cf. I Peter 4:7), doing one's duty and fulfilling one's ministry (II Tim. 4:5). The *sober* person lives deeply. His pleasures are not primarily those of the senses, like the pleasures of the drunkard for instance, but those of the soul. He is by no means a Stoic. On the contrary, with a full measure of joyful anticipation he looks forward to the return of the Lord (I Peter 1:13). But he does not run away from his task! Note how both here and also in I Peter 5:8 the two verbs *to be watchful* and *to be sober* are used as synonyms.

The apostle's exhortation, then, amounts to this: "Let us not be lax and unprepared, but let us be prepared, being spiritually alert, firm in the

---

[99] This is not the proper place to discuss the question whether or not this verb is used in its literal or in its metaphorical sense (or perhaps a combination of the two) in Matt. 26:41 and Mark 14:38.

faith, courageous, strong, calmly but with glad anticipation looking forward to the future day. Let us, moreover, do all this because we belong to the day and not to the night." The opposite course of action, namely, to be asleep spiritually and morally (instead of being on guard), and to be drunk spiritually and morally (instead of being sober), befits people who belong to the night (the realm of darkness and sin), just as even in the natural realm it is generally at night that sleepers sleep and that drunkards are drunk. (It is clear, of course, that here in verse 7 the words *sleepers, sleep, drunkards,* and *are drunk* are used in their primary, literal sense.)

8b. It befits the man who is of the day to be watchful and sober: **putting on a breastplate of faith and love, and for a helmet (the) hope of salvation.**

The question may be asked, "How is it that Paul suddenly and somewhat unexpectedly comes up with these articles of defensive armor: breastplate and helmet?" The answer given by A. T. Robertson (*Word Pictures,* Vol. IV, p. 35) may well be correct: "The idea of *watchfulness* brings the figure of a sentry, on guard and armed, to Paul's mind. . . ."

By the exercise of calm and stedfast faith in and love for God in Christ — which in the midst of a wicked world becomes *an aggressive testimony* — the watchful and sober person wards off the poisonous arrows of temptation. He puts on *faith* ("a *certain* knowledge of God and of his promises . . . and a hearty confidence that all his sins are forgiven him for Christ's sake") and *love* (the yielding of the self to God, the object of his delight, in the spirit of joy and gratitude) just like a warrior would put on his breastplate.

Faith and love (genitives of apposition) constitute the Christian's coat of mail. The readers understood this illustration. The *breastplate* protected the sentry's breast, shoulders, and back. It was made of various materials, for instance, leather, quilted cloth, linen (Herodotus III. xlvii), brass, iron (I Sam. 17:5; Rev. 9:9) or at times even gold (I Macc. 6:2). The warrior Goliath wore a scale-armor coat (I Sam. 17:5). The soldiers of Antiochus Eupator had chain coats (I Macc. 6:35). Compare today's "bullet-proof vest."

What is important to note, in this connection (yet, is generally overlooked) is that Paul calls *active* faith and love a piece of *defensive* armor, a breastplate! How perfectly true is this comparison, for in matters of religion (and often also in so-called secular matters) the best defence is an offense; the most positive protection is an attack. The believer's spontaneous and aggressive testimony of faith in and love for God in Christ keeps him from the dissolute habits of the world. The *work* resulting from faith and the *exertion* prompted by love — the "walking by faith" — keep one from "fulfilling the lust of the flesh" (Gal. 5:16).

To *faith* and *love,* Paul adds *hope,* just as he did in 1:3. Here too, just like in 1:3, he expands the third element in the series; hence, "and for a helmet the hope *of salvation* (objective genitive)," etc. To be sure, *in principle* believers in Thessalonica were already in possession of salvation. But this is *full* salvation, the salvation which was going to be theirs at the coming of the Lord Jesus Christ.

Paul is fond of this word *salvation* (σωτηρία). He uses it again and again (in addition to its use in the present passage see also 5:9; II Thess. 2:13; II Tim. 2:10; 3:15; then Rom. 1:16; 10:1, 10; 11:11; 13:11; II Cor. 1:6; 6:2 twice; 7:10; Eph. 1:13; Phil. 1:19, 28; 2:12). This salvation is a. *negatively:* rescue from the guilt, pollution, and punishment of sin (specifically, it is often represented as a deliverance from the wrath of God which rests upon sin and which will one day be revealed; cf. 1:10; II Thess. 1:8, 9; Eph. 2:3, 5; Phil. 1:28) this rescue being a result of Christ's objective substitutionary atonement; and b. *positively:* that sum-total of every spiritual endowment which God grants to his people on the basis of the redemptive work of his Son. Both the negative aspect of this salvation (deliverance from wrath) and the positive aspect (for instance, "living together with him") are mentioned here in the immediately following context (see on verses 9 and 10). Since salvation is here an eschatological concept, it is understandable that the apostle speaks about *"the hope* of salvation," for *hope* ever looks to the future. It is the confident and firmly anchored assurance that the full inheritance will one day be ours.

This hope is the Christian's *helmet.* The helmet of iron and brass (I Sam. 17:5, 38; II Chron. 26:14; cf. I Macc. 6:35) afforded a measure of protection for the head, as did the breastplate for the heart. Much more did hope — and the endurance inspired by hope, cf. 1:3 — preserve the believer in safety over against the seduction of the world. Here too the assault upon the fortress of darkness by those Christians who endured to the very end, ever ready to testify, was their best defence. On the entire armor of the Christian read Eph. 6:10-20.

9, 10. As already remarked, Paul expands the concept *salvation* (or, if one prefers, "hope of salvation") in the following two verses: **For God did not appoint us for wrath but for the obtaining of salvation through our Lord Jesus Christ, who died for us, in order that whether we wake or whether we sleep we may live in fellowship with him.**

This passage indicates the reasonable character of the aforementioned hope. This hope is not visionary. It will be fulfilled, as is clear from the fact that God did not *appoint* (this verb combines duty and destination) us for *wrath* (to be revealed at Christ's return, 1:10; cf. II Thess. 1:8-10), but for *the obtaining* [100] of *salvation* (see on verse 8 above) through our *Lord Jesus Christ* (see on 1:1).

---

[100] As this noun (περιποίησις, which at times means *possession,* Eph. 1:14; I Peter 2:9) is clearly used in the active sense in II Thess. 2:14 (cf. Heb. 10:39) and as both

While the expression *the obtaining* places the emphasis on that which, according to God's purpose, is *our* duty, the immediately added phrase "through our Lord Jesus Christ" indicates that it is only through *him* (his death for us, his power operating in us) that we are able to carry this out. Paul is fond of this juxtaposition of the divine and the human element in the acquisition of salvation (cf. Eph. 2:8; 2:10; Phil. 2:12, 13).

When the apostle mentions the Lord Jesus Christ as the cause of our salvation, he immediately thinks of the Savior's *death* for us, inasmuch as that is basic. This death *concerns* us. Literally we read, ". . . who died *with reference to* (περί) us (though there is also some textual support for another preposition, ὑπέρ, for the meaning of which see N.T.C. on John 10:11. The Good Shepherd gave his life *for the benefit of* the sheep). Paul says "for *us.*" In this *us* he includes all believers, whether they be readers or writers or anyone else who can lay claim to the name *believer*. Specifically, he is thinking here of the same two groups which he has mentioned before (see on 4:13-18): the survivors and the departed ones. The purpose (or the result, it makes little difference in this connection) of Christ's death for his own is that whether at his coming we be *waking* or *sleeping* the sleep of death (καθεύδωμεν cf. Mark 5:39), we may together live in fellowship with him. Compare and see on 4:17.

This is the simplest explanation. Those who are *awake* are those who are *alive*, the survivors, the ones who according to 4:15 are "left until the coming of the Lord." And those who are *sleeping* are the *dead*, the departed, the ones who according to 4:15 "fell asleep" (namely, *in* or *through* Jesus Christ).[101]

11. The relation between 5:10 and 11 is a close parallel to that between 4:17 and 18. Just as in chapter 4 the clause, "And so shall we always be

---

there and also here it occurs in a context of exhortations, I see no good reason to depart from the translation favored by most of the versions.

[101] It is simply impossible to interpret the verb *to sleep* here in 5:10 as in verses 6 and 7. Clearly, here in verse 10 the verb has reference to believers ("we"), but in verse 6 it refers to the lost condition of unbelievers, that is, of "the rest," those who are not watchful and sober; and in verse 7 it has reference to the natural repose of sleep. It is also true, of course, that the verb here used for *to sleep* (first pers. pl. pres. subj. of καθεύδω) is not the same as the one used in 4:13-15 (gen. pl. pres. pass. part., and acc. pl. aor. pass. part. of κοιμάω). The latter verb has reference to blessed departure, falling asleep in and through Jesus. In distinction from it, the verb used here in 5:10 refers merely to being physically *dead* at Christ's return. And similarly — for it stands to reason that the two verbs must correspond — it will not do to derive the meaning of the verb *to wake* (first pers. pl. pres. subj. of γρηγορέω) from verse 6 (*to be watchful* morally and spiritually). Here in 5:10 the meaning is simply to be physically *alive* when Jesus comes. Cf. Rom. 14:8. The translators have caught the distinction in the use of these verbs. Hence, for example, in verse 6 they translate "let us *watch*" but in verse 10 (the same verb) "whether we *wake*" (thus A.V., A.R.V., and somewhat similarly most modern translators). Though some interpreters find fault with this, we cannot join them.

with the Lord" was followed by "Therefore encourage one another with these words," so here in chapter 5 the clause "In order that . . . we may live in fellowship with him" is followed by **Therefore encourage one another and build up one the other, as in fact y o u are doing.**

That last expression, "as in fact y o u are doing" has been explained in connection with 4:10. By instructing one another and by encouraging one another with the comfort which is found in the preceding paragraph (such comfort as is contained in assurances like "Y o u are not in darkness," "Y o u are all sons of day," "For God did not appoint us for wrath but for the obtaining of salvation through our Lord Jesus Christ . . . in order that we may live in fellowship with him"), believers at Thessalonica will be doing very valuable personal work: *building up* one the other; for the church and also the individual believer is God's edifice, God's temple, I Cor. 6:19.

Synthesis of 4:13 — 5:11

See p. 108. *Instruction. Paul writes to the Thessalonians instructing them how Christ will come again*

4:13-18 *with impartiality toward all believers, sothat survivors will have no advantage over those who have fallen asleep*

The conversion of the Thessalonians was of very recent date. The danger of a relapse, be it ever so temporary, into *pagan customs* was not imaginary. One of these was the manner of grieving for the dead. As most pagans saw it, there was no hope *at all* for the dead body and no *substantial* hope for the departed soul. Moreover, whatever flickering expectation there may have been of a happy life hereafter — and the inscriptions on tombstones, the letters of condolence, etc., voice despair rather than confidence — there was no solid foundation for it. And in this latter sense it was absolutely true that the heathen had *no hope!*

But surely the man who believes in a Jesus "who died *and arose again*" should not "grieve as do the rest, who have no hope." He should accept the precious truth that there is a glorious future in store for every Christian, and this not only for the soul but also for the body. "Those who *fell asleep* (entered upon their rest from labor, with the certainty of a glorious awakening) through Jesus God will bring with him." In no sense whatever will those who remain alive, who are left until the coming of the Lord, have any advantage over them. When Christ at his descent from heaven shouts the command for the dead to arise and when the archangel by sounding God's trumpet issues a similar order, and proclaims the final and everlasting meeting of God with his people, then *first of all* the spirits of the already departed believers will rejoin their bodies which will arise gloriously, *and not until this has happened* will those children of God who at Christ's coming are still living on earth begin to "rise to worlds unknown." The survivors "shall be caught up *together with*" those who previously fell asleep. *Together* — there is here no favoritism or partiality of any kind! — they shall ascend in clouds to meet the Lord in the air. And *so* — that is, glorious in soul and body, as *one* Church Universal and Triumphant — shall they always be with the Lord. The readers should encourage each other with these words.

5:1-11 *with suddenness, taking people by surprise, though believers will be (and should ever exert themselves to be) fully prepared*

In addition to worry with respect to a possible disadvantage which departed believers might suffer at Christ's return, there was also curiosity anent the exact time when that coming again would take place. *How long* did God's children still have to wait? Just *when* was Jesus going to arrive?

Basing his answer on previous teaching which had come straight from the mouth of the Lord, Paul states that the readers have no need of further information on this subject. If they will but reflect, they will recall that they have been repeatedly shown that, according to the word of the Lord (Matt. 24:43), the day of his return will be "like a thief in the night." He will come very suddenly, taking people by surprise.

As to the wicked, the Lord will come upon them while they are saying, "Peace and safety." They will be *wholly unprepared*. Hence, sudden destruction will come upon them.

In this respect *believers* are different. Moreover, they should *endeavor* to be different, for by God's grace they are filled with the light of salvation. Says Paul, "We belong neither to night nor to darkness," the night and the darkness of sin and unbelief. He continues, "Accordingly, let us not sleep as do the rest, but let us remain *watchful* and *sober*." He means, "Let us be prepared, spiritually alert, firm in faith, courageous, strong, calmly and with glad anticipation looking forward to the future day." Thus, believers will be putting on "the breastplate of faith and love, and for a helmet the hope of salvation." They must never hesitate to keep alive this glorious hope, ever bearing in mind that "God did not appoint us for wrath but for the obtaining of salvation through our Lord Jesus Christ, who died for us, in order that whether at his return we are still living on earth or have fallen asleep in the Lord, we may live forever in fellowship with him."

Summary of I Thessalonians 5:12-28

Paul Writes to the Thessalonians

Exhorting Them How They Should Conduct Themselves
This Section comprises *the Apostle's Exhortation.* Proper Behavior:

5:12, 13   with respect to the elders of the church

5:14   with respect to:
the disorderly
the fainthearted
the weak
"everyone"

5:15   with respect to those who have injured them

5:16-18   with respect to God

5:19-22   with respect to the Holy Spirit and his gifts (also: with respect to would-be prophets)
This is followed by

5:23, 24   a solemn wish for sanctification and preservation, the wish being immediately followed by the promise;
Next comes:

5:25-28   a trio of urgent requests:
for intercessory prayer
for extending greetings by means of the holy kiss, and
for the public reading of this letter. The Benediction.

12 Now we request y o u, brothers, to appreciate those who labor among y o u and are over y o u in the Lord and admonish y o u, 13 and to esteem them very highly in love because of their work. Be at peace among yourselves.

14 And we urge y o u, brothers, admonish the disorderly, encourage the faint-hearted, help the weak, exercise patience toward everyone.

15 See to it that no one renders to anyone evil for evil, but always pursue that which is good with reference to one another and with reference to all.

16 Always be joyful.

17 Ceaselessly pray.

18 In all circumstances give thanks, for this is the will of God in Christ Jesus for y o u.

19 The Spirit do not quench.

20 Prophetic utterances do not despise, 21 but test all things: to the good hold on; 22 from every form of evil hold off.

23 And may he, the God of peace,
sanctify y o u through and through,
and without flaw may be y o u r spirit,
and y o u r soul-and-body
without blame at the coming of our Lord Jesus Christ
may it be kept.

24 Reliable is the One who calls y o u, who will also do it.

25 Brothers, do pray for us.

26 Greet all the brothers with a holy kiss.

27 I solemnly charge y o u before the Lord to have this epistle read to all the brothers.

28 The grace of our Lord Jesus Christ be with y o u.

5:12-28

5:12, 13. Now we request y o u, brothers, to appreciate those who labor among y o u and are over y o u in the Lord and admonish y o u, and to esteem them very highly in love because of their work.

For the relation of 5:12-28 to 4:1-12; 4:13-18; and 5:1-11 see on 4:1. The watchfulness and soberness enjoined in the immediately preceding paragraph (5:1-11) must become evident in every walk of life. That is the gist of the present section. Detailed directions follow. They are striking because of their brevity. Paul knows how to say much in few words. Though it is, perhaps, impossible to separate the church as an organization from the church as an organism, and to say: *this* instruction pertains to the former and *that* to the latter, yet it may be safely affirmed that at least in verses 12 and 13 it is the church viewed as an organization that receives special attention.

The opening words, "We request y o u, brothers," are similar to what is found in 4:1; see on that verse. In order to understand what follows it must be borne in mind that Timothy had just returned (3:6) and had given a detailed report on "The Thessalonian Situation." It has already become clear that most of what he reported was very favorable. However, it has also been shown that some of the news was of a different nature. See on 4:1-8, 11. Moreover, also here in chapter 5 the immediate context speaks about "disorderly persons" (verse 14). Evidently some of them were loathe to obey the rules laid down by the religious authorities (see also on 4:8). This is the reason why Paul writes, "We request y o u, brothers, *to appreciate* [102] those who labor among y o u," etc. It is clear that the two verbs "to appreciate" and "to esteem (very highly)" are used synonymously.

When Paul speaks about "those who labor among y o u and are over y o u in the Lord and admonish y o u" he has in mind not three different kinds of leaders but one and the same group. The use of only one article preceding all three participles points in this direction. These leaders are characterized as:

a. *laborers or toilers,* that is, men who exert themselves in the interest of their brothers, performing much spiritual labor (explaining the gospel, applying it to concrete situations, warning, admonishing, helping, encouraging, etc.) for their benefit and amid great difficulty. Paul often used this verb (κοπιάω) when he was thinking of work that required strenuous effort and resulted in weariness. He used it in connection with manual labor (I Cor. 4:12; Eph. 4:28; II Tim. 2:6; cf. the noun in I Thess. 1:3; 2:9; II Thess. 3:8) and also with reference to religious work (Rom. 16:12 twice; I Cor. 5:10; Gal. 4:11; Phil. 2:16; 16:16; I Tim. 4:10; 5:17). In the Pauline phraseology not only the church-officer but also the voluntary worker, Col. 1:29, and in a sense every wide-awake member, is a *laborer.* His *exertion* is prompted by love.

b. *superintendents or managers* ("those who are over y o u"), and this "in the Lord," that is, by virtue of appointment by him and qualifications derived from him. Cf. I Tim. 3:4, 12 for an analogous use.

c. *admonishers,* that is, those who *put* (their brothers) *in mind* (νουθετέω from νοῦς and τίθημι) to obey God's ordinances. In the New Testament Paul is the only one who uses this word (besides 5:12, 14 and II Thess. 3:15 also Acts 20:31; Rom. 15:14; I Cor. 4:14; Col. 1:28; 3:16). The admonisher may be Paul himself (Acts 20:31) or any member of the church (Rom. 15:14; Col. 3:16).

Although, as has become evident, the first and the third participles (that is, *laborers* and *admonishers*) apply not only to men who have been invested with an office in the church but also to any other wide-awake member, yet the use of the second participle together with its modifier (*super-*

---

[102] The meaning *to appreciate* (for εἰδέναι) is paralleled in extra-canonical literature (see M.M. p. 440), though this is not what the verb generally signifies. It most frequently indicates *to know by reflection, based on intuition or information;* in distinction from γινώσκω which means *to know by observation or experience.* See also N.T.C. on John 8:28. However, it is easy to see how the meaning *to appreciate* developed from the basic connotation.

intendents, "those who are over y o u in the Lord") would seem to point in the direction of officers. We seem to have a parallel passage in I Tim. 5:17, where those who *rule* well (perfect participle of the same verb) are *the elders.* Note also how in that passage (just as here in I Thess. 5:12) these elders are further described as "those who *labor,*" namely, in the word and in teaching.

It will not do to say that I Tim. 5:17 cannot be adduced as proof because the system of church-organization by then had reached a much higher and more complicated development. To offset that argument it should be borne in mind that Paul was a great organizer (Acts 20:17; Phil. 1:1; Titus 1:5), and that even on his First Missionary Journey he was already appointing "elders in every church" (Acts 14:23). Certainly, if there were elders in the church at Thessalonica — and it is highly probable that there were! — these are meant here in I Thess. 5:12; at least they are included.

Paul requests that *because of their work* (and not solely because they are divinely appointed leaders) these men be esteemed *very highly,*[103] and this in the spirit of love.

Be at peace among yourselves,[104] Paul continues. In connection with what immediately precedes, this must mean, "Stop y o u r carping. Instead of continually criticizing the leaders, follow their directions, so that peace (here: absence of dissension) results."

14. In view of the fact that in urging the Thessalonians to show respect for their leaders Paul was thinking especially about the disorderly persons who had made this admonition necessary, it is not surprising that the next instruction begins as it does: **And we urge y o u, brothers, admonish the disorderly, encourage the fainthearted, help the weak, exercise patience toward everyone.**

In the congregation at Thessalonica there were three groups that needed special attention: the disorderly, the fainthearted, and the weak.

The words *disorderly* (ἄτακτος-οι, III Macc. 1:19 in the LXX) and *fainthearted* (ὁλιγόψυχος-οι — the "little souls"[105] —, Is. 35:4 in the LXX) occur nowhere else in the New Testament. The word *weak* (ἀσθενής-εῖς, i.e., without strength) occurs frequently, and is used with respect to both physical debility (Matt. 25:39, 43, 44; Luke 10:9; Acts 4:9; 5:15, 16) and moral and spiritual illness (Rom. 5:6; 14:1; I Cor. 8:7, 9, 10; 9:22; 11:30; etc.).

---

103 The Greek adverb is very picturesque: ὑπερεκπερισσῶς over-abundant (also used in 3:10 and in Eph. 3:20). Note the piling up of prefixes in this word: the ocean of esteem having reached its outermost *peri*meter, reaches even *higher* and begins to flow *outward,* overflowing its banks.
104 That the reading, "Be at peace *with them*" (i.e., with the leaders) is better than the one preferred by N.N. has not been proved.
105 Cf. German *die Kleinmüthigen,* Dutch *de kleinmoedigen.*

We have met each group before. Thus, *the disorderly* persons — that is, those who are out of step, like soldiers who do not keep the ranks — are the fanatics, meddlers, and loafers (4:11, 12; 5:12, 13; and cf. II Thess. 3:10). *The fainthearted* are probably those who worried about their departed friends and relatives and/or about their own spiritual condition (4:13-18; 5:4, 5, 9). And *the weak* could well be those who were characterized by a tendency toward immorality (4:1-8). Thus interpreted, each passage is explained in the light of others within the same epistle, and no novelties are introduced. It is, of course, readily admitted that this representation may not be exact. Thus, for example, the third group ("the weak") may also have included individuals who, though spiritually immature, were not particularly in danger of trespassing the bounds of propriety in matters pertaining to sex. Besides, the three groups may overlap to some extent.

It is clear as day that these admonitions are addressed to *the entire congregation* — note the word *brothers* (see on 1:4) — that is, in each case, to all the members except those specifically mentioned in the admonition. Thus, all except the disorderly must admonish the disorderly; all except the fainthearted must encourage the fainthearted, etc. Mutual discipline must be exercised by all the members. It is wrong to leave all this to pastors and elders.

As to the present imperatives [106] here employed, first of all Paul bids the brothers *to admonish* the disorderly. For the verb see on verse 12 above. The admonition might take the form suggested by Paul himself in 4:11, 12; 5:12, 13. It stands to reason that the faint-hearted must be *encouraged* (see on 2:11 and N.T.C. on John 11:31). The weak must be *helped*, that is, must not be abandoned. The brothers should "cling to" [107] them, rendering all the necessary spiritual and moral assistance.

Thus instead of quickly rejecting anyone, whether he be disorderly, faint-hearted, or weak, *patience* (or *longsuffering*, μακροθυμία) should be shown to everyone. Cf. Gal. 5:22; Eph. 4:2.[108]

---

[106] It is tempting to render all of these as durative, progressive, or linear, as is done by several commentators and translators. This would yield the rendering, "Keep on admonishing the disorderly, continue to encourage the fainthearted, never stop helping the weak," or something similar. However, in crisp imperatives of this character it is not always established that the continuative idea is predominant. In certain cases the present tense may be aoristic.

[107] The verb is ἀντέχω. See my doctoral dissertation, "The Meaning of the Preposition ἀντί in the New Testament," p. 68. The original notion of being *opposite* or *in front of* a person or object (oppositeness, the local sense), by an easy transition leads to that of being physically close, which in turn may suggest the idea of moral and spiritual closeness. This closeness may be one of attitude (for example, love or loyalty), or of practical helpfulness, the one not excluding the other. Cf. Matt. 6:24; I Thess. 5:14; Tit. 1:9.

[108] Trench (*op. cit.* liiii) has a fine discussion on the three synonyms μακροθυμία (longsuffering), ὑπομονή (endurance), and ἀνοχή (forbearance). He defines the

15. Not only is it the duty of the entire membership to exercise this virtue, patience or longsuffering, but the brotherhood must also see to it that each individual member cultivates it and manifests this grace toward everyone. Hence, there follows: **See to it that no one renders to anyone evil for evil, but always pursue that which is good with reference to one another and with reference to all.**

The impatient person retaliates when he is injured. He *"renders* (ἀποδῷ: gives back) evil for [109] evil."* Paul condemns this practice (see also Rom. 12:17, 19; cf. I Cor. 4:12; 6:7) and so does Peter (I Peter 3:9), in complete harmony with the injunction of Jesus: to love not only those who love us but even those who hate us and who are, in that sense, our enemies (Matt. 5:44).

It is not true, however, that in forbidding the exercise of pesronal vengeance Jesus laid down a principle that was *entirely* new and in striking contrast with the spirit and teaching of the Old Testament. The commandment — "eye for eye, tooth for tooth, hand for hand, foot for foot, burning for burning, wound for wound, stripe for stripe" (Ex. 21:24, 25; cf. Lev. 24:20; Deut. 19:21) — relates to the *public* administration of criminal law (see Lev. 24:14), and was issued in order that the practice of seeking *personal* revenge might be discouraged. What Jesus is opposing in Matt. 5:38-42 was not the Old Testament law but its Pharisaic misinterpretation. What the Lord taught, and what Paul in substance repeats, *is entirely in line with* (is a further development of) such Old Testament passages as Lev. 19:18; Deut. 32:35; Prov. 20:22; and 24:20. To be sure, there is an advance here (i.e. in Matt. 5:43-48). Revelation also in this respect is progressive. The idea that one should never render evil for evil, no not to *anyone,* was never as strikingly expressed as it was by Jesus when he said, "Love y o u r enemies." Also in this respect Jesus "came to fulfil" the law (Matt. 5:17), and also in this respect Paul (here in I Thess. 5:15) enforces a principle which he derived from the Lord.

Instead of "rendering evil for evil" it is the believer's duty to pursue that which is *good* — that is, *beneficial* — , and this not only with reference

---

first (used here in I Thess. 5:14) as "patience in respect of persons," while the second is "patience in respect of things."

From the passages in which Paul uses μαχροθυμία (longsuffering) it is clear that he views it as being not only *a divine attribute* (one pertaining to God, Rom. 2:4, or to *Christ,* I Tim. 1:16), of which even "vessels of wrath" are the objects (Rom. 9:22), but also *a Christian virtue* (II Cor. 6:6; Eph. 4:2; Col. 1:11; 3:12), which should adorn every believer, and specifically also every Gospel-worker, whether he be an apostle (like Paul, II Tim. 3:10) or his special representative (II Tim. 4:2). As a Christian virtue it is, of course, a fruit of the Spirit (Gal. 5:22).

[109] As I have pointed out in my doctoral dissertation, "The Meaning of the Preposition ἀντί in the New Testament," pp. 92, 93, ἀντί has here the sense "in exchange (or: in return) for" as in Gen. 44:4 and many other passages in which it is the equivalent of the Hebrew *tachath.*

to one another (fellow-believers) but even with reference to all (believers and unbelievers alike; cf. 3:12). This good which the believers must *pursue* (eagerly seek after) is *love,* as is clear from a comparison of the present passage with 3:12; Rom. 13:10; and I Cor. 14:1.

16-18. While in verses 12-15 Paul has shown what should be the attitude of the Thessalonians toward their leaders, to fellow-members character-ized by particular shortcomings, to those who have injured them, and finally to one another and to all, in verses 16-18 he sets forth what should be their inner attitude and how this inner attitude should express itself with reference to God. Hence, we now have the following three beautiful, closely related, and tersely expressed admonitions:

Always be joyful.

Ceaselessly pray.

In all circumstances give thanks.

The Thessalonians were no strangers (see on 1:6) to the "joy unspeak-able and full of glory" (I Peter 1:8), the "great joy" which resulted from the incarnation of Christ and from the redemption wrought through his cross. Yet with persecution from without and disturbances within, there was a danger (humanly speaking, of course!) that this joy would disappear. Hence, Paul, who himself again and again rejoiced in the midst of perse-cution and hardship (3:7-9; cf. Phil. 3:1; 4:4, 10), urges his readers to *always* be joyful.

Of course, in seasons of distress and grief he alone is able to find relief and even be joyful (in view of Rom. 8:28, 35-39) who at the Father's throne makes all his wants and wishes known. Hence, the directive "Always be joyful" is immediately followed by "Ceaselessly pray." The most compre-hensive word for *prayer* (προσευχή, προσεύχομαι) is used here. For synonyms see the striking passage Phil. 4:6. What Paul means is: there must be no decline in the regularity of the habit of "taking hold on God" in the midst of all circumstances of life. Cf. Rom. 12:12; Eph. 6:18; Col. 4:2. The apostle could afford to say this, for he himself gave the example (3:10; II Thess. 1:11; Eph. 1:16; 3:14).

When a person prays without giving thanks, he has clipped the wings of prayer, sothat it cannot rise. Hence, the trio of admonitions concludes with, "In *all circumstances* give thanks." This phrase *in everything* (ἐν παντί probably with χρήματι understood) includes affliction, for even in the midst of all *these* things ("tribulation, anguish, persecution, famine, naked-ness, peril, or sword") believers are not merely conquerors but "more than conquerors" (super-invincibles), inasmuch as all these things actually help them to reach their predestined goal! See Rom. 8:35-37.

For this is the will of God (not merely the word of Paul, Silas, and Tim-othy) **in Christ Jesus for y o u.** The will of God, as clearly set forth by

138

means of the redemptive work and revelation of Jesus Christ, is this very thing, namely, that believers should always be joyful, should ceaselessly pray, and should in all circumstances give thanks.

19-22. The next little series of admonitions has to do with the Holy Spirit and his gifts:

The Spirit do not quench.

Prophetic utterances do not despise, but test all things: to the good hold on; from every form of evil hold off.

Upon the early church the Holy Spirit had bestowed certain *special gifts* or *charismata*. Among them were: ability to perform miracles of healing, speaking in tongues, and prophesying.

Although according to some interpreters there was nothing miraculous about the latter, we do not share this opinion.[110] The Church in its infancy had no complete Bible (Old and New Testament). It had no extensive body of Christian literature, such as we have today. Christian hymnology, too, was still in its infancy. Numerically also, the Church was rather insignificant. It was, moreover, the object of scorn and derision from every side. In that situation God graciously provided special supports or endowments, until the time would arrive when these were no longer needed. One of these gifts was that of prophesying.

As the term — and its derivatives — implies (for in this case the etymological sense continues to cling to it), a *prophet* (προφήτης from πρό *forth*, and φημί to *speak*) is "a person who speaks forth." And what he speaks forth or openly declares is the will and mind of God. He is[111] a "forthteller," and not necessarily (though sometimes also) a "fore-teller."

Now, although this particular gift of prophesying was one of the greatest of the charismata, ranking even above that of the ability to speak in tongues — for, the prophet's message as contrasted with the utterance of the man who spoke in a tongue, was readily understandable (I Cor. 14:1, 2, 4, 5, 6) —, yet it was held in low esteem by some of the members of the Thessalonian church. This was deplorable in view of the fact that by making light of prophetic utterances these members missed the "edification, encouragement, and consolation" (I Cor. 14:3) brought by the prophet. Moreover, by means of despising the prophetic utterances, their Giver, the Holy Spirit, was being dishonored. In the early Church the

---

[110] Lenski (*op. cit.*, p. 360), for example, denies that prophesying belongs to the extraordinary charismata. He points to the fact that in Rom. 12:7 this kind of prophesying heads the list of gifts, none of which were miraculous. But over against this stands the fact that in I Cor. 12:10 prophesying is mentioned in one breath with such gifts as the working of miracles and the ability to speak in tongues; and according to I Cor. 14:24, 25 by means of prophesying the secrets of the heart of the outsider who enters the religious meeting are laid bare, so that he falls on his face and declares, in utter astonishment, "God is really among y o u."

[111] See A. T. Robertson, *Word Pictures*, Vol. IV, pp. 37, 38.

gift of prophesying was like a brightly burning flame. It must not be *quenched* or *extinguished!* (for the verb cf. Matt. 12:20; 25:8; Mark 9:48; Eph. 6:16; Heb. 11:34). Hence, we read, "The Spirit do not quench. Prophetic utterances do not despise." The objects are placed first for the sake of emphasis. It is as if Paul were saying, "By making light of the utterances of the prophets among y o u, y o u are belittling the work of no One less than the Holy Spirit."

The reason for this disparagement of prophetical utterances can readily be surmised. Wherever God plants wheat, Satan sows his tares. Wherever God establishes a church, the devil erects a chapel. And so, too, wherever the Holy Spirit enables certain men to perform miracles of healing, the evil one distributes his "lying wonders." And wherever the Paraclete brings a *true* prophet upon the scene, the deceiver presents his *false* prophet. The easiest — but not the wisest — reaction to this state of affairs is to despise *all* prophesying. Add to this the fact that the fanatics, the meddlers, and the loafers at Thessalonica may not have appreciated some of the utterances of the true prophets, and it is readily understood why by some in the congregation prophetic utterances had fallen into disfavor.

Paul, therefore, states what course of action the congregation should take: "Prophetic utterances do not despise, but *test* (on the verb see I Thess. 2:4) all things." The standard by which the true prophet can be distinguished from the false is that the former will declare nothing that is contrary to what God has made known previously, in his special revelation.[112] Cf. Deut. 13:1-5; Rom. 12:6. In the new dispensation the criterion would be the revelation of God through the testimony of Christ and of the apostles. Besides, in the early Church some men seem to have been gifted with rare proficiency in separating genuine from false prophesying (see I Cor. 12:10: "and to another the ability to distinguish between spirits").

Once a true verdict has been reached, the practical rule must apply: "to the good *hold on* (κατέχετε); from every *form* (or *kind,* not *appearance* here) of evil *hold off* (ἀπέχεσθε). Note: *every* form, whether the wicked and uninspired utterance concerns doctrine or life. It is probable that this *every* is even broader, to be taken absolutely.

When verses 19-22 are studied together, as a unit, it becomes apparent immediately that the rule *"Test* all things" cannot mean "Try everything once," or "Enter every place of wickedness and find out for yourselves what it is." In the given context it simply means that, instead of despising each and every prophetical utterance, one should test whatever presents itself as such. The good should be accepted; *every* kind of evil (without any

---

[112] Cf. G. Ch. Aalders, *De Profeten Des Ouden Verbonds,* Kampen, 1918, pp. 224-235. On the indicated pages the author discusses the pro and the con of the various criteria that have been suggested as means for distinguishing the true prophet from the false.

exception; hence, whether it be *evil advice* — given by a false prophet — *or any other form of evil*) must be avoided.

What follows is a concluding wish and a few urgent requests, such as one expects to find at the close of this letter; then the benediction.

23. **And may he, the God of peace,**
sanctify y o u through and through,
and without flaw may be y o u r spirit,
and y o u r soul-and-body
without blame at the coming of our Lord Jesus Christ
may it be kept.

In this passage the author points to the source of power for the believer. It is as if he wished to say, "In y o u r own strength y o u cannot fulfil the precepts which I have just issued. Y o u need God, *the God of peace* (cf. Rom. 15:33; 16:20; II Cor. 13:11; Phil. 4:9; II Thess. 3:16; Heb. 13:20), a peace established through the cross, a peace which implies spiritual prosperity in the fullest sense (see on 1:1). May this God *sanctify* y o u, that is, may he separate y o u from the life of sin and cause y o u to be dedicated to him (cf. Rom. 15:16; I Cor. 1:2; 6:11; 7:14; Rev. 22:11; and see above on 3:13; 4:3, 7; also N.T.C. on John 17:17, 19) *through and through*. This "through and through" (ὁλοτελεῖς, from ὅλος *whole*, and τέλος *end*) is a rare word, occurring only here in the New Testament. It is a plural adjective, sothat the literal meaning of the word in connection with the noun which it modifies is *y o u whole*, that is, "the whole of each of y o u, every part of each of y o u" (A. T. Robertson, *Word Pictures,* Vol. IV, p. 38). (M.M., p. 447, points out that both here in I Thess. 5:23 and in a decree of Epaminondas the adjective has adverbial force.)

Now this process of sanctification occurs during the present life, the life here on earth. Paul expresses a closely related wish which pertains to the judgment day. The two thoughts constitute a unit. He expresses the wish — which has the solemnity of a prayer — that also "at the coming of our Lord Jesus Christ" (see on 2:19), when others will be sentenced to everlasting damnation for both soul and body (the entire person), the spirit of the believers at Thessalonica (together with all other believers, of course) may be without flaw; indeed that their soul-and-body may be preserved from this terrible condemnation, that is, may be kept *blamelessly* (2:10; cf. 3:13).

So far there is no great difficulty. The *main* idea is clear. The problem arises in interpreting .the details. See grammatical footnote [113] which because of its length has been placed at the end of this chapter (on pp. 146-150). If one wishes an answer to the question, "Was Paul a trichotomist?" "Does I Thess. 5:23 teach that man consists of three parts, spirit, soul, and body?" he should read that note.

141

The *entirety-idea* is stressed throughout the passage. This is shown by the forward position of the word "entire" or "without flaw," and also by such expressions as "through and through" and "y o u r soul and body." Though certain people in Greece and Macedonia might hold the body in low esteem and might consider it to be merely a prison from which the soul must be liberated, and though the Thessalonian believers, mourning the loss of dear ones, might be wondering whether the buried bodies would in any way come to share in the glory of Christ's return (see on 4:13-18), Paul assures the readers that God in Christ is a perfect Savior.

24. A wonderful expression of assurance follows. What Paul has expressed so strikingly is a wish, indeed, but not a *mere* wish. It is a wish which, by God's sovereign grace, will attain certain fulfilment:

Faithful is he who calls y o u, who will also do it.

The Thessalonians need have no fear. The One who *calls* (ὁ καλῶν timeless present participle) them (see on 2:12; 4:7; II Thess. 2:14) will also certainly complete what he has begun with respect to them (cf. Phil. 1:16). He will surely sanctify and preserve them. He is *faithful* (πιστός), to be trusted (cf. I Cor. 1:9; 10:13; II Cor. 1:18; II Thess. 3:3; II Tim. 2:13). What he promises he does.

25. The man who, in the midst of his herculean labors, in II Cor. 11:29 exclaims, "Who is weak, that I am not weak?" and who prefaces that remark with a long list of sufferings and hardships which he had to endure, feels the need of prayer. The circumstances which surround him at Corinth are by no means easy. See on 3:7. Besides, he (together with Silas and Timothy, of course) believes in the efficacy of prayer. It is, therefore, not surprising that here (and in several of the epistles) we find this stirring request, **Brothers, do pray for us.** Cf. II Thess. 3:1; Rom. 15:30; Eph. 6:19; Col. 4:3. The emphatic position of the word "Brothers" (see on 1:4) — sothat the propriety of the request is based, as it were, upon the love which obtains between those who are members of the same spiritual family — adds to its earnest and urgent character.

26. Greet all the brothers with a holy kiss.

Just as someone living today will write, "Tender my kindest greetings to" this or that person, so Paul, Silas, and Timothy ask that they be remembered to "all the brothers," that is, to every member of the congregation, including even those who were displaying tendencies in the direction of fanaticism or of meddlesomeness or of idleness. None is to be skipped.

The form of this greeting is the "holy kiss" (cf. Rom. 16:16; I Cor. 16:20; II Cor. 13:12). This was the kiss *of love* (cf. I Peter 5:14) and *of peace* (see *Constitutions,* quoted below). It was *holy* because it was a symbol of spiritual oneness in Christ. It was, moreover, a seal of *Christian* affection, the feeling which members of one and the same spiritual household cherish for one another.

Among the early references to this kind of kiss are the following:

"As many as are convinced and believe that what we teach and say is true, and pledge themselves to be able to live accordingly, are instructed to pray and to entreat God with fasting for the remission of their past sins, while we pray and fast with them. Then they are brought by us to a place where there is water, and they are regenerated in the same manner in which we ourselves were regenerated. For, in the name of God, the Father and Lord of the universe, and of our Savior Jesus Christ, and of the Holy Spirit, they then receive the washing with water. . . . After we have thus baptized the one who has been convinced and has given his assent to our teaching, we bring him to the place where those who are called *brothers* are gathered, in order that we may offer hearty prayers in common for ourselves, for the baptized person, and for all others in every place. . . . *Having ended the prayers, we salute one another with a holy kiss.* Then bread and a cup containing wine mixed with water are presented to that one of the brothers who was presiding" (Justin Martyr — about the middle of the second century A. D. — *First Apology*. LXI. LXV).

"Who [i.e., what *un*believing husband] will, without some suspicion, dismiss her [i.e., his wife who is a believer] to attend that Lord's Supper which they defame? Who will permit her to creep into prison, *to kiss a martyr's bonds? nay, indeed, to meet any one of the brothers to exchange the kiss?*" (Tertullian — about 207 A. D. — *To His Wife* II. iv).

"Let the younger women also sit by themselves, if there be a place for them; otherwise, let them stand behind the women. Let married women who have children be placed by themselves; but let the virgins and the widows and the old women stand or sit before all the rest. And let the deacon be the disposer of the places, that every one who enters may go to his proper place, and may not sit at the entrance. In like manner, let the deacon watch the people, that nobody whispers or sleeps or laughs or nods. . . . After this let all arise together, and looking toward the east . . . pray to God eastward. . . . After the prayer is over, let some of the deacons attend upon the oblation of the Eucharist. . . . Let other deacons watch the multitude and keep them silent. But let that deacon who is at the highpriest's right hand say to the people, 'Let no one have any dispute with another; let no one come in hypocrisy.' *Then let the men give the men, and the women give the women, the Lord's kiss*" (*Constitutions of the Holy Apostles* — about the third century A. D. — II. vii).

"And after this [prayer for the faithful] let the deacon say, Let us attend. And let the bishop salute the church, and say, The peace of God be with y o u all. And let the people answer, And with thy spirit."

"And let the deacon say to all, *Salute one another with a holy kiss. And* let the clergy salute the bishop, the men of the laity salute the men, the women (salute) the women. And let the children stand by the reading-desk. And let another deacon stand by them, that they may not be disorderly" (*Constitutions of the Holy Apostles,* VIII. xi).

"*Let us salute one another with a holy kiss.* Let us bow our heads to the Lord" ("*The Divine Liturgy of James, the Holy Apostle and Brother of the Lord*" — date, origin, and authorship disputed — , II).

Of interest, in this connection, is also the remark of Augustine: "People complain about being led out of the dark night of ruinous unbelief into the light of life-giving faith. Held fast by the evil spirit, they grumble because other people stream into the church to render a pure worship to God, where, for the sake of modesty, men are on one side and women on the other" (*Concerning the City of God* — written 413-426 A. D. — , II. xxviii).

27. I solemnly charge y o u before the Lord to have this epistle read to all the brothers. This solemn charge or adjuration is not surprising. The contents of the epistle is important, both with respect to teaching (for example, anent the Second Coming) and with respect to admonition. It is very well possible that some of the disorderly persons, upon hearing that a letter from the missionaries had arrived and suspecting that it contained some admonitions intended especially for them, might wish to be absent when it was read aloud to the congregation. So Paul stresses the fact that by all means *every* person in the church must hear the letter! The adjuration implies a threat of divine punishment if this be not done. Yet, the charge contains no bitterness, note the term of endearment: *brothers.*

28. The grace of our Lord Jesus Christ be with y o u. With variations this benediction occurs *at* or *near* the close of *all* of Paul's epistles (i.e., *all* if its occurrence in Rom. 16:20 is authentic). It is entirely in harmony with the spiritual character of the salutation at the beginning. For the various concepts and for the force of both see on 1:1.

Synthesis of 5:12-28

See p. 132. *Exhortation. Paul writes to the Thessalonians, exhorting them how they should conduct themselves with respect to all classes and at all times.*

A close study of I Thessalonians reveals the fact that a mighty conflict between the forces of light and those of darkness is presupposed throughout. At times (in certain words and phrases) it arises to the surface.

Arrayed on one side are, first of all, God the Father, the Lord Jesus Christ, and the Holy Spirit; then Paul, Silvanus, and Timothy, who are carrying on their spiritual labors by means of this letter and also through the elders of the church. Finally, there is the brotherhood in general.

Here again a distinction is made between those whose faith, love, and hope are bearing much fruit (and who are therefore examples to others), and those who, though regarded as brothers, are characterized by shortcomings that call for special consideration. Thus, there are the disorderly persons (fanatics, meddlers, and loafers), the fainthearted, and the weak.

But there are also those who had been endowed with special gifts, for example, that of prophesying, and — as could be expected — there were the would-be prophets.

Furthermore, reference is made to "those who believe in Macedonia and Achaia" and to "the churches of God that are in Judea." From this it is clear that the various local churches, though autonomous, do not stand entirely by themselves. There is an organic bond between them, the bond of faith, love, and hope. The idea of the *one,* holy, catholic Church (the theme of Ephesians) begins to emerge already in I Thessalonians! See especially 1:7-9; 2:14; 2:19; 4:10. The Thessalonian believers love (and have become an example to) those in Macedonia and Achaia. They have become imitators of those in Judea and are enduring the same hardships. Along with others, moreover, they constitute Paul's glory-wreath. Here is the idea of the Church Militant.

But the Church Militant, in turn, stands in the closest possible relation to the Church Triumphant. At Christ's Return those who previously fell asleep, *together with* those who are then still living on earth will be caught up in clouds to meet the Lord in the air, and to remain with him forever.

On the other side are Satan, the idols, the pagans who afflict believers, and those who instigate the pagans. These pagans "do not know God," are living in darkness, are morally and spiritually asleep, have no firmly-anchored hope, and are destined for sudden destruction (everlasting punishment).

The wicked instigators are the impenitent Jews, who are "contrary to all men" and on whom the wrath of God has come "to the uttermost."

Such are the two armies. Again and again believers receive the bracing assurance of complete victory at the coming of the Lord Jesus Christ.

Now the present, closing section of I Thessalonians contains specific exhortations showing what should be the attitude of the Thessalonians with respect to several of the groups and persons mentioned in the preceding, namely, towards:

verses 12, 13	the elders of the church
verse 14	the disorderly
	the fainthearted
	the weak
	"everyone"
verse 15	those who have injured them
verses 16-18	God

145

verses 19-22 the Holy Spirit and his gifts (also: would-be prophets). This is followed by

verses 23, 24 a solemn wish for sanctification and preservation, the wish being immediately followed by the promise;

       by

verses 25-28 a trio of urgent requests (for intercessory prayer, for extending greetings by means of the "holy kiss," and for the public reading of this letter); and finally by

       the benediction.

---

113 If a. the nominative, singular, neuter *adjective* "without flaw" or "entire" or "sound" (ὁλόκληϱον) is either treated as an adverb (some call it an adverb) or as an adjective belonging to all three nouns (spirit, soul, body); and b. this word is given a totally different place in the sentence than it has in the original, being now placed next to the word "without blame" (or "blamelessly"), as if also in the original the two occurred in close co-ordination, a rendering results which changes a *little* problem into a *big* one. The rendering to which I refer is:

"And may your spirit and soul and body be preserved entire, without blame. . . ." (A.R.V., cf. A.V. and R.S.V. neither of which is any better).

Naturally, the question now arises, "Did Paul believe that human nature consists of three parts: spirit, soul, and body? In other words, was he a trichotomist?" The deeper question is, "Just what did Paul mean when he wrote I Thess. 5:23 (especially the words in dispute)?"

Among the answers or solutions which have been offered the following are, perhaps, the most important:

a. Paul was evidently a trichotomist. He clearly divides human nature into spirit, soul, and body.

b. Paul's readers were trichotomists. Paul accommodates himself to their view. Had he simply written, "And may your soul and body be kept sound and blameless," the readers would have asked, "Must not our *spirits* be preserved also?" In order to avoid this erroneous conclusion — that *the spirit* did not need to be guarded — the apostle writes as he does.

c. Paul does not distinguish at all between *spirit* and *soul* in the present passage. He is speaking rhetorically. We do the same thing today when we tell an audience to put its "heart and soul" into a certain worthwhile project.

d. Paul, in using the word *spirit,* meant the Holy Spirit, or that portion of the divine Spirit which dwells permanently in each regenerated individual. To this Holy Spirit, who dwells in (but is never part of) the human nature, he, as a true dichotomist, adds "soul and body" as constituting the human nature.

e. When Paul mentions both spirit and soul, he indicates *not two* substances but *one* and the same immaterial substance. However, he views this substance first from the aspect of its relation to God — as a recipient of divine influences and as an organ for divine worship ("spirit") —, then from the aspect of its relation to the lower realm — as the seat of sensations, affections, desires, etc. ("soul"). To this *one* immaterial substance, viewed from *two* aspects, *Paul adds the body.* It is in this sense that he writes, "and may your spirit and soul and body be kept sound and blameless."

f. Paul does not have in mind a series of three co-ordinate elements: "spirit and soul and body." On the contrary, the first concept is "your entire person." To this, by way of explanation, the apostle adds, "both your soul and body."

With respect to these six theories our own opinion is as follows:

Theory a.

This can be dismissed at once. The fact that Paul was not a trichotomist is clear from such passages as the following: Rom. 8:10; I Cor. 5:5; 7:34; II Cor. 7:1; Eph.

2:3; Col. 2:5. Apart from I Thess. 5:23 he nowhere employs trichotomistic language with respect to the nature of man. The conclusion seems valid that also in the present passage he does not write as a trichotomist.

Theory b.

This accommodation theory, besides being questionable as to the ethics implied, lacks a solid historical basis. The readers surely were not Neo-Platonists!

Theory c.

The illustration employed is not very appropriate. When we tell an audience to put its "heart and soul" into a certain project, we immediately recognize the synonymous character of these two terms. But when *within one and the same clause* (as this theory implies) we co-ordinate *three* terms, *the third of which is clearly of a totally different nature from the second* (the third being *body*, the second being *soul*), the question is legitimate whether perhaps the first (*spirit*) should not also be distinguished in meaning from the others. Besides, Paul elsewhere frequently uses the term *soul* (ψυχή, whence ψυχικός "natural" or "unspiritual" I Cor. 2:14) in a sense different from *spirit* (πνεῦμα, whence πνευματικός "spiritual" I Cor. 2:15). It must not be taken for granted, therefore, that every distinction between *spirit* and *soul* is *here* (in I Thess. 5:23) completely absent from his mind.

The summary of the first table of the law, Mark 12:30, far from proving theory c. to be correct, would rather seem to establish the very opposite, for certainly here heart, soul, mind, and strength do not all mean exactly the same thing!

Theory d.

This is definitely wrong, though we admit that it is advanced by really great exegetes. Paul, Silas, and Timothy would not be expressing the wish that the Holy Spirit (or "a portion of the Holy Spirit") might be kept sound and blameless! Nor would they be hoping that the third person of the Trinity might be without a flaw!

Theory e.

This is probably the best of those so far reviewed. It has much in its favor: it permits Paul to remain a dichotomist, which is correct (as has been shown). It is also correct in indicating that the first and the second terms of the triad (hence, πνεῦμα and ψυχή) are at times to be distinguished in the manner stated in the theory. If we had to choose between the five theories discussed so far, this would be our choice. In fact, as we see it, in some respects this theory is also better than theory f. (below), for example, in that it does not render the adjective *sound* (ὁλόκληρον) as if it were in the attributive position.

Nevertheless, the *translation* proposed here ("and may your spirit and soul and body be kept sound and blameless") has the following debatable features:

(1) It co-ordinates the words "sound" and "blameless," placing them next to each other, which does not seem to harmonize with the intention of the original.

(2) It interprets the conjunction "and" (καί) which occurs between the second and the third terms of the triad as *adding* two different substances (soul, body), but it views the "and" (καί) which connects the first and the second as merely indicating that *the same substance* is considered from two different aspects. Although this may be possible, it is not the usual manner in which one would interpret two identical conjunctions in an expression consisting of three terms which one considers to be co-ordinate, *all occurring in the same clause,* and which one thus translates: "your spirit *and* soul *and* body."

(3) It connects the adjective *sound* with all three nouns (spirit, soul, body), but it does not show why in the original it is *in the singular!* (However, this objection is not formidable. It happens more often that in such a series, the number of the adjective which modifies all the nouns in the series simply agrees with the first or last noun mentioned.) Or if the word "sound" is considered to be an adverb modifying the verb "be kept" (some interpreters view it as such), it is not made

clear why it should be an adverb *here* while elsewhere in the Greek Bible it is always an adjective (see in the LXX: Lev. 23:15; Deut. 27:6; Josh. 9:2; Ezek. 15:5; Zech. 11:16; Wisd. Sol. 15:3; I Macc. 4:47; IV Macc. 15:17: *whole* stones, *entire* righteousness, *complete* sabbaths, etc.).

I accept theory e. in part, not entirely.

Theory f.

According to this theory, proposed long ago, and recently presented in strengthened form by Charles Masson in a well-written article ("Sur I Thessaloniciens 5:23," *RThPh* 33 (1945), 97-102) the passage in question should be translated somewhat as follows:

> "And may the God of peace himself
> sanctify y o u wholly;
> and may y o u r entire person,
> y o u r soul and y o u r body,
> be kept irreproachable
> for the day of the coming
> of our Lord Jesus Christ."

This theory avoids many of the objectionable features of the others but, as I see it, introduces some new difficulties. The points which distinguish it from the preceding are the following: it experiences no difficulty with respect to the number and gender of the word *sound* or *entire* (ὁλόκληρον); it views that word as an adjective, which is probably correct. However, it considers πνεῦμα, as used here in I Thess. 5:23, to mean *person*, and it offers as proof the parallelism between

"The grace of our Lord Jesus Christ be with y o u r *spirit*" (Gal. 6:18; Phil. 4:23; Philemon 25)

and

"The grace of our Lord Jesus Christ be with y o u" (I Thess. 5:28), noting that in such liturgical passages (and it considers I Thess. 5:23 to belong to this category) "y o u r spirit" means "y o u" or something closely akin to it (the entire person of the believer, both soul and body). It seeks support from the immediately preceding line ("sanctify y o u wholly" corresponding to "may y o u r entire person . . . be kept"); and it considers καί . . . καί to mean "both . . . and" (cf. Rom. 11:33).

A final feature, which requires special mention, is the fact that, according to Masson, when the original is read as he reads it, verse 23 "divides itself into two strophes, each containing two stitches, whose parallelism in the number of syllables, as also in the assonances of initial and final syllables, compose an easily perceptible rhythm."

While we acknowledge our indebtedness to Masson and to those before him who have advanced this view, we, nevertheless, cannot go along with them all the way. In addition to minor differences in translation, which become immediately evident when our rendering for the entire verse is compared to that offered by the proponents of this theory, two differences stand out above all the rest:

The first is this: *in the Greek original* the word which Masson, etc., correctly render "entire" is in the predicate position. Hence, as I see it, the original does not really say, "And may y o u r entire spirit," but "And entire (or "and without flaw") may be y o u r spirit." The Berkeley Version correctly retains the predicate position of the adjective when it translates: "May your spirit be without flaw and your soul and body maintained blameless."

The second point which requires additional comment concerns the theory's rendering of the term πνεῦμα. It favors the translation "person" in the sense of *soul and body*. But does this Greek word πνεῦμα ever have that meaning anywhere else in the New Testament? The simple fact is that it does not.

It will be profitable in this connection to give a review of the uses of the two terms in question, namely, πνεῦμα and ψυχή. (The third term, σῶμα, is clear enough.)

(1) There is first of all the meaning *wind* (John 3:8; Heb. 1:7 plural). The original has πνεῦμα.

(2) The closely related concept *breath, breath of life, life, animating principle* is represented both by πνεῦμα (II Thess. 2:8, fig.; Rev. 11:11; 13:15?; and cf. Matt. 27:50; Luke 8:55; 23:46; John 19:30; Acts 7:59; James 2:26) and by ψυχή (Matt. 2:20; 6:25a; 6:25b; 16:26a; 16:26b; Mark 3:4; Luke 6:9, etc.), though mostly by the latter.

(3) The meaning *living being, self, person,* especially frequent in passages which can be traced back to Hebrew originals, but by no means confined to such passages, is always ψυχή. Under this heading some would include only the following: Matt. 11:29; Mark 8:36; Acts 2:41, 43; 3:23; 7:14; 27:37; Rom. 2:9; 13:1; I Cor. 15:45; I Peter 3:20; and Rev. 16:3. Others, on the basis of a comparison of parallel passages, would add such references as Matt. 20:28; Mark 10:45, cf. I Tim. 2:6; John 10:11, 15, 17; and many more (note "my soul" is "I" in Matt. 12:18; and "my soul" is "thy Holy One" and is "he" in Acts 2:27, 31).

(4) *Soul* or *spirit.* The original has ψυχή and πνεῦμα.

(5) *Incorporeal* or *disembodied being.* With the possible exception of the disputed meaning of ψυχή in Rev. 6:9 and 20:4 (which, as I see it, properly come under this heading, but not all agree) this meaning is in the New Testament everywhere represented by πνεῦμα. The following subdivisions can be recognized: spirit in general (Acts 23:8, 9), God as Spirit (John 4:24), Christ as Spirit (I Cor. 15:45), the human soul apart from the body (Heb. 12:23; I Peter 3:19), ghost (Luke 24:37, 39), angel (Heb. 1:14), demon, more than forty passages for this last subdivision of (5) (Matt. 8:16; 10:1; 12:43, etc.).

(6) *The Holy Spirit and/or his gifts.* There are about one hundred twenty passages in which "the Holy Spirit" ("Spirit of God," — "of the Lord," — "of Jesus," — "of Christ," — "of Jesus Christ," "the seven Spirits") is definitely mentioned. In an approximately equal number of passages the term "Spirit" in all probability refers to the Holy Spirit, though in several cases this is disputed. In all cases which come under this sixth heading the word used is πνεῦμα (Matt. 1:18, 20; 3:11; 12:32; etc.).

(7) *Frame of mind, disposition, efficient source, influence, life-imparting energy.* With the exception of a couple disputed instances where one of these closely related connotations may be represented by ψυχή, the word is always πνεῦμα (Matt. 5:3; Luke 1:17; I Cor. 4:21; Gal. 6:1, etc.).

With the exception of (1) all these meanings are also found in the writings of Paul. At present, however, we are concerned only with (4). It is striking that Paul nearly always uses πνεῦμα when this concept is indicated. Yet he also uses ψυχή (I Thess. 2:8, unless this should fall under heading 3; I Thess. 5:23).

The question arises, Did Paul distinguish between πνεῦμα and ψυχή? The two words have in common that both refer to the invisible element in man, viewed as the principle of thinking, willing, desiring. It must be granted that there are several passages in the New Testament where the distinction in meaning is so small that the two may be said to be interchangeable or nearly so. Nevertheless, close study of these terms in all their occurrences points to the fact that *basically* there is a distinction between them. Whenever this distinction has not yet faded away, it amounts to this, that when πνεῦμα is used *mental* activity comes into prominence, while ψυχή frequently points in the direction of *emotional* activity. It is the *spirit* (πνεῦμα) which perceives (Mark 2:8), plans (Acts 19:21), and knows (I Cor. 2:11). It is the *soul* (ψυχή) that is sorrowful (Matt. 26:38). The *spirit* (πνεῦμα) prays (I Cor. 14:14), the ψυχή loves (Mark 12:30). Also, ψυχή is often more general, broader in scope, indicating the *sum-total* of life which rises above the physical, while πνεῦμα is more restricted, indicating the human spirit in its relation to *God,* man's self-consciousness or personality viewed as the subject in acts of worship or in activities related to worship, such as praying, bearing witness, serving the Lord.

In my study of all the Pauline passages in which πνεῦμα is used I have not found a single one in which it has the meaning "person," in the sense of one's soul and body.

It has become evident that I am not satisfied (at least not *wholly* satisfied) with theory f.

Having now discussed the six theories, none of which I am ready to accept in its entirety, though I admit that some contain valuable elements, I will state my own view:

a. The trichotomistic appearance of the passage is considerably reduced as soon as it is seen that the words in dispute are found not in one clause but in two clauses:

hence not: "And may your spirit and soul and body be kept . . ."

but

"And without flaw may be y o u r spirit,
And y o u r soul-and-body

. . . .

May it be kept."

But thus rendering the passage we can do justice to its grammatical syntax and even to its word-order (see the original).

b. Every trace of trichotomy which still remains can be obliterated in one of two ways:

(1) by considering the word "soul" to have the same meaning as "spirit," the change from "spirit" to "soul" having been introduced for stylistic reasons. This eliminates trichotomy.

(2) by accepting the position that although both "spirit" and "soul" refer to *the same* immaterial substance (hence, no trichotomy here either!), this substance is viewed first (in one clause) from the aspect of its relation to *God* — the "spirit" being man's power of grasping divine things, his invisible essence viewed as a recipient of divine influences and as an organ of divine worship — ; then, in the next clause, from the aspect of its relation to *the lower realm*, as the seat of sensations, affections, desires. This could well be the true element in theory e.

If a choice must be made, I would prefer this second alternative. It is in harmony with the distinction between the two words which is present elsewhere (as has been shown). There is also an interesting parallel in a somewhat similar passage, Heb. 4:12, where it is obvious that the two words have distinct meanings.

The main point has been proved, namely, that, either way, every trace of trichotomy has disappeared!

Commentary
on
II Thessalonians

Outline of II Thessalonians 1

Theme: *The Revelation of the Lord Jesus from Heaven*
has a twofold purpose:

(1) To be glorified in the saints, including those at Thessalonica, for whom, because of their increase in faith and love, and their continued endurance amid persecution, Paul feels impelled to thank God, and for whom he prays.

(2) To render vengeance to the disobedient.

CHAPTER I

1 Paul and Silvanus and Timothy to the church of the Thessalonians in God
our Father and the Lord Jesus Christ; 2 grace to y o u and peace from God
the Father and the Lord Jesus Christ.

3 We are obliged to give thanks to God always for y o u, brothers, as is fitting, because y o u r faith is growing beyond measure, and the love of each single
one of y o u for one another is constantly increasing, 4 so that we on our part boast
of y o u in the churches of God, of y o u r endurance and faith in all y o u r persecutions and in the afflictions under which y o u are holding up, 5 an evident indication of God's righteous judgment, in order that y o u may be deemed worthy of
the kingdom of God, for which y o u, too, are suffering; 6 (God's *righteous* judgment, we say) if, indeed, (it is) righteous in God's estimation (as it certainly is) to
repay with afflictions those who afflict y o u, 7 and (to grant) y o u who are being
afflicted rest with us at the revelation of the Lord Jesus from heaven with the
angels of his power in flaming fire, 8 inflicting vengeance on those who do not
know God, even on those who do not obey the gospel of our Lord Jesus, such as
will pay the penalty of everlasting destruction away from the face of the Lord and
from the glory of his might, 10 when he comes in order to be glorified in his saints
and to be marveled at in all who believe — for our testimony to y o u was believed
— in that day.

11 With this in view we are also praying always for y o u, that our God may
count y o u worthy of the call, and that he by his power may bring to fulfilment
(y o u r) every resolve prompted by goodness and (y o u r every) work resulting from
faith, 12 in order that the name of our Lord Jesus may be glorified in y o u, and
y o u in him according to the grace of our God and of the Lord Jesus Christ.

1:1-12

**1:1, 2. Paul and Silvanus and Timothy to the church of the Thessa-
lonians in God our Father and the Lord Jesus Christ; 2 grace to y o u
and peace from God the Father and the Lord Jesus Christ.**

This superscription differs from that found in I Thess. 1:1 in two respects
only:

(1) It has *"our* Father" instead of *"the* Father." Thus the fact that both
writers and readers have one and the same Father is here definitely expressed, though it was also implied in I Thess. 1:1.

(2) After the clause "grace to y o u and peace" it adds a phrase which

153

makes explicit *the source* of grace and peace, showing that it comes *"from* God the Father and the Lord Jesus Christ." In I Thess. 1:1 this source was implied in the statement that the church was (founded and still existing) *"in* God the Father and the Lord Jesus Christ."

For the rest, see on I Thess. 1:1.

3. We are obliged to give thanks to God always for y o u, brothers, as is fitting.

For the meaning of, "We give thanks to God always," see on I Thess. 1:2. However, here in II Thess. 1:3 the writers do not state, "We give thanks to God always," but *"We are obliged"* (ὀφείλομεν) to do so. They feel impelled to express their gratitude to God. They cannot do otherwise. And this subjective necessity is in harmony with the objective necessity: "as is *fitting"* (ἄξιον).

The idea advanced by some commentators that the substitution of, "We are obliged to give thanks," for "We give thanks" implies a degree of reluctance or hesitancy, and that this "somewhat faltering manner of expression" must be explained in the light of 2:2; 3:6, 10, 11 — passages which indicate that the mental attitude and conduct of some had grown worse instead of better — impresses us as an instance of reading too much into the text. Also open to serious question is the view according to which the replacement of "for y o u *all"* (I Thess. 1:2) by the simple "for y o u" (here in II Thess. 1:3) must be explained similarly. That Paul is not trying to omit any true "brother" is rather clear from what immediately follows (note the words "each single one of y o u"): **because y o u r faith is growing beyond measure, and the love of each single one of y o u** (literally, "of each one of y o u all") **for one another is constantly increasing.** Clearly in this entire passage — whether it be read in the original or in the translation makes no difference — the writers reveal themselves as men who are elated (see also on 2:13; 3:4) rather than reluctant, exuberant rather than hesitant. The presence in the congregation of a few members who were not living in accordance with the rules cannot be denied. In fact, it constituted a real problem, more so even than when the first epistle was written. But in the jubilant passage which we are now discussing the disorderly persons are kept in the background for the moment. What we have here is irrepressible joy, a joy which in the form of sincere and humble thanksgiving is directed to the Giver of all good things.

The reason for the constant thanksgiving is that the faith of the Thessalonians *is growing beyond measure* (ὑπεραυξάνει) or *very much,* and that the love of each single brother *is constantly increasing* (πλεονάζει), which was exactly what Paul had wished and prayed for so earnestly (see on I Thess. 3:12; 4:1, 10). It is true that in the present passage *faith* and *love* are mentioned, *not hope.* Contrast I Thess. 1:3, where all three are mentioned. But to infer from this omission (as some interpreters do) that in Paul's judgment the Thessalonians had lost their hope is unwarranted. Such a conclusion brings one into conflict with what is clearly stated in II Thess. 2:16: "who gave *us* (both readers and writers) *good hope.*" Besides, Paul immediately adds (verse 4) that he boasts of the *endurance* which the readers are showing; and is not *endurance* inspired by hope? See on I Thess. 1:3.

It is certainly true that the Thessalonians needed further instruction with respect to things to come (see 2:1-12), but their hope was by no means dim. On the contrary, it was buoyant, and it sustained them sothat they were able to endure persecution. Verse 3 must not be interpreted as if verse 4 did not exist! *The only correct way to interpret a passage is to read on and on.* If that is done, we shall not commit the error of saying that Paul praises the Thessalonians for their faith and love but not for their hope.

4. One of the results of the readers' growth in faith and increase in love is now stated: **sothat we on our part boast of y o u in the churches of God, of y o u r endurance and faith in all y o u r persecutions and in the afflictions under which y o u are holding up.**

The perfectly natural and easy manner in which the term *endurance* is here introduced seems to imply that it was already presupposed in verse 3. Faith full-grown implies hope, and hope produces endurance.

Paul, Silas, and Timothy *are boasting* (i.e., they *"spoke with pride"*) about the Thessalonians. In connection with this boasting four facts are pointed out:

(1) *Its authors:* "we on our part" (αὐτοὺς ἡμᾶς). Cf. Rom. 9:3; 15:14; II Cor. 12:13. The idea seems to be one of contrast, not one of resemblance. In other words, the meaning is not, "we, like others who have heard about y o u" (in which case we would have expected καὶ ἡμᾶς), nor is it "we of our own accord," but "we on our part over against y o u on y o u r part." The missionaries must have heard from the Thessalonians since the first epistle was written. Naturally, the genuine believers in the recently established church were rather restrained in speaking about their own spiritual condition. They were humble, ready to admit that even the most devout among them were still far removed from the goal of spiritual perfection, and that some in the congregation conducted themselves in such a manner that the others felt ashamed. Over against this, Paul, by way of encouragement, says, *"We on our part* boast of y o u."

(2) *Its personal object:* "y o u," i.e., the Thessalonians.

(3) *Its impersonal object:* "y o u r endurance and faith in all y o u r persecutions and in the afflictions under which y o u are holding up."

This indicates *the qualities* in the readers which had given rise to the boasting. The missionaries spoke with pride about the Thessalonians because they *were holding up under* (they manifested the grace of ὑπομονή, endurance; see on I Thess. 1:3; 4:14) all their distresses, armed, as they were, by faith in God and in his promises. These distresses are here characterized as *persecutions* (used by Paul also in Rom. 8:35; II Cor. 12:10; II Tim. 3:11), which is the more specific term, and *afflictions*, which is the more general term. The latter may also indicate the result of the persecutions. These afflictions are the "tribulations" caused by the pressure which the enemy exerts upon the children of God. See N.T.C. on John 16:33. Paul commends the Thessalonians for *holding up* (ἀνέχεσθε) under these trials. The expression *"all* y o u r persecutions" seems to indicate that of late these hardships had increased rather than decreased.

(4) *Its place or sphere:* "the churches of God." See on I Thess. 1:7, 8; 2:14. That Paul was in rather close contact with these churches appears again and again. Anxiety for all the churches pressed upon him daily (II Cor. 11:28). Is he thinking here of other churches in Macedonia, of Corinth and other churches in Achaia (cf. II Cor. 1:1), and of the churches in Asia Minor? We do not know. We do know that it was Paul's custom to boast of one church to another (II Cor. 8:1-6; 9-2; contrast Phil. 4:15).

5. an evident indication of God's righteous judgment, in order that y o u may be counted worthy of the kingdom of God, for which y o u, too, are suffering.

Paul calls this unflinching attitude on the part of the Thessalonians (their endurance and faith amid all persecutions and afflictions) an *indication* (ἔνδειγμα) or "proof positive" of God's righteous judgment. The very fact that God *rewards* his children with fortitude indicates that he is a *righteous* God, who, accordingly, will also manifest this righteousness in the final judgment, which judgment will have as its purpose to state openly that his loyal followers are worthy of entering his everlasting kingdom.

For the sake of this kingdom not only Paul, Silas, Timothy and many others *outside* of Thessalonica are suffering but so are also the believers *at* Thessalonica. They gladly endure tribulation in order that one day they may enter into the kingdom of perfection, in which God will be all in all, and his sovereign rule will be joyfully recognized and obeyed.[114]

---

[114] The exegesis here given is based upon the following conclusions with respect to points of grammar.

a. ἔνδειγμα is either accusative in apposition with verse 4b (somewhat like λατρείαν in Rom. 12:1) or else it is to be regarded as a predicate nominative (after ὅ ἐστιν understood). In either case it refers not to the persecutions and afflictions as such, as if Paul were saying that these tribulations which believers had to endure were an evidence of God's righteous judgment, but to the believers' faith and endurance amid all their persecutions and afflictions.

b. The κρίσις refers, indeed, to the *final* judgment, and not to God's verdict here and now with respect to the genuine character of the endurance and faith of the

Let not the Thessalonians doubt this benevolent purpose of God with respect to them, namely, to count them worthy of entering the kingdom. Let them have no fear (cf. I Thess. 5:4, 5, 9). Let them bear in mind that God is not only Judge but *righteous* Judge, who rewards faith and obedience, and who ever keeps his promise. The righteous character of God's judgment is emphasized in the immediately following verses:

6, 7. (God's *righteous* judgment, we say) if, indeed, (it is) righteous in God's estimation (as it certainly is) to repay with afflictions those who afflict y o u, and (to grant) y o u who are being afflicted rest with us at the revelation of the Lord Jesus from heaven.

Here Paul shows that God's kindly purpose with respect to the Thessalonians (to count them worthy of entering the kingdom) is in harmony with the basic principle of recompense, according to which those who persecute God's people will suffer punishment, and those who are persecuted because of their faith will receive a reward.

The apostle is so thoroughly convinced of the absolutely indisputable character of this basic principle that he can afford to say, "If . . ." Note, however, that he does not merely say, "If," but "If, *indeed!*" (εἴπερ), and that the condition is assumed to be true (first class conditional sentence). Hence, clearly to convey the full force of the original, one should add to the words, "If, indeed, (it is) righteous in God's sight" something like "as it certainly is."

Even today we use *such* if-clauses again and again. We use them when we are sure that the statement included in the if-clause is beyond dispute; for instance:

Thessalonians. (On the noun *judgment* and the verb *to judge* see N.T.C. on John 3:19, 17.)

Proof: the following verses (6-10) clearly indicate that Paul is thinking of the judgment "at the revelation of the Lord Jesus from heaven." *One should read on and on.*

c. εἰς τό, as often in Paul, is best taken in its telic sense; cf. the parallel thought expressed in verse 10. The judgment day arrives in order that the saints may be deemed worthy of the kingdom, and in order that Christ may be glorified in his saints.

d. The verb καταξιόω means not "make" but "count" worthy. For evidence see M.M., p. 330.

e. As in I Thess. 2:12 (see on that verse) so also here the expression "the kingdom of God" indicates the redeemed society of the future which will gladly recognize and obey God's rule. This future sense is clear from the entire context (verses 6-10). Also elsewhere in Paul's epistles this kingdom is an inheritance which believers will receive by and by, and from which those who practice immorality, uncleanness, etc., will be excluded (I Cor. 6:9, 19; Gal. 5:21; Eph. 5:5). Flesh and blood cannot inherit it (I Cor. 15:50). Nevertheless, this future kingdom is foreshadowed in the present, into which believers have been translated (Col. 1:13). Its citizens even now possess "righteousness and peace and joy in the Holy Spirit" (Rom. 14:17). It is "not in word but in power" (I Cor. 4:20).

f. For the meaning of ὑπέρ see N.T.C. on John 10:11.

"If the sun rose yesterday, it will rise tomorrow."

"If I am poor, I am not dishonest."

"If the mail was delivered yesterday, it will be delivered today." In each case such an "if" means "on the valid assumption that."

Hence, the sense of verses 6 and 7 in relation to verse 5b is: "On the valid assumption that it is a divine rule that the persecutor is punished and that the persecuted is rewarded, God will reward y o u on the coming judgment-day by counting y o u worthy to enter his glorious kingdom."

God's righteousness is manifested in a twofold manner. On the one hand, it is *retributive:* God *repays (gives in return;* see on I Thess. 3:9) with *afflictions* (see N.T.C. on John 16:33) those who afflict believers. On the other hand, it is *remunerative:* he grants those who are being afflicted *rest* (ἄνεσιν, from ἄνεσις, literally *let-up*), gracious *relief* (II Cor. 2:13; 7:5; 8:13) from all the hardships they have borne on account of their valiant battle for the truth.

In a touching manner the passage is so worded that association with others *in suffering* for the cause of Christ (note verse 5: "y o u, *too,* are suffering") is balanced by association with others *in enjoyment of rest* ("rest *with us,*" that is, with Paul, Silas, Timothy, and, of course, with all other believers).

This rest — freedom from every form of bondage, and everlasting peace in the presence of the God of love — will be granted to believers "at the revelation of the Lord Jesus from heaven."

Paul is fond of this word *revelation* (ἀποκάλυψις, literally *uncovering, the removal of the veil*). Often he uses it in the sense of a disclosure of divine truth (Rom. 2:5; 16:25; I Cor. 14:6, 26; II Cor. 12:1, 7; Gal. 1:12; Eph. 3:3). In the present instance, however, the term has reference to the glorious manifestation of the Lord at his second coming. So also in I Cor. 1:7. Then the veil which now hides him from our view will be taken away, for we shall see him in his majestic descent *from heaven* (see on I Thess. 4:16). The expression "at the revelation of the Lord Jesus from heaven" means "when the Lord Jesus will be revealed, coming from heaven." [115]

---

[115] It is clear that I take the genitive to be objective or perhaps objective-subjective; certainly not only subjective (as Van Leeuwen maintains, *op. cit.,* p. 409) as in Gal. 1:12. The Lord Jesus (for the meaning of "Lord" and "Jesus" see on I Thess. 1:1) is represented here in II Thess. 1:7 as being revealed. My reasons for accepting this position are as follows:

(1) This is in harmony with the context (see verse 10: he comes "to be marveled at").

(2) It agrees with Christ's own manner of speaking (which must have been transmitted to Paul). Thus according to Luke 17:30 Jesus spoke about "the day when the Son of man *is revealed.*"

(3) "The revelation of the Lord Jesus" (cf. similar expressions in I Peter 1:7, 13) is "the revelation *of his glory.*"

It is true, of course, that the Lord reveals himself. Hence, it is a revelation of

This is the Parousia (see on I Thess. 2:19; see also N.T.C. on John 21:1). **With the angels of his power in flaming fire** ("in fire of flame" = "flaming fire" is perhaps the best reading; contrast Acts 7:30 "flame of fire").

That the Lord at his coming will be accompanied by the angels (in whom his power is made manifest) had been proclaimed by Jesus himself (Matt. 13:41, 42; 25:31; cf. Jude 15; Rev. 14:19). Their function will be twofold: "first, to gather the weeds, binding them in bundles to be burned," and also "to gather the wheat into my (the Lord's) barn."

The addition of the phrase "in flaming fire" indicates the Lord's holiness manifested in judgment (cf. Ex. 3:2; 19:16-20; Is. 29:6; 66:15, 16; Ps. 50:3; 97:3). The passage which must have been vividly present to Paul's consciousness when he wrote this is Is. 66:15, 16:

"For behold, Jehovah will come with fire, and his chariots will be like the whirlwind; to render his anger with fierceness, and his rebuke with flames of fire. For by fire will Jehovah execute judgment. . . ."

The picture is very vivid. We can almost see the angelic host, the Lord himself in the center. Moreover, this is not merely a picture; it is reality! It is by no means established that the mass of fire with its flames shooting in all directions is a "mere" symbol of judgment. To be sure, not until these events become actual history shall we know how much of this description must be taken literally and how much figuratively, and it is useless to speculate. On the other hand it is also true that the seer on Patmos describes how at Christ's coming the earth and the heaven flee away (Rev. 20:11); and II Peter 3:7, 11, 12 states that the universe will be purged completely by a great conflagration ("the heavens being on fire shall be dissolved, and the elements shall melt with fervent heat"). To explain the phrase "in flaming fire" as indicating that the descending host of angels will itself be a flaming fire does not satisfy. The "in" is that of investiture: the host — with Christ leading in the center — is invested in, surrounded by, fire. The three prepositional phrases are clearly parallel. The revela-. tion of the Lord Jesus is:

a. from heaven

b. with the angels of his power

c. in flaming fire.

To speak about a "mere" symbol in such connections is never right. The reality which answers to the symbol is always far more terrible (or far more glorious) than the symbol itself. Human language is stretched almost to

---

himself, by himself (objective-subjective), but the emphasis is on the idea that it is a revelation in which his glory *is disclosed* (objective).

(4) Thus viewed we get an antithesis between the Christ and the Antichrist: Christ is revealed when he returns in glory, and then also the Antichrist ("the man of sin," "the lawless one") will be revealed (see on II Thess. 2:3, 6, 8).

its breaking-point in order to convey the terrible character of the coming of the Lord in relation to the wicked:

8. inflicting vengeance on those who do not know God, even on those who do not obey the gospel of our Lord Jesus.

The Lord comes in order to "inflict vengeance" (cf. Deut. 32:35; Is. 59:17; Ezek. 25:14). On whom? Two answers are possible, depending on what translation one adopts, whether, "inflicting vengeance on those who do not know God, *and on those* who do not obey the gospel of our Lord Jesus," or "inflicting vengeance on those who do not know God, *even on those* who do not obey the gospel of our Lord Jesus." In the former case two classes are indicated: a. pagans who have never heard the gospel and b. Jews and pagans who have rejected the gospel. In the latter case the reference is to only one class, namely, those who, having heard the gospel, refuse to obey it. In view of the fact that in the entire context the blind heathen who have never come into contact with the message of salvation are never alluded to, and that those who in their wilful disobedience persecute God's children are definitely in the apostle's mind (see verses 4, 6, 9), we accept the latter alternative.

Not ignorance of the gospel but disobedience was the sin of the persecutors. It is true that the wicked are here described as "those who *do not know* God." They do not know him as their own God. They do not call on his name. They hate him; hence, they also hate *his gospel* (the gospel which proclaims him, and which he proclaims). Cf. Jer. 10:25; then N.T.C. on John 7:17; II Thess. 3:14; Rom. 10:16.

9. With reference to the persecutors Paul continues: such as will pay the penalty of everlasting destruction away from the face of the Lord and from the glory of his might.

The attention is once more focussed on the cruel individuals who, in their hatred of God and of the gospel, make life hard for sincere believers. They are *such people as* (οἵτινες is a qualitative relative pronoun, not the same as "who") will pay the penalty of *everlasting* (actually never-ending; see N.T.C. on John 3:16) *destruction.* The very fact that this "destruction" (cf. I Thess. 5:3; I Cor. 5:5; I Tim. 6:9) is "everlasting" shows that it does not amount to "annihilation" or "going out of existence." On the contrary it indicates an existence "away from the face of the Lord and from the glory of his might."

While "everlasting life" manifests itself in the blessed contemplation of the face of the Lord, sweet fellowship with him, closeness to him (Rev. 22:4; cf. Ps. 17:15; Matt. 5:8), a most wonderful together-ness (I Thess. 4:17), "everlasting destruction" — which is the product of God's *vengeance* (see verse 8 above) — is the very opposite. Just as the "blessing" (?) of Esau consisted in this, that his dwelling would be *away from* the fatness of the earth, and *away from* the dew of heaven (Gen. 27:39 correctly translated), so the punishment which all the persecutors of God's people will suffer will be everlasting existence *away from* (ἀπό) Christ, banished forever from his favor. Cf. Rom. 9:3. The language employed here reminds one of the recurring refrain of Is. 2:10, 19, 21, or of the well-known stanza:

"To live apart from God is death,
  'Tis good his face to seek;
My refuge is the living God,
  His praise I long to speak." (Based on Ps. 73:27.)

This banishment from loving fellowship with Christ implies expulsion from "the glory (radiant splendor) of his might" as it is manifested in the salvation of the saints.

10. The terrible separation will become publicly evident **when he comes in order to be glorified in his saints and to be marveled at in all who believed — for our testimony to y o u was believed — in that day.**
The meaning of Christ's second coming for those who by sovereign grace have placed their trust in him is here set forth. In a sense this may be viewed as a continuation of the thought begun in verse 7. According to that verse, God's children will receive *rest* when the Lord Jesus is revealed. Here in verse 10 we are shown that this rest which they will enjoy means glory for *him*. He will be glorified *in* (not merely *among*) them; that is, they will reflect his light, his attributes as, in principle, they do even now (II Cor. 3:18). Every vestige of sin will have been banished from their soul. They will mirror forth his image and walk in the light of his countenance (Ps. 89:15-17). In this *he* will rejoice. In this the angels, too, in seeing it, will rejoice. And in this each of the redeemed, seeing the reflection of Christ's image in all the other redeemed, will rejoice. Moreover, not only will Christ rejoice in the reflection of his own image in them, but he will also rejoice in their joy! Cf. Zeph. 3:17. And his rejoicing in *their* joy will reflect glory on him! Thus, take it in any sense, he will be glorified in his saints. Cf. Is. 49:3; see also N.T.C. on John 12:28. He *will be marveled at* (viewed with glad astonishment and with grateful wonder; hence, *praised*) in all who believed.
On the one hand, the redeemed are here viewed as *saints* (set apart by God for his service); on the other, as *believers*, men who have placed their trust in the Lord. The first term emphasizes the fact that *their* salvation is basically *God's work*. The second sets forth that *they*, nevertheless, *actively embrace* the Christ.
"*When* (ὅταν) he comes" means "when he returns on that day which to us is indefinite." Yet to God it is well-known: it is *that specific day* (note emphatic position at the end of the sentence), namely, the day of Christ's

return unto judgment. Cf. Is. 2:11, 17, 20; Matt. 24:36; II Tim. 1:12, 18; 4:8.

The expression "For our testimony (cf. I Cor. 1:6; 2:1) to y o u was believed" is clearly parenthetical. What Paul, Silas, and Timothy wish to say may be paraphrased as follows:

"The enemies of God who so bitterly persecute y o u will pay the penalty of everlasting destruction, away from the face of the Lord and from the glory of his might, when he comes in order to be glorified in his saints and to be marveled at in *all* who believed; and please notice that we said, 'In *all* who believed.' That includes *y o u,* Thessalonians; yes, it includes both those of y o u who have already fallen asleep in Jesus and those (if any) who will remain alive until the return of the Lord. It includes *all* sincere believers without exception. Hence, it includes y o u, for our testimony to y o u was believed."

This was a word of comfort for the congregation as a whole, but especially for those who wondered about the state of their salvation and about the lot of those believers who had departed from this life. See on 4:13-5:11.

11. With this in view we are also praying always for y o u, that our God may count y o u worthy of the call. That ıs, with a view to the realization of the expectations mentioned in verses 5-10 (namely, that on the day of judgment y o u may be counted worthy of entering the kingdom, that y o u may then receive rest, that he may at his coming be glorified in y o u, etc.) Paul, Silas, and Timothy are *giving thanks* not only (see on verse 3 above) but are *also* (καί) *praying.* They do not skip a single day — note praying *always,* and see on I Thess. 1:2 — but are continually remembering the needs of the Thessalonians before the throne of grace.

Now it stands to reason that if on the day of judgment the Thessalonians are to be counted worthy of inheriting the kingdom, they must *here and now* conduct themselves in harmony with the Gospel-call [116] which they have received. If our life is Christ, our future will be gain; otherwise not. Hence, *the content* (naturally also the purpose) of the prayer is "that God may count y o u worthy" (see on verse 5 above) of his gracious invitation extended to y o u by means of the preaching of the gospel, already in principle savingly applied to y o u r hearts by the Holy Spirit; in other words, that in the estimation of God y o u may live and act as it becomes those who have received the call which y o u have received. Cf. Eph. 4:1.

But since *in their own power* men are unable to live in such a manner

---

[116] In the New Testament κλῆσις is always the divine call to salvation: Rom. 11:29; I Cor. 1:26; 7:20; Eph. 1:18; 4:1, 4; Phil. 3:14; II Tim. 1:9; Heb. 3:1; II Peter 1:10. In agreement with Lenski (*op. cit.,* p. 394) we see no need of interpreting the term as used here in II Thess. 1:11 in any other way than as indicating the effective Gospel call. For a different interpretation see Van Leeuwen, *op. cit.,* p. 414.

that God can count them worthy of the call, it is immediately added, **and that he by (his) power may bring to fulfilment (y o u r) every resolve prompted by goodness and (y o u r every) work resulting from faith.** Note the combination: *resolve and work.* The first is incomplete without the second. *Delight* (εὐδοκία, used by Paul also in Rom. 10:1; Eph. 1:5, 9; Phil. 1:15; 2:13, *good pleasure*) in doing something that is to God's honor, even to the point of *resolve* or *determination* to do it, is fine; but it must be translated into *action;* it must be brought to fulfilment. For the type of genitive employed in such expressions as "resolve *prompted by goodness* (ἀγαθωσύνης admiration for the good)" and "work *resulting from* (and sustained by) *faith* (πίστεως)" see on I Thess. 1:3. It is hardly necessary to point out that Paul has in mind *the believer's resolve* (cf. in Rom. 10:1; Phil. 1:15) and *the believer's* (not God's) work. If that is the meaning when the latter phrase is used in I Thess. 1:3 (see on that passage), why not here? Moreover, since the two phrases ("resolve prompted by goodness" and "work resulting from faith") form a pair, it follows that not only the latter but also the former refers to the Thessalonians, not to God; (εὐδοκία refers to *God's* good pleasure in Eph. 1:5, 9; Phil. 2:13; cf. Matt. 11:26; Luke 2:14; 10:21).

In thought the word *every* (πᾶσαν, feminine) must be connected both with *resolve* (εὐδοκίαν, feminine) and with *work* (ἔργον, neuter): "every resolve" and "every work." The missionaries are constantly praying that in the case of the Thessalonians no resolution that springs from the good disposition which the Holy Spirit has created in their souls be left unfulfilled, and that no faith-inspired work be left unfinished. They are praying that God may accomplish this "by (his) power" (ἐν δυνάμει), the power of his grace working within them. Cf. Rom. 1:29; Col. 1:4; I Cor. 1:24; and see on I Thess. 1:5.

It is foolish to ask, "But if Paul already knew from the evidences — faith, love, endurance (see verses 3, 4 above) — that God on the day of judgment would count them worthy of entering the kingdom, then why does he with a view to this final verdict still pray for their further sanctification?" The answer is not, "Because, after all, he was afraid that they might still fall away from grace." In that case he could not have said what he did say in verse 5. The true answer is, "Paul knew from the evidences that *as a result of constant prayer* (their own prayer-life and the prayers of others for them) the Thessalonians would live and act as it becomes those who have received the call, sothat on the day of judgment God would count them worthy of entering the kingdom." In the chain of salvation, which connects one eternity with another, constant prayer and daily sanctification are indispensable links.

12. Moreover, the missionaries are interested in something else besides the salvation of the Thessalonians. They desire that *every* resolve prompted by goodness and *every* work resulting from faith be brought to fulfilment and that the readers may finally be counted worthy of entering the state of ultimate perfection *in order that* (ὅπως) an even higher goal may be attained, as is expressed in verse 12: **in order that the name of our Lord Jesus may be glorified in y o u, and y o u in him according to the grace of our God and of the Lord Jesus Christ.**

What it means for our Lord Jesus to be glorified in his disciples (or saints) has been explained in connection with verse 10 above. Here in verse 12, however, it is *the name* of the Lord that is glorified. . Christ's name is Christ himself as he has revealed himself: for example, as God's Anointed One, the Savior and Lord of his own. Hence, when they share in his anointing, accept his salvation, and recognize his Lordship, then his *name* is glorified in them. And this, in turn, reflects glory on them. (We accept the rendering "in him," though "in it" – i.e., *in the name* – is also possible, with very little difference in meaning.)

This "he in y o u" and "y o u in him" is probably based directly upon the teaching of Jesus. See N.T.C. on John 17:10, 22; then also on John 15:4. It indicates the closeness of the fellowship between the Lord and those who are his own. His work in their hearts reflects glory on him. Their nearness to him means glory for them. Moreover, the glory which they receive is not given according to the standard of human merit, for then there would be none. It is given according to the standard of "the grace of our God and of the Lord Jesus Christ." That *grace* (see on I Thess, 1:1) is derived from God our Father as the Fountain, and, being mediated through *the Lord Jesus Christ* (see on I Thess. 1:1), may be said to be derived also from him.

The translation preferred by some, namely, "according to the grace of our God and Lord Jesus Christ," sothat the entire expression would refer to the second person of the Trinity, and sothat it would be another proof-text for the deity of Christ, has little in its favor. In the epistles to the Thessalonians (I Thess. 1:1, 2; II Thess. 1:2) grace is pictured as proceeding from a twofold source, namely, God our Father and the Lord Jesus Christ. There is no solid reason to introduce a change here. It is definitely not true that grammar necessitates such a change.[117]

---

[117] Sharp's Rule is valuable, but on this one condition: that it be applied only to such cases to which it applies by right, not to proper names which may be definite even without the article. Thus A. T. Robertson, who wrote a delightful chapter on Sharp's Rule ("The Greek Article and the Deity of Christ" in *The Minister and his Greek New Testament,* New York, 1923, pp. 61-68; cf. Gram.N.T., pp. 785, 786) admits that the argument in favor of interpreting what follows the final τοῦ in II Thess. 1:12 as referring to only one person is weakened by the fact that κύριος is often employed as a proper name without the article. See also his *Word Pictures,*

Synthesis of Chapter 1

See p. 152. *The Revelation of the Lord Jesus from Heaven has a two-fold purpose: to be glorified in the saints and to render vengeance to the disobedient.*

After the usual introduction (verses 1 and 2) Paul writes that he feels impelled to express his gratitude to God for the readers' growth in faith and love. He (and, of course, his partners with him) boasts of the Thessalonians whenever he contacts anyone from the other churches. He regards the readers' endurance and continued faith amid persecution and affliction to be a reward for their loyalty, according to the usual manner in which God rewards holy endeavor with strength to increase in it. The fact that here and now God fulfills his promise causes the apostle to look forward with courage to the day of the final judgment, fully trusting that also then God's righteousness will become evident, and the readers will be deemed worthy of the kingdom in perfection.

This action on the part of God is in harmony with the divinely established principle that a man reaps what he sows. Accordingly, God afflicts the afflictors, and grants rest to those who rest in his promises. Thus, for unbelievers the revelation of the Lord Jesus from heaven with the angels of his power in flaming fire will have as its purpose the rendering of vengeance. This vengeance will be in the form of "everlasting destruction away from the face of the Lord and from the glory of his might." But for believers its purpose will be that he may be glorified and marveled at in them, the splendor of his attributes being reflected in them. This will be the portion of *all* his saints, including the Thessalonians, for they, as well as others, have accepted the missionaries' testimony.

With a view to "the great assize" and its glorious reward Paul never lets a day go by without praying for the readers, in order that the work in them begun may by God's grace be fully done: that pious resolutions may become actions, and that these actions may be completed. Thus the name of the Lord Jesus will be glorified. And this, too, will be glory for *them*, in accordance with the standard of "the grace of our God and of the Lord Jesus Christ."

Vol. IV, p. 46. We disagree, therefore, with Lenski, *op. cit.*, pp. 398, 399, and we agree with most other interpreters.

Outline of II Thessalonians 2

Theme: *The Revelation of the Lord Jesus from Heaven*
will be preceded by the falling away and by the revelation of
the man of lawlessness:

2:1-3a   The two events that will precede Christ's return: the falling
away and the revelation of the lawless one. Groundless alarm
condemned.

2:3b-12   The lawless one's:
verse 3b perverse character
verse 4 God-defying activity
verses 6-8a present concealment and future revelation
verse 8b decisive defeat
verses 9, 10a relation to Satan and to Satan's power to deceive
verses 10b-12 sin-hardened, hell-bound followers.

2:13-16   Contrast between the destiny of the lawless one and his followers, on the one hand, and that of the readers, on the other.

CHAPTER II

2 1 Now concerning the coming of our Lord Jesus Christ and our gathering together to (meet) him, 2 we request y o u, brothers, not to be easily shaken from y o u r (normal state of) mind or disturbed, either by spirit or by word or by letter as from us, to the effect that the day of the Lord has arrived. 3 Let no one deceive y o u in any way; for (that day will not arrive) unless there comes the apostasy first of all and there be revealed the man of lawlessness, the son of perdition, 4 the one who opposes and exalts himself against everything (that is) called God or worshiped, so that he seats himself in the sanctuary of God, proclaiming himself to be God. 5 Do y o u not remember that, while still with y o u, I used to tell y o u these things?

6 And what is now holding (him) back y o u know, in order that he may be revealed in his appropriate season. 7 For the mystery of lawlessness is already at work, (but *as mystery*) only until he who now holds (him) back, be taken out of the way.[118] 8 And then shall be revealed the lawless one, whom the Lord Jesus will slay with the breath of his mouth, and will utterly defeat by the manifestation of his coming; 9 (that one) whose coming is according to the energy of Satan, attended by all power and signs and wonders of falsehood 10 and by all deceit that originates in unrighteousness for those who are perishing because they did not accept the love for the truth that they might be saved. 11 And for this reason God sends them a deluding energy that they should believe in the falsehood; 12 in order that all may be condemned who did not believe the truth but delighted in unrighteousness.

2:1-12

2:1, 2. Now concerning the coming of our Lord Jesus Christ and our gathering together to (meet) him, we request y o u, brothers, not to be easily shaken from y o u r (normal state of) mind or disturbed.

Paul had written about the sudden character of Christ's (second) *coming* (Parousia; see on I Thess. 2:19) and about the necessity of being prepared for it (I Thess. 5:1-11). Apparently this message had been misinterpreted, as if "sudden" coming meant "immediate" coming. Paul had also made known to the Thessalonians what the Lord had revealed to him *regarding*

---

[118] Or: "only (there is) one who now holds (him) back, until he be taken out of the way." Thus, either the rendering favored by the margin of the A.R.V., or the one found in the text of that version may be correct. Essentially, however, there is no difference: the resultant meaning is the same.

(ὑπέρ, see on John 10:11) the "gathering together to (meet) him" (I Thess. 4:13-18). He had stressed the impartial character of this great future event: survivors would have no advantage over departed ones. *Together* the two groups (now united) would ascend to meet the Lord in the air to be with him forever. But though this teaching must have comforted the readers, the comfort had to some extent been offset by the excitement about the "imminent" coming. Believers were behaving like ships that have become the victim of waves and winds and are being blown hither and thither. It seems that in the case of some the Parousia had become the main subject of conversation, the one important and ever-recurring theme for discussion. People were "losing their heads" over it, so that some decided to stop working altogether. They were perturbed because of it, terribly "shaken up," yes, *"shaken* (σαλεύω, σαλευθῆναι from σάλος, the rolling swell of the sea, cf. Luke 21:25) from their (normal state of) mind."

Hence, soothingly Paul addresses the readers as "brothers" (see on I Thess. 1:4), and *requests* them (cf. I Thess. 4:1; 5:12) not *to be suddenly shaken* (aor. infinitive) or, as a result, *continually disturbed* (present infinitive, cf. Matt. 24:6; Mark 13:7; Luke 24:37); specifically, not to be alarmed *so easily,* that is, **either by spirit or by word or by letter as from us.**[119] It seems that after I Thessalonians had been read to the assembled congregation, there was no dearth of "interpreters." One individual would be telling everybody about an "inspired message" or "prophetic voice" ("spirit") which he had received (or so he thought); another would draw attention to himself by asserting, "Paul must mean this, for I heard the *word* from his own lips while he was here with us," and a third would circulate the news that "someone" had received *a letter* from Paul, in which the latter expressed his views in such or such a manner. In view of 3:17 the idea that someone had even sent a forged letter (a letter purporting to be from Paul) — though open to certain objections — cannot be lightly dismissed.

The substance of all these would-be interpretations (whether by spirit or by word or by letter as from us) is expressed in the words: **to the effect that the day of the Lord has arrived.** These excited people were convinced that "the day of the Lord" (that is, of his return for judgment and of the signs which would *immediately* precede that arrival) was here already. A few more days, weeks, or months at the most, and Jesus *himself* would make his appearance upon the clouds of heaven. His "day" had arrived.

3a: Says Paul, **Let no one deceive y o u in any way.** The cause of the agitation which menaced the hearts and minds of the Thessalonians was doctrinal error. They were being *deceived, led astray, deluded* (ἐξαπατάω,

---

[119] It is impossible to determine whether "as from us" modifies the immediately preceding item only ("by letter as from us"), the two preceding items, or all three. *The preceding two* seems most natural, but certainty is lacking.

used only by Paul — Rom. 7:11; 16:18; I Cor. 3:18; II Cor. 11:3; I Tim. 2:14 —, though the form without the strengthening prefix ἐκ occurs also in James 1:26). Hence, they are warned that they should not allow themselves to be misled *in any way*, whether by "spirit, word, letter" or anything else whatever.

The reason why the readers should not allow themselves to be deceived and alarmed is stated in the words: **for (that day will not arrive) unless there comes the apostasy first of all.** The words included between parentheses are not found in the original, but can easily be derived from the preceding context. We have here another instance of abbreviated expression.

The fact that the day of the Lord would be preceded by *the* apostasy (falling away, rebellion) — an apostasy about which the readers had received previous instruction (see on verse 5) — had been clearly predicted by the Lord while he was still on earth (Matt. 24:10-13). During the old dispensation the predicted final apostasy had been foreshadowed again and again by defection of Israel from the living God. A most striking instance of apostasy occurred during the reign of that cruel and wicked forerunner of the Antichrist, namely, Antiochus Epiphanes (who ruled from 175-164 B. C.). He was determined to wipe out the religion of Israel root and branch:

"In those days there came forth out of Israel. transgressors of the law, who persuaded many, saying, Let us go and make a covenant with the Gentiles that are round about us. . . . And they made themselves uncircumcised, and forsook the holy covenant, and joined themselves to the Gentiles, and sold themselves to do evil. . . . And many of Israel consented to his worship, and sacrificed to the idols, and profaned the sabbath. . . . And the king's officers, *that were enforcing the apostasy*, came into the city of Modein to sacrifice" (I Macc. 1:11, 15, 43; 2:15).

Here at Modein, not far from Jerusalem, there lived at that time an aged priest, Mattathias. When the commissioner of Antiochus requested that he take the lead in offering a pagan sacrifice, he not only refused to do this but slew both the commissioner and an apostate Jew who was about to comply with the request. That deed of courage marked the beginning of the splendid era of Maccabean revolt.

What the apostle Paul is now saying, here in II Thess. 2:3, amount to this: Just like the first coming of Christ was preceded by a period of apostasy, so also the second coming will not occur until a similar apostasy has taken place. In this case, however, the apostasy will be a falling away from (yes, and open rebellion against) the God who climaxed his love by a deed of infinite sacrifice in the interest of sinners, namely, the giving of his only-begotten Son.

The passage with reference to the coming apostasy by no means teaches that those who are God's genuine children will "fall away from grace."

There is no such falling away. The Good Shepherd knows his own sheep, and no one shall ever snatch them out of his hands (see N.T.C. on John 10:28; see also on I Thess. 1:4). But it does mean that the faith of the fathers — a faith to which the children adhere for a while in a merely formal way — will finally be abandoned altogether by many of the children. In that sense the apostasy will be very real, indeed.

It will be a defection on the part of those who have been reached by the gospel (cf. I Peter 4:17; Ezek. 9:6), and it will be on a large scale: *"many shall stumble . . . many false prophets shall arise and shall lead many astray . . . the love of many shall wax cold"* (Matt. 24:10-13).[120] The use of the term *apostasy* here in II Thess. 2:3 *without an accompanying adjective* points to the fact that, by and large, the visible Church will forsake the true faith.

> **3b, 4. . . . And there be revealed the man of lawlessness,**
> **the son of perdition,**
> **the one who opposes and exalts himself against everything**
> **(that is) called God or worshiped,**
> **sothat he seats himself in the sanctuary of God,**
> **proclaiming himself to be God.**

The movement of apostasy will soon have a leader, namely, "the man of lawlessness" (ὁ ἄνθρωπος τῆς ἀνομίας). This is probably the best reading, though there is also rather strong support for the reading "the man of sin" (ἄνθρωπος τῆς ἁμαρτίας). In view of the fact that "sin is lawlessness" (I John 3:4), this makes no essential difference. It is important to note, in this connection, that just like the apostasy will not be merely passive but active (not merely a falling away from but also a rebellion against God and his Christ), so also the man of lawlessness will be an active and aggressive transgressor. He is not called "lawless" because he never heard God's law, but because he openly defies it!

A few misconceptions with reference to this "man of sin" must be removed first of all.

(1) *He is not to be identified with Satan.*

The very fact that his coming is "according to the energy of Satan" (verse 9) shows that he is not himself Satan. To call him "the devil incarnate" is wrong.

---

[120] Both of these points are also stressed by Calvin:
Apostasiam ergo vocat Paulus perfidam a Deo defectionem: nec eam unius hominis vel paucorum, sed quae longe lateque in maiore hominum multitudine grassetur. Nam quum apostasia sine adiectione nominatur, non potest restringi ad paucos. Iam non alii possunt intelligi apostatae, quam qui prius nomen Christo et evangelio dederunt. Praedicit ergo Paulus generalem quandam visibilis ecclesiae defectionem (*op. cit.*, pp. 196, 197).

(2) *He must not be identified with "the beast out of the sea" of Rev. 13 and 17.*

There is, indeed, a close connection between these two:

a. "The man of lawlessness" stands in close connection with Satan, and so does "the beast out of the sea" (II Thess. 2:9; cf. Rev. 13:4).

b. "The man of lawlessness" opposes God and exalts himself, proclaiming himself to be God; similarly "the beast out of the sea" opens his mouth for blasphemies against God, and welcomes the honor of being worshiped by a sinful world (II Thess. 2:4; Rev. 13:5-8).

c. "The man of lawlessness" is a "son of perdition" and suffers total defeat when Christ appears upon the clouds of heaven; so also the beast out of the sea goes into perdition (II Thess. 2:8; cf. Rev. 17:8; 19:20).

It is not surprising, therefore, that many authors simply identify the two. Yet this identification is "wholly without foundation." [121] In Revelation the four beasts of Daniel's prophecy (Dan. 7) are combined into one composite beast. Now it should be evident that if even the separate beasts of Daniel's prophecy certainly indicate *kingdoms,* and *not only* individuals (the reference to individuals is not *entirely* absent), the *composite* beast of Revelation cannot refer to only one person. On the contrary it must refer to antichristian government whenever and wherever it manifests itself.[122]

To get the complete picture we must therefore combine II Thess. 2 and Rev. 13 and 17. It then becomes clear that in all ages antichristian power manifests itself, and it is our duty to resist it with might and main. Again and again this dominion of antichrist suffers defeat. It will suffer its greatest defeat at the end of this present age when, symbolized under "the beast out of the sea" under its eighth head, it will be under the control of a terrible blasphemer, namely, the man of lawlessness, the personal antagonist mentioned and described in II Thess. 2. Revelation (chapters 13 and 17) and II Thess. (chapter 2) supplement each other. The one pictures a movement, the other its final leader. This brings us to the more general proposition:

(3) *He is not an abstract power or a collective concept, but definitely an eschatological person.*

The principle of lawlessness, always present, will finally become embodied in "the man of lawlessness." But this does not mean that the two — the principle and the man — are one and the same. It is true that the

[121] A. Pieters, *The Lamb, the Woman, and the Dragon,* Grand Rapids, Mich., 1937, p. 205.
[122] See my Commentary on the book of Revelation, namely, *More Than Conquerors,* Grand Rapids, Mich., seventh edition 1954, pp. 175-179, 199-206; also my article "Is the Beast out of the Sea the Personal Antichrist?" in *The Banner,* April 7,. 1950. Also J. E. H. Thomson "Antichrist," article in I.S.B.E.; S. Greydanus, *Kommentaar op het Nieuwe Testament,* Vol. XIV, p. 406; K. Dijk, *Het Rijk der Duizend Jaren,* Kampen, 1933, p. 236. Contrast the view expressed by V. Hepp, *De Antichrist,* 1919.

real and final "man of lawlessness" has his precursors; but what is pictured here in II Thess. 2 is not a precursor but "the man of sin" himself.

We base this view not so much on the terms *"man* of sin" or *"son* of perdition" which expressions because of their Semitic character and meaning may not be conclusive for the thesis that "the man of lawlessness" here in II Thess. is a *person,* but on the fact that the entire description which is here given is of a personal character. The man of lawlessness "opposes," "exalts himself," "seats himself in the temple of God," "proclaims himself to be God," and will be "slain." Also, there is every reason to believe that the man of lawlessness described by Paul is the same person as the antichrist mentioned by John. Now Christ is a person. Hence, in all probability, the antichrist ("counter-Christ") is also a person. Therefore, "the man of lawlessness," being the antichrist, is also very likely a person. Like Christ himself, "the man of lawlessness" performs signs and wonders, has his "Parousia" and his "revelation." It would be strange, therefore, if "the man of sin" were not a person. But *is* "the man of lawlessness" to be identified with the antichrist? Our reasons for identifying the two are as follows:

a. "The man of lawlessness" will be revealed immediately before the coming of Christ. The antichrist *concerning whom the readers have received previous information* will come "at the last hour" (II Thess. 2:8; I John 2:18).

b. The "mystery of lawlessness" is already at work. Even now "there are many antichrists" (II Thess. 2:7; I John 2:18). In both cases the thought is as follows: though believers are correct in expecting one definite individual at the end of the age, an individual in whom wicked opposition to Christ will become crystallized, they should rather fix their attention upon the "many" antichrists already present in their own day and age, upon the fact that the mystery of lawlessness is in operation even now.

c. The coming of "the man of lawlessness" is according to Satan's energy, with great signs and miracles, all of them false. Similarly, antichrist is called the liar and deceiver (II Thess. 2:9; I John 2:22; II John 7).

However, not only is "the man of lawlessness" a person; he is a person who belongs to the *end-*time; hence, he is an *eschatological* person. This is clear from verses 3 and 8.

To be sure, by speaking about a whole *line* of antichrists one is doing justice to a Scriptural idea (I John 2:18; cf. II Thess. 2:7). Moreover, this idea has a practical advantage over that of *the one, final* antichrist. The *line-*idea — antichrists in *every* age — against which the church must *ever* be on its guard, furnishes a very useful and proper theme for sermonizing. But a careful reading of II Thess. 2:3, 4, 8, and 9 should suffice to convince anyone that we are here dealing with a precise prediction of a certain, definite person who will receive his doom when Christ returns. Other explanations may be philosophical; they are not exegetical.

This naturally leads to the next proposition:

(4) *He is not to be identified with the line of Roman emperors.*

Here for once I cannot agree with Dr. B. B. Warfield, staunch defender of the faith, whose views on matters theological generally command the utmost respect. It was his opinion that the man of lawlessness is to be identified with the line of such Roman emperors as Caligula, Nero, Vespasian, Titus, and Domitian (see his *Biblical and Theological Studies,* edited by S. C. Craig, Philadelphia, 1952, p. 472). But, as has been indicated, the entire context here in II Thess. 2 is eschatological. It has to do with "the end" of the present dispensation. The "man of lawlessness" is the one who will immediately precede Christ's second coming (verse 3), and will be "slain by the breath of Christ's mouth" when the Lord returns gloriously (verse 8). This fact is an insurmountable obstacle in the path of the "Roman emperor" theory. It also annihilates the theories discussed below, namely, that "the man of lawlessness" is Nero Redivivus, the pope, or some vague mythological figure.

(5) *He is not Nero Redivivus* (Nero brought back to life).

Neither the entire line of Roman emperors nor any one particular Roman emperor is meant here. Thus, for example, Antichrist is not Nero.

It was Kern (in *Tübinger Zeitschrift für Theologie,* 2 [1839], p. 145 ff.) who revived the *old* theory — Augustine was acquainted with it! —: "the man of lawlessness is Nero Redivivus." He thought that the origin of the idea was the widespread and superstitious fear in the early church that the monster of cruelty was about to reappear upon the scene. The Nero Saga seems to have manifested itself in two forms. According to the first, the emperor did not really *die* in 68 A. D., but merely *hid* himself; according to the second (which became prevalent especially after 88 A. D.), he was really dead, but would rise again.

But in addition to the cogent argument already presented (see under (4) above), the most decisive answer is this, that the theory, according to which whoever wrote II Thess. 2 actually meant to say that Nero would return and that he was being held in check temporarily by Vespasian and his son Titus, must be considered "impossible of acceptance" by anyone who believes in an infallible Bible, for Nero never returned! This is the answer which we give to Kern, Baur, Weizäcker, Holtzmann, Schmiedel, and all their followers.

But if "the man of sin" is not the Roman *emperor,* could he be the Roman *pope?*

This introduces the next proposition:

(6) *He is not the pope.*

The notion according to which the antichrist is the pope can be traced to . . . the pope himself! It was Gregory I ("the Great," 550-604) who said that whoever arrogates to himself the title of "universal priest" is a forerunner of antichrist. He made this statement in an epistle in which he denounced the claims of the contemporary "patriarch" of the East. The idea was kept alive throughout the middle ages, and was uttered in whispers here and there whenever any occupant of the papal See manifested his arrogance or lust for power. Wyclif even wrote a treatise *Concerning Christ and his Adversary, Antichrist.* He defended the proposition, The pope is the antichrist, giving twelve reasons.

Naturally, the idea was eagerly seized upon by many of the leaders of the Reformation. Thus, on October 11, 1520, Luther wrote that he felt much more at ease since he had become thoroughly convinced that the pope is the antichrist. The marginal explanations of the Dutch "authorized" or "official" version (Staten-Bijbel) of 1637 are very interesting in this respect. (We happen to own one of these heavy, antique Bibles with covers of wood and hinges of brass; ours was published in 1643 at "Amstelredam" = Amsterdam.) At times the comments become almost amusing, so consistently is everything that pertains to "the man of sin," "the antichrist," "the beast out of the sea," "the beast out of the earth" (Revelation, chapter 13) applied to the pope and his entire machinery. Thus, the fire which the "beast" causes to come down out of heaven is said to represent the pope's excommunication-edict. The "miracles" of which the Roman Catholic boasts, its sacraments, and especially (among these) the mass, are all read back into the pages of Holy Writ. And the number "666" (Rev. 13:18) is interpreted to mean "Lateinos," for the pope is the head of the Latin church!

But if one should find this a bit amusing, it certainly is not any more so than is the statement in the *Preface* to our own A.V. in which "the most high and mighty prince, James, by the grace of God, king of Great Britain, France, and Ireland, Defender of the Faith, etc." is given credit for having by means of a tract dealt "such a blow to that Man of Sin [meaning the pope] as will not be healed."

The Westminster Confession speaks very positively, "There is no other head of the Church but the Lord Jesus Christ: nor can the Pope of Rome, in any sense be the head thereof; but is that Antichrist, that man of sin and son of perdition, that exalteth himself in the Church against Christ, and all that is called God" (XXV. vi).

But though the proposition "the pope is the antichrist" is still being defended, it finds no support on II Thess. 2. It stands to reason that if the man of sin is a definitely eschatological person, he cannot be the first pope, nor the second, nor the third, etc., neither can he be the collective concept "the papacy." It is true, of course, that any man (be he a religious or a political dictator) who arrogates to himself attributes and prerogatives which pertain to deity possesses *anti-christian traits.* He may be called "an antichrist," one among many of the final antichrist's precursors.

174

In such a man the mystery of lawlessness is already at work. But to call the pope *the* antichrist is contrary to all sound exegesis. Though we Protestants justly deplore whatever idolatry, Maryolatry, superstition, and worship of tradition is found in the Roman Catholic Church, evils against which we must warn with increasing vigor and earnestness, we have no right to condemn *everything* that is found in that church. We should strive to be fair and just, lest while condemning the evils of Rome we close our eyes to the many and very serious evils that are creeping into all sections of the Protestant Church. The proposition, "The pope is *the* antichrist," while inexcusable — though understandable! — even during the days of intense struggle which marked the birth of Protestantism, is no less inexcusable today. And the verdict of some, namely, that those who are not ready to identify the man of sin of II Thess. 2 with the pope have never experienced in their hearts and lives the truth of "justification by faith" impresses us as a rather unkind judgment.

In liberal circles the tendency to interpret Biblical concepts in the light of uncanonical and even pagan origins has asserted itself also with respect to the term now under discussion. This brings us to the final proposition:

(7) *He is not the Chaos-dragon of the Babylonians nor is he to be identified with the apocryphal and pseudepigraphical perversion of the term "Belial."*

To begin with the first, this refers to the Babylonian creation-epic with its story of the struggle between the Chaos-dragon, Tiamat, on the one hand, and the god of light, Marduk, on the other. It has been pointed out again and again, however, that the legendary elements which characterize this wholly mythical and "impossible" tale contrast most strongly with the sober description that is found in the Bible with reference to God's great opponents, Satan and antichrist. In this connection, moreover, one should ever distinguish between *form* and *contents,* between a *term* and the *use* which is made of it. To be sure, inspired authors make use at times of the terminology of ancient and current superstition. Thus, the author of the book of Revelation introduces a *dragon.* But this dragon is not Tiamat, whom Marduk cleaves asunder like a fish, after he has with a javelin cut her heart in pieces. (By the critics reference is also made to such passages as Ps. 74:13; 89:10; Job 41:1, but each passage should be interpreted in the light of its own specific context and background.)

Moreover, of late the entire attempt to derive Biblical teachings from *Babylonian* sources, an attempt which was never very successful and has been refuted more than once, has received another jolt in the discovery of the *Ras Shamra* tablets. These were found in 1929 at the ancient Phoenician city of Ugarit on the coast of Syria. These tablets present a wealth of information with respect to the *Canaanite* background of the Old Testament. They contain several variations on the theme of the slaying of a dragon. Hence, now the critics are beginning to revise their views once more, and are saying that, after all, the religion of Israel may have been influenced more directly by that of Canaan than by that of Babylon. One wonders what theory will be advanced next?

There is also the closely related one which attempts to derive the "man-of-sin" concept from apocryphical and pseudepigraphical perversions of the Old Testament term Belial or Beliar (I Sam. 2:12; II Chron. 13:7; cf. II Cor. 6:15). After a thorough study G. Vos comments as follows:

"This recurrence upon the apocalyptic and pseudepigraphical literature to discover the antecedants of the antichrist figure does not carry much convincing force. Of course, it cannot *a priori* be denied that an amount of superstitious folklore was current in Jewish circles before the Pauline epistles were written. Only that these current beliefs of such gross and rudimentary form were the source from which the N.T. antichrist doctrine was drawn and from which it can be satisfactorily explained is hard to believe. . . . *No clearly traceable and safe road leads back into the past to discover the man-of-sin concept except that via the prophecy of Daniel.*" [123]

Having reviewed the various misconceptions regarding the nature of "the man of sin" and the origin of the idea, it can now be positively stated that the apostle's use of the concept is capable of being traced to a canonical book. It is, indeed, true, as conservatives have always maintained, that many of the features in Paul's description of the great and final prince of wickedness are derived from the book of Daniel:

(1) "The man of lawlessness," cf. Dan. 7:25; 8:25.

(2) "the son of perdition," cf. Dan. 8:26.

(3) "the one who opposes," cf. Dan. 7:25

(4) "and exalts himself against everything (that is) called God or wor-shiped," cf. Dan. 7:8, 20, 25; 8:4, 10, 11.

(5) "sothat he seats himself in the temple of God, proclaiming himself to be God," cf. Dan. 8:9-14.

---

[123] G. Vos, *The Pauline Eschatology*, Princeton, 1930, pp. 103-105. See also *Sib. Or.,* book III; IV *Esdras* 5:4, 6; *Apoc. Bar.,* ch. 40; and *Asc. Isa.,* ch. 4.

For the "Babylonian-derivation" theory see F. Delitzsch, *Babel and Bible* (transla-tion of *Babel und Bibel*), New York, 1903, especially pp. 47-49; then, E. König, *Die moderne Babylonisierung der Bibel*, Stuttgart, 1922, especially pp. 22-26.

And for information with respect to the *Ras Shamra* texts see R. de Vaux, "Les textes de Ras Shamra et l'Ancient Testament," *RB* 46 (1937), 526-565; René Dus-saud, *Les découvertes de Ras Shamra et l'Ancien Testament*, Paris, second edition, 1941, vol. I; A. Lods, "Quelques remarques sur les poèmes mythologiques de Ras Shamra et leurs rapports avec l'Ancien Testament," *RHPR* 16 (1936), 112-117; Julian Obermann, *Ugaritic Mythology*, New Haven, 1948; H. F. Hahn, *Old Testa-ment in Modern Research*, Philadelphia, 1954, especially pp. 110-117. This author points out that the *distinctive* features of Old Testament religion were of greater significance than those which it had in common with other religions, and that even those elements which might be called derivative had been transformed into vehicles for *distinctive* beliefs.

This is not surprising, for "the little horn" of *Dan. 7*, the one which came up after the ten horns, is the antichrist, and "the little horn" of *Dan. 8*, the one which came up out of one of the four notable horns, is Antiochus Epiphanes, antichrist's most notorious forerunner, the one who desecrated Jerusalem's temple by erecting a pagan altar over the altar of burnt-offering, and by sacrificing upon it (which was an "appalling horror" in the estimation of every true believer).

Moreover, in Matt. 24:15 (cf. Mark 13:14) "the desolating abomination" ("appalling horror") of which Jesus speaks is derived from Dan. 11:31; 12:11 (probably not directly from 9:27). History, in a sense, repeats itself. Better: prophecy attains multiple fulfilment. The underlying thought is ever the same. God's city and sanctuary are desecrated, whether by Antiochus Epiphanes and his sacrilegious offerings (Dan. 8:9-14; cf. "Gog" in Ezek. 38, 39), by Roman armies with their idolatrous standards (Luke 21:20; Mark 13:14); or finally by the antichrist himself.

Now with respect to the final antichrist as pictured by Paul, our present passage (II Thess. 2:3b, 4) states the following:

He is "the man of lawlessness" (a Semitism), that is, the man in whom opposition to God's law will as it were be embodied, the very personification of rebellion against God's ordinances.

He is also "the son of perdition" (another Semitism), the final Judas, see N.T.C. on John 17:12. Cf. David's remark to Nathan, "The man who has done this is *a son of death*" (i.e., must certainly die); and cf. also Matt. 23:15: "a son of hell." The man of lawlessness is pictured here as the utterly lost one, designated unto perdition. Contrast "sons of light" in I Thess. 5:5.

Furthermore, he is described as "the one who opposes." This word (ἀντίκειμαι, here ὁ ἀντικείμενος) is found eight times in the New Testament (Luke 13:17; 21:15; I Cor. 16:9; Gal. 5:17; Phil. 1:28; II Thess. 2:4; I Tim. 1:10; I Tim. 5:14). It is used both as a verb (finite) and as a participial substantive (so here). The man of sin is *the adversary* of God, of God's law, of God's people, etc. As such he immediately reminds one of his master, Satan, who is "the great adversary."

In very close connection with this opposing activity stands the fact that this adversary who will appear in the end-time "exalts himself against everything (that is) called God or worshiped." In his reckless audacity and ferocious insolence he *uplifts* himself (ὑπεραιρόμενος) not only against the only true God who has revealed himself in Jesus Christ and against all so-called gods, but also against all sacred objects, against whatever stands in connection with religious cults. The reference is probably to such objects as temples, places set aside for divine worship, altars, religious statues. He rages against them all. He recognizes only one god (*he* would spell it with a capital: God), namely, himself! Hence, he seats himself in *the sanctuary* (the term ναός in its primary·sense, in distinction from ἱερόν, generally refers to the shrine itself rather than to the entire building-complex) of God, that is, *in the church* (see I Cor. 3:16; 6:19; II Cor. 6:16; Eph. 2:21; and see N.T.C. on 2:19-22), for the term ναός is here clearly used metaphorically. He arrogates to himself authority over God's true people. Of course, they will not recognize this violent usurper, and will refuse to render homage to him. The result will be great tribulation for them (Matt. 24:15, 21, 22, 29). "Standing where he ought not" he *proclaims* or *publicly declares* himself to be God. In the Greek of that day and age the verb (ἀποδείκνυμι) is used of proclaiming an appointment to public office. Thus we are told, "The expectation and hope of the world, Nero!, has been *declared* (ἀποδέδεικται) Emperor" (M.M., p. 60), a quotation which also illustrates emperor-worship. But even Antiochus Epiphanes, that is, "Antiochus (the) Illustrious (God)" or "Antiochus (the) God who reveals himself," demanding divine homage but not altogether ignoring Zeus, was not as blasphemous as the final man of lawlessness will be, for the latter will recognize only *one* deity, namely, himself, will seat *himself* (will *not merely* deposit *his image*) in God's shrine, and will demand divine adoration for himself alone.

It is instructive to note that the explanation which I have given with respect to the "man of sin" passage is in line with that which was favored by the earliest ecclesiastical writers. These understood it as being a .prophecy with reference to a definite person who would live on earth at the close of history and would be utterly discomfited by Christ at his return. The church should never have departed from this interpretation. Here are a few quotations:

The *Didache* ("Teaching of the Twelve Apostles")

". . . As lawlessness increases they shall hate each other and shall persecute and betray, and then shall appear the deceiver of the world as a Son of God, and shall do signs and wonders. . . . And then shall appear the signs . . . first, the sign spread out in heaven, then the sign of the sound of the trumpet, and thirdly the resurrection of the dead" (XVI. iv-vi).

Justin Martyr, *Dialogue with Trypho*

"What brainless men! For they have failed to understand what has been proved by all these passages, namely, that two advents of Christ have been announced, the first, in which he is shown as suffering, without glory, without honor, subject to crucifixion, and the second, in which he shall come from the heavens in glory, when the man of apostasy who utters arrogant things against the Most High, will boldly attempt to perpetrate unlawless deeds against us Christians" (CX).

Augustine, *De Civitate Dei* ("Concerning the City of God")

Commenting on II Thess. 2:1-11 he says: "There can be no doubt that what is here said refers to Antichrist and the day of judgment, or as Paul calls it, the day of the Lord. . . ." (XX. xix).

In the same chapter he points out that even in his day the interpretation which points away from *the one, final* antichrist to a whole multitude of antichrists was beginning to become popular; also, that he regards the Nero Redivivus theory, in both forms, to be farfetched.

Having now discussed the nature of the man of sin at some length, we may summarize the idea expressed in verses 3 and 4 as follows:

The day of Christ's glorious coming will not arrive until the apostasy has become a fact and the man characterized by utter disrespect for law, the man who is most certainly doomed, is revealed, sothat both he himself and his program of activities are there for all to see, *the veil* which now hides him from view (for as yet he is only an idea in the mind of Satan) *having been removed.*

5. Hence, the Thessalonians must not be deceived into thinking that the day of the Lord is here. In fact, they have no excuse for so thinking. Says Paul, **Do y o u not remember that, while still with y o u, I used to tell y o u these things?**

This is a kind of mild rebuke. It is as if Paul is saying, "If y o u had only reflected more often and more earnestly on what I repeatedly told y o u while still with y o u, y o u would not have been so confused with reference to this point, and y o u would not have become so excited and unsettled." Note: *"I used to tell"* (not merely, "I told"). Evidently the doctrine concerning such matters as the apostasy, the man of sin, the coming of Christ, and the rapture had received more than scant attention in the preaching of Paul at Thessalonica. The singular pronoun implied in the verb (*"I* used to tell" and not *"We* used to tell") shows that although Silas and Timothy are intimately associated with Paul in writing this letter, as they had also been in bringing the gospel to Thessalonica, it is nevertheless, Paul who in both of these activities is to be regarded as the leading spirit.

6, 7. Paul continues: **And what is now holding (him) back y o u know, in order that he may be revealed in his appropriate season. For the mystery of lawlessness is already at work, (but *as mystery*) only until he who now holds (him) back be taken out of the way.**

Grammatically it is also possible to translate: "And now y o u know what is holding him back." So the question is, "Does *now* modify the participle (holding back) or the verb (y o u know)?" The logic of the entire

passage (cf. verse 7 with verse 6) seems to point in the direction of connecting it with the participle. The contrast seems to be between the two concepts *"now* held back or restrained" and *"then* revealed."

That "the mystery of lawlessness" is already at work we understand
readily. Even in Paul's day rebellion against God and his ordinances was
present in the world. Yet, it was not evident that one day this spirit of
lawlessness would become incarnate in "the man of lawlessness." This was
still a *mystery* (cf. Rom. 11:25; I Cor. 15:51; Eph. 5:22); that is, a truth
unknown apart from divine special revelation. In the wicked opposition to
the gospel, shown by some of those who knew the way, Paul, as a result of
divine special revelation and illumination, saw a clear sign of that sinister
movement which one day would culminate in the reign of the antichrist.
What the apostle writes may be compared with John's statement that the
spirit of the antichrist is in the world already, and that even now there have
arisen many antichrists (I John 4:3; 2:18).

Far more difficult to answer is the question, "What is meant by *that
which* or *he who* is now holding (him) back" from becoming revealed as
"the man of lawlessness"?

In order to approach this question properly, it is necessary first of all to
determine the right translation. In the works of commentators the verb
in question (χατέχω) has been translated in three different ways: a. *to hold
back* or *restrain,* b. *to hold* or *hold fast,* and c. *to hold sway* or *rule.*

Beginning with the last, the meaning might then become:

"And what is now holding sway (namely, the mystery of lawlessness) y o u
know, in order that he (Christ) may be revealed in his appropriate season.
For the mystery of lawlessness is already at work, only until he who now
holds sway (namely, Satan) be taken out of the way."

We can dismiss this at once. Not only is it hard to fit this meaning into
the present context, but also: although the verb is of rather frequent occurrence in the New Testament, not once (in any of the other New Testament passages) does it have this meaning (*to hold sway*).

The second meaning (*to hold fast*) and the first (*to hold back, to restrain*)
are closely related, and in the end probably yield the same resultant interpretation of the entire passage. With an appeal to such passages as Job 7:12
(placing a guard over a sea-monster), Rev. 20:1-3 (binding the dragon for
a thousand years), and passages from the apocrypha, the view is defended
that the man of lawlessness is here compared to a mythological being (a
dragon or a sea-monster) which is being held fast for the time being. However, it should be borne in mind that the "dragon" in Rev. 20 is a symbol,
and represents not Satan's *instrument* but Satan *himself.* And even then
the resultant meaning of the symbol is the *restraint* upon Satan, sothat he
can deceive the nations no more until the thousand years are finished.
Hence, an appeal to Rev. 20, *if* legitimate, would seem to support the trans-

lation *hold back, restrain* as readily as *hold, hold fast.* Something similar can be said with reference to the Job 7:12 passage; while the apocryphal passages yield little that is of any value in this connection. Besides, if the man of sin is being *held fast,* he is being held fast with a purpose, and in the present context (in view of what immediately follows in verses 8 and 9) that purpose is *to restrain* him for the present from being revealed.

In the New Testament the various meanings of the verb may be classified as follows (though with respect to a few there is some doubt):

(1) *to possess, have, hold:* I Cor. 7:30; II Cor. 6:10.

(2) *to take possession of:* Luke 14:9.

(3) *to hold fast or keep:* Luke 8:15; Rom. 7:6 (but some would classify this under the fourth heading); I Cor. 11:2; 15:2; I Thess. 5:21 (see on that passage); Heb. 3:6, 14; 10:23. It is possible that the sense of the word as used in Acts 27:40 is not far removed from this. They "held for" (or "made for") the beach.

(4) *to hold back, restrain, detain:* Luke 4:42 (the multitude *would have held him back,* to prevent him from leaving them); Rom. 1:18 (wicked men *hold back* or *suppress* the truth); Philemon 13 (Paul would have liked *to detain* Onesimus). In the present context this meaning makes excellent sense. It has abundant support in the papyri (see M.M., pp. 336, 337).

Adopting meaning (4) as the most natural in the present context, we are face to face with the problem of identifying the restrainer. On this point, however, the Thessalonians were ahead of us in their knowledge of eschatology. *They* knew. *We* do not. Augustine in his day frankly confessed that even with the best efforts he was not able to discover what the apostle meant (*Concerning the City of God.* XX. xix).

Some interpretations are wrong even on the surface (such as, "Paul," "God," "the Holy Spirit"). God or the Holy Spirit are not "taken out of the way" (which, in spite of objections that have been advanced, is probably a good English equivalent of the Greek idiom ἐκ μέσου γίνεσθαι); cf. also Col. 2:14.

Of all the theories advanced so far the one which seems to have most in its favor is that according to which the restrainer is "the power of well-ordered human rule," "the principle of legality as opposed to that of lawlessness" (see Ellicott's *Commentary* on this passage). According to this view Paul intends to say that as long as law and order still obtain, the man of lawlessness is unable to appear upon the scene of history with his program of unprecedented unrighteousness, blasphemy, and persecution. In favor of this view note the following:

a. It has the context somewhat in its favor: "the man of *lawlessness*" is being held back by the reign of *law.*

b. It explains how Paul can speak both of *"that which* restrains" and *"he who* restrains." Think of the empire and the emperor, of justice and the judge, of law and the one who enforces it.

c. It (or something on this order) is the most frequently expressed view of the church fathers. Tertullian, commenting on this passage, states: "What obstacle is there but the Roman state?" (*On The Resurrection of the Flesh* XXIV).

d. It receives support from the fact that Paul was proud of his Roman citizenship, which helped him again and again, also right here in Corinth where the letter was written (Acts 18:12-17). Moreover, in a well-known chapter of another epistle he speaks of the power of the Roman state as "a minister of God to thee for good," and of the rulers as "a terror not to good but to evil conduct" (Rom. 13).[124] We may safely say, therefore, that the apostle viewed government and its administrators as a restraint upon evil.

e. It is a reasonable theory also in view of the fact that in a sense Roman law and order did not die when Rome fell. In the civilized world of today it is still in force. However, when the basic structure of justice disappears, and when fake-trials and fake-confessions become the order of the day, the stage is set for the revelation of the man of lawlessness.

The theory according to which Michael [125] or some other angel binds, restrains, or holds back the antichrist (those who favor it appeal to such passages as Dan. 10:13 and Rev. 20:1-3) does not explain how such an angel can be called both "he who" and "that which" restrains. Nevertheless, the two theories last mentioned — namely, a. that the restrainer is law and order and those who enforce it, and b. that the restrainer is an angel — may not be as far apart as they appear to be. Are not the dispositions of rulers influenced by angels? (See Dan. 10:13, 20.)

We repeat, however, that the view which we have characterized as being in our opinion the best which has been offered so far may not be the right one. Certainty on this point is not available.

Accordingly, the sense of the entire passage (verses 6 and 7) seems to be this: Satan, while perfectly aware of the fact that he cannot himself become incarnate, nevertheless would like to imitate the second person of the Trinity also in this respect as far as possible. He yearns for a man over whom he will have complete control, and who will perform his will as

---

[124] Some have even discovered a word-play in the fact that Claudius was the reigning emperor when this was written; so they connect Claudius with the verb *claudo,* to close, stop, *restrain,* making Claudius the restrainer! This impresses us as being rather far-fetched.

[125] V. Hepp, *De Antichrist,* p. 102, criticized by A. Pieters, *op. cit.,* p. 197.
　W. Neil (in *The Moffatt New Testament Commentary*) is of the opinion that the restrainer is perhaps Michael, perhaps Elijah, "more probably someone or something somehow" (The Epistle of Paul to the Thessalonians, New York, 1950, pp. 172, 173).

thoroughly as Jesus performed the will of the Father. It will have to be a man of outstanding talents. But as yet the devil is being frustrated in his attempt to put this plan into operation. Someone and something is always "holding back" the deceiver's man of lawlessness. This, of course, happens under God's direction. Hence, for the time being, *the worst* Satan can do is to promote the spirit of lawlessness. But this does not satisfy him. It is as if he and his man of sin bide their time. At the divinely decreed moment ("the appropriate season") when, as a punishment for man's willingness to cooperate with this spirit, the "some one" and "something" that now holds back is removed, Satan will begin to carry out his plans:

8. And then shall be revealed the lawless one. This "then" is in contrast with the "now" of verse 6: "now" "the lawless one" is being held back, but "then" he will be revealed. "The lawless one" is the same as "the man of lawlessness" introduced in verse 3, that is, the final antagonist, the one who openly defies all of God's ordinances, the antichrist. When the proper time arrives, Satan's scheme will become outwardly realized. *The mystery* will be replaced by *the man*. The lawless one will appear on earth and will become revealed in his words and actions.

In order to encourage believers, who might otherwise be filled with unjustifiable alarm, Paul immediately adds: **whom the Lord Jesus will slay with the breath of his mouth, and will utterly defeat by the manifestation of his coming.**

There will not be a long drawn-out conflict, with victory now apparently with the lawless one, then with the Christ, this "round" going to Satan, that to the Christ. The issue will be settled in a moment. The Lord Jesus (see on I Thess. 1:1) will very summarily and decisively put an end to antichrist and his program. The entire description is symbolical. The two clauses are parallel, though this does *not* necessarily mean that they are *completely identical* in meaning. The first clause stresses what will happen to the lawless one himself: he will be slain (which in this connection has been interpreted to mean that he will be punished with everlasting death, but the idea that he will first be put to death physically must not be excluded). The Lord will merely blow upon him, so swift will be his destruction. The second clause also indicates what will happen to him, perhaps with the added idea: in relation to his program of activities. Also in this respect he will be "abolished," "utterly defeated," "put out of commission," "rendered useless," "made inoperative or inactive" (καταργέω; a verb very frequently used by Paul and almost confined to him in the New Testament; for the particular shade of meaning in the present connection see especially such passages as Rom. 3:31; 4:14; I Cor. 1:28; Gal. 3:17; Eph. 2:15; II Tim. 1:10). In parallel relationship to "breath of his mouth" stands "manifestation of his coming." The very *appearance* (ἐπιφάνεια, epiphany, elsewhere in the New Testament only in the pastorals: I Tim. 6:14; II Tim. 1:10; 4:1, 8; Titus 2:13) of Christ's coming (Parousia; see on I Thess. 2:19), the first gleam of the advent, will suffice to abolish the lawless one, to put him out of commission.

The *thorough, swift,* and *sudden* character of antichrist's defeat is here pictured in symbolic language. The decisive character of his downfall is the one, main thought. Merely by Christ's *breath and appearance* "the man of lawlessness" will be discomfited. More should not be read into the passage. For example, one should not begin to embellish the interpretation by arguing that "the breath of his (Christ's) mouth" means the Word of God, that this Word is always effective, etc. If further commentary is needed, one should read Is. 11:4 and Rev. 1:16.[126]

9, 10. Having comforted the readers with the thought of the decisive intervention of the Lord Jesus when he comes to judge, sothat the passage with reference to the final antagonist has been robbed of its terror for those who believe, Paul now gives a further description of the character of the lawless one and of his activity. One might say that the description already begun in verse 4 is here continued; however with this difference: while verse 4 pictured antichrist's relation to the realm divine, verses 8 and 9 set forth his relation to the kingdom of evil:

(that one) whose coming is according to the energy of Satan, attended by all power and signs and wonders of falsehood and by all deceit that originates in unrighteousness for those who are perishing because they did not accept the love for the truth that they might be saved.

The coming or parousia of the lawless one (for the meaning of the term see on I Thess. 2:19) *is* (prophetic present: it will certainly be) in complete accordance with the powerful activity of Satan, his master. That "energy of Satan" will be its standard of comparison. Hence, this coming will be attended by (or: invested with) all power and signs and wonders; that is, there will be a mighty display of *power* (δύναμις cf. *dynamite*); there will be *signs* (σημεῖα), supernatural feats which point away from themselves to the one who performs them, namely, the devil-controlled antichrist (see also N.T.C. on John 2:11); and *wonders* or *marvels* (τέρατα), the same astonishing performances viewed now from the aspect of their unusual character and their effect upon those who behold them. But all of this display (power, signs, wonders) will spring from *falsehood,* from the desire to deceive.[127] Hence,

---

[126] On the latter passage I have commented as follows: "Do not destroy the unity of the symbol. For example, do not interpret the sharp two-edged sword that proceeds out of Christ's mouth as indicating the sweet and tender influences of the Gospel in its mission of conversion. Notice that in 2:16 we read: 'and I will do battle against them with the great-sword of my mouth.' This is addressed to those who *refuse* to repent" (*More Than Conquerors,* p. 71).

[127] There is no good reason to restrict "of falsehood" to the noun which immedi-

there follows, "and by all *deceit* that originates in unrighteousness." The noun *deceit* is also used by Paul in Col. 2:8 ("philosophy and vain deceit"; and see the compound verb, derived from the same stem, in II Thess. 2:3). The deceit will be inspired by *unrighteousness*. This is not surprising, for the antichrist is energized by the devil himself. See also N.T.C. on John 8:44.

Now this coming of the final antagonist, with his lying power, signs, and wonders, though observed by both believers and unbelievers, has the effect of deceiving *those who are perishing* (i.e., those who then will be perishing); cf. I Cor. 1:18; II Cor. 2:15; 4:3. The cause of their perishing lies not in God but in themselves. They are perishing *because* [128] they *did not accept* (past tense from the aspect of the days just before the final judgment) the love for the truth.

But what is meant by the expression "the love for the truth"? We answer as follows:

When the Gospel is proclaimed, the hearers are urged to accept *Christ and all his benefits*. These benefits are not only objective, such as heaven, the resurrection-body, etc., but also subjective, such as love and hope. Those hearers who perish do so because they have rejected what they have been urged to accept, in this case: "the love *for the truth*" (objective genitive) as it is in Christ (the Gospel-truth). The purpose of their accepting it would have been "that they might be saved." It is true that in his own power no man can accept "the love for the truth." That, however, is not the emphasis here. Here what is stressed is *man's guilt*. When man is lost, it is ever his own fault, never God's.

11. And for this reason God sends them a deluding energy, that they should believe the falsehood. That is, the men of the end-time, who will harden themselves against the earnest exhortation to repent and to receive the love for the truth, will suffer the penalty of being hardened. God sends (i.e., will certainly send) them an "energy of (i.e., unto) delusion." It will be a power working mightily within them, leading them even farther astray, sothat they will believe antichrist's lie. See N.T.C. on John 12:36b-43.

God is love. He is not a cruel monster who deliberately and with inward delight prepares people for everlasting damnation. On the contrary, he

---

ately precedes or to two of the three nouns. It is true that *power* is singular, and that *signs* and *wonders* are plural, but all three terms are co-ordinated by ". . . and . . . and . . ." They evidently constitute one group.

[128] Van Leeuwen states that ἀνθ' ὧν is of infrequent occurrence in the LXX (*Kommentaar op het Nieuwe Testament*, Vol. X, p. 435). It occurs about eighty times, however, and is the Greek equivalent of more than fifteen Hebrew words or phrases with meanings such as: on account of, because, according as, forasmuch as, after that, inasfar as, as a consequence of the fact that, in return for the fact that, in consequence of, as often as. The predominant meaning is *because*, i.e., *in return for the fact that*. One thing is given in the place of another.

earnestly warns, proclaims the gospel, and states what will happen if people believe, also what will happen if they do not believe. He even *urges* them to accept the love for the truth. But when people, of their own accord and after repeated threats and promises, reject him and spurn his messages, then — and not until then — he hardens them in order that those who were not willing to repent may not be able to repent but may believe the falsehood that "the man of lawlessness" is God, the only God, and that everyone should obey him.

When Pharaoh hardens his heart (Ex. 7:14; 8:15, 32; 9:7), God hardens Pharaoh's heart (Ex. 9:12). When the king of Israel hates God's true prophets, then the Lord permits him to be deceived by placing a lying spirit in the mouth of other prophets (II Chron. 18:22). When men practice impurity, God gives them up in the lusts of their hearts to impurity (Rom. 1:24, 26). And when they stubbornly refuse to acknowledge God, he finally gives them up to a base mind and to unclean behavior (Rom. 1:28).

12. So it will also be in the end-time. God will send a deluding energy into the hearts of those who stubbornly refused to accept his redemptive truth; and this in order that they may be condemned: **in order that all may be condemned who did not believe the truth but delighted in unrighteousness.**

This refers to the final judgment. Then all the deluded ones *shall be judged,* i.e., *condemned* (for the verb κρίνω see N.T.C. on John 3:17). This sentence of condemnation will be just and fair, for those upon whom it is pronounced, far from consenting to the redemptive truth of God, *have placed their delight* (εὐδοκήσαντες see on 3:1) in its very opposite, namely, *unrighteousness* (see on verse 9 above). This very antithesis between *truth* and *unrighteousness* (see also Rom. 1:18; 2:8; I Cor. 13:6) indicates that man's intellect cannot be separated from his will and his emotions. When a person really accepts God's truth, he will practice righteousness; when he does not but accepts the lie of antichrist (neutrality is impossible!), he will *delight in* unrighteousness.

The true believer must never be afraid of belonging to the minority. It is the remnant that shall be saved. *All* others will be condemned.

---

13 But we are obliged to give thanks to God always for y o u, brothers beloved by the Lord, because God chose y o u from the beginning to salvation through sanctification by the Spirit and belief in the truth; 14 to which (salvation) he also called y o u through our gospel, with a view to obtaining the glory of our Lord Jesus Christ. 15 So then, brothers, stand firm and cling to the traditions which y o u have been taught by us, whether orally or by letter.

16 Now may he, our Lord Jesus Christ and God our Father, who loved us and graciously gave (us) everlasting encouragement and good hope, encourage y o u r hearts and strengthen (them) in every good work and word.

2:13, 14. But we are obliged to give thanks to God always for y o u, brothers beloved by the Lord, because God chose y o u from the beginning to salvation through sanctification by the Spirit and belief in the truth; to which (salvation) he also called y o u through our gospel, with a view to obtaining the glory of our Lord Jesus Christ.

Over against (note δέ) *the damnation* which awaits Satan's followers stands *the salvation* which is in store for God's children. This thought is developed in the present passage, which is full of rich concepts. However, as all of these have been discussed before, and some at considerable length, a reference to the place where this material can be found should suffice:

For "we are obliged to give thanks to God always for y o u" see on II Thess. 1:3.

For "brothers beloved by the Lord" cf. on I Thess. 1:4.

For "because God chose y o u" see on I Thess. 1:4.

For "salvation" see on I Thess. 5:8, 9.

For "sanctification" see on I Thess. 4:3, 7.

For "belief" see on II Thess. 1:3, 4, 11; I Thess. 1:3.

For "truth" see on II Thess. 2:10, 12.

For "calling" see on I Thess. 1:5; 2:12; 4:7; 5:24.

For "with a view to obtaining" see on I Thess. 5:9.

For "glory" see on I Thess. 2:12.

For "our Lord Jesus Christ" see on I Thess. 1:1.

On the basis of the explanation of these various concepts and of the context here in II Thess. 2:13, 14, we can now paraphrase the thought of the present passage as follows:

"We — Paul, Silas, and Timothy — cannot do otherwise than ceaselessly thank God for y o u, brothers in the faith (who are the objects of God's special love), because in his sovereign, immutable election God from the beginning chose y o u to salvation — which is negatively, rescue from the guilt, pollution, and punishment of sin; positively, the entrance into the inheritance reserved for God's children — ; a salvation which becomes y o u r possession through the work of the Holy Spirit, that is, *through sanctification* — a process of causing y o u to become increasingly detached from the world and attached to Christ until his image is completely formed in y o u — *and through y o u r active, vital consent* to the body of redemptive truth revealed in Christ; to which final and complete salvation God also called y o u, having effectively applied to y o u r hearts the gospel which we preached to y o u and which we urged y o u to accept in order that y o u might one day share in the glory of our Lord Jesus Christ."

We accept the reading, "God chose y o u *from the beginning*" (ἀπ' ἀρχῆς) and not, "God chose y o u *as first-fruits*" (ἀπαρχήν). Both readings are well attested, and the conception of believers as "first-fruits" is entirely Biblical

(Jas. 1:18; Rev. 14:4 [129]) and even Pauline (Rom. 8:23; 11:16; 16:5; I Cor. 15:20, 23; 16:15). However, Paul never uses it in connection with the idea of election or choosing. On the other hand, the idea that God *chose* his own (or *decreed* something) "before the ages" (I Cor. 2:7), "from the ages" (Col. 1:26), "before the foundation of the world" (Eph. 1:4) is definitely Pauline. To this would correspond the rendering "chose y o u from the beginning" (i.e., from eternity) here in II Thess. 2:14. Also, the thought here expressed, namely, that God *called* men to a salvation to which *he had before chosen* them is both logical and Pauline (Rom. 8:30).

15. Paul is now summing up and drawing a conclusion. **So then, brothers, stand firm and cling to the traditions which y o u have been taught by us, whether orally or by letter.**

In view of all that has been said (note "so then"), particularly with respect to dangers from the side of Satan and with respect to the blessed prospect of those who adhere to the faith, the Thessalonians are now urged to lay aside their doubts and fears and to *stand firm* (Rom. 14:4; I Cor. 16:13; Phil. 1:27; 4:1) and *cling* — that is, to remain standing firm and to keep on clinging (note present imperatives which here as often are undoubtedly continuative) — to *the traditions,* that is, to the authoritative teachings that have been handed down (I Cor. 11:2; Gal. 1:14; Col. 2:8; and see on 3:6), whether *orally,* that is, by word of mouth while Paul, Silas, and Timothy were working among them and afterward while Timothy visited them, or *by letter* (I Thessalonians, but note "by us," hence, not by any letter *purporting* to come from Paul; see on verse 2 above).

For the idea of *standing firm* see the beautiful passage I Cor. 16:13; also on I Thess. 3:8. On the matter of transmitting traditions or teaching that has been received see also Rom. 6:17; 16:17; I Cor. 15:1-11; Phil. 4:9; Rev. 2:14, 15.

16, 17. **Now may he, our Lord Jesus Christ and God our Father, who loved us and graciously gave (us) everlasting encouragement and good hope, encourage y o u r hearts and strengthen (them) in every good work and word.**

Now (δέ is here only slightly adversative; it can be translated *now*) the Thessalonians will not be able to stand firm and to cling to the traditions unless God in Christ encourages and strengthens their hearts. It is for that reason that the command is here followed by the expression of a solemn and effective wish. For the combination "our Lord Jesus Christ" and "God our Father" with singular verb to stress the unity of essence and of purpose,

---

[129] For the Old Testament background of the idea of the first-fruits and for its meaning in Rev. 14:4 see my *More Than Conquerors,* Grand Rapids, Mich., seventh edition, 1954, pp. 183-185. Naturally those who favor the idea that II Thessalonians was addressed to "the Jewish community" favor "first-fruits" here. See footnote 7.

see on I Thess. 3:11. However, here in II Thess. 2:16, 17, "our Lord Jesus Christ" is mentioned first (before "God our Father"), perhaps because of the reference to Christ in the almost immediately preceding context (verse 14).

Although it is certainly true that the aorist participles ("the One having loved" and "graciously having given") comprehend all the blessings of redemption without exception — beginning from eternity and never ending —, nevertheless this does not mean that in the mind of Paul certain central facts did not stand out clearly; such as, "he chose us," "he gave his Son (also *himself*) for us," "he gave us the Holy Spirit," etc. The main idea, however, is that, as a result of these gifts, "the-Lord-Jesus-Christ-and-God-our-Father," conceived as One, has given everlasting (that is, never-ending) *encouragement* and *good hope* to the readers. In view of their fears and doubts (see on 2:1-12; cf. I Thess. 4:13-5:11) this *help* was, indeed, needed. For the meaning of the word *encourage* (παρακαλέω) see on I Thess. 2:3; also N.T.C. on John 14:16. The encouragement is not only for the present life. It will also be imparted on the final day of judgment. In fact, although *comfort* or *consolation* amid sorrow will not be needed nor imparted in heaven — the land of never-ending delight —, nevertheless even there God in Christ will ever "encourage" the redeemed by giving them glory upon glory. The *good* hope of which Paul speaks is a hope that is well-founded, namely, upon God's promises, Christ's redemptive work, etc., is full of joy, never ends in disappointment, and has its object in God Triune. When, by God's sovereign grace, the words of II Thessalonians (for example, with respect to the *"rest"* in store for God's children, the *"victory"* of Christ over Satan, the divine *"election"* and *"calling"* of the readers) are taken to heart, the readers will experience everlasting encouragement and good hope. Objectively (also subjectively, but only *to a certain extent*) they have it even now. Subjectively it will *then* be applied to their hearts *in full measure*. Of course, such encouragement and good hope never ends in man. Here, too, the circle must be completed. Everlasting encouragement and good hope result in gratitude and a desire to please the Giver. Hence, Paul writes, "Now may he . . . encourage y o u r hearts (the central organ of y o u r life) *in every good work and word.*" Such works and words are those which redound to God's honor. Thus, the circle has again been completed. What came from God has, by way of thanksgiving, returned to him!

Synthesis of Chapter 2

See p. 166 *The Revelation of the Lord Jesus From Heaven will be preceded by the falling away and by the revelation of "the man of lawlessness."*

The latter's destiny and that of his followers contrasted with that of the readers.

Verses 1-3a *The two events that will precede Christ's Return*

In this chapter the apostle warns the readers against acting as if the end of the world had arrived, and against believing that he himself had said or written anything that could have lent color to this notion. He declares that two events will occur first, namely, a. the apostasy — that is, the world-wide falling away from (and rebellion against) God's ordinances — and b. the arrival of "the lawless one."

Verses 3b-12 *The lawless one*

a. His perverse character (verse 3b)

He will be the hell-bound, personal embodiment of the spirit of antagonism to God's law.

b. His God-defying activity (verse 4)

He will strive to dethrone God and to enthrone himself. In his reckless audacity and ferocious insolence he will uplift himself not only against the true God and all so-called gods but also against all sacred objects. He will endeavor to wield dominion over God's people. He has his prototype in everyone who aspires to be God, for example, in the king of Babylon (Is. 14), the king of Tyre (Ezek. 28), and especially Antiochus Epiphanes.

c. His present concealment and future revelation (verses 6-8a)

At present he is being held back. Though present in the mind of Satan, something and someone (perhaps law and order and those who enforce it) is for the time being preventing the antichrist from appearing on the scene of history. However, the spirit of lawlessness, interpreted in the light of God's revelation which clears up this mystery, holds in its womb the lawless one. It cannot but issue in his revelation when the proper time arrives. As soon as the restrainer is taken out of the way, the predicted final antagonist will be seen. When law and order, founded on justice, are removed, then the man of lawlessness will be made manifest.

d. His decisive defeat (verse 8b)

The Lord Jesus, returning on the clouds, will intervene decisively in the interest of his people. Messiah's very breath (cf. Is. 11:4), the first gleam of his advent, will suffice to destroy the lawless one and to cut short the realization of the latter's program. (This indicates that the lawless one belongs to the end-time.)

e. His relation to Satan and to Satan's power to deceive (verses 9, 10a)

The coming of the great opponent will be attended by astounding performances, aimed to delude the masses on their way to perdition. The energy of the devil will operate in and through the son of perdition.

f. His sin-hardened, hell-bound followers (verses 10b-12)

His followers will perish by their own fault, for they will have willfully rejected the love for the truth, and of their own accord will have taken

190

delight in unrighteousness. God, accordingly, will punish them by sending them a deluding energy that they should believe antichrist's falsehood
and should suffer everlasting damnation.

Verses 13-16 *Contrast between the destiny of the lawless one and of his
followers, on the one hand, and that of the readers, on the other*

These verses are transitional in character. Inasfar as they draw a sharp
contrast between the perdition of antichrist and his followers (see the preceding verses), on the one hand, and the everlasting salvation of the
"brothers beloved by the Lord," on the other, they belong to the present
section. Nevertheless, the change in style (from didactic and revelatory
to congratulatory and hortatory) shows that this paragraph may also be
considered in connection with the contents of chapter 3. Note the simi-
larities:

a. Expression of thanks to God and (by implication) of confidence in
the readers (2:13, 14; cf. 3:4)

b. Exhortation (2:15; cf. the exhortations in 3:1, 6, 12-15)

c. Expression of a wish which has the solemnity of a prayer (2:16; cf.
3:5, 16).

In dividing the material of II Thessalonians into sections or thought-
units it is therefore not an error either to consider 2:13-16 along with the
preceding twelve verses of chapter 2, or along with the contents of chapter
3. There is overlapping here.

Paul comforts the readers with the thought that the sentence of condemnation will not rest on *them,* for *they* have been chosen from eternity. In
this sovereign election *not only the end* was foreordained but *also the
means* through which it would be brought about. The end is salvation,
and the means are "sanctification by the Spirit and belief in the truth."
In fact, the divine, inward calling may also be considered as one of the
means, for the readers had been called "with a view to obtaining the glory
of our Lord Jesus Christ."

Accordingly, the brothers are urged to stand firm and to cling to the
traditions which they have been taught by the writers, whether orally or
by letter.

The pendulum swings back once more to emphasis upon the divine
factor. The wish expressed in verse 16 (see the explanation) is very touching.

Outline of II Thessalonians 3

Theme: *The Revelation of the Lord Jesus from Heaven*

is a firmly anchored hope whose contemplation should result not in disorderliness but in calm assurance, stedfast endurance, and strength-imparting peace.

3:1 and 2   A request for intercession

3:3-5   Calm assurance and stedfast endurance required and promised

3:6-15   Disorderliness condemned

3:16-18   Conclusion: "Now may he, the Lord of peace, give you this peace." Closing benediction.

CHAPTER III

3 1 For the rest, brothers, pray for us, that the word of the Lord may run its race and be crowned with glory [130], just as it did among y o u; 2 and that we may be rescued from those unrighteous and evil men, for (true) faith is not everyone's portion. 3 Yet, faithful is the Lord, who will strengthen y o u and guard y o u from the evil one. 4 Moreover, we have confidence in the Lord about y o u, that what we command, y o u are doing and will continue to do. 5 And may the Lord direct y o u r hearts to the love of God and to the endurance of Christ.

6 Now we command y o u, brothers, in the name of the Lord Jesus Christ, that y o u stay away from every brother who conducts himself in a disorderly manner and not in accordance with the tradition which y o u received from us. 7 For y o u yourselves know how y o u ought to imitate us, because we did not conduct ourselves in a disorderly manner (when we were) among y o u, 8 neither did we eat anyone's bread without paying for it, but with toil and hardship we were working for a living by night and by day, in order not to be a burden to any of y o u; 9 not because we have no right (to be supported by y o u) but in order that we might offer ourselves as an example for y o u to imitate. 10 For also when we were with y o u, *this* we used to command y o u, "If anyone does not want to work, neither let him eat." 11 For we hear that some among y o u are conducting themselves in a disorderly manner, not busy workers but busybodies. 12 Now such people we command and urge in the Lord Jesus Christ that by quietly working for a living they eat their own bread. 13 But as for y o u, brothers, do not become weary in well-doing. 14 Now if anyone does not obey our word expressed in this letter, note that man, and do not get mixed up with him, in order that he may become ashamed. 15 And do not consider him an enemy, but admonish him as a brother. 16 Now may he, the Lord of peace, give y o u this peace at all times and in all ways. The Lord (be) with y o u all.

17 The greeting by the hand of me, Paul, which is a token of genuineness in every epistle; so I write. 18 The grace of our Lord Jesus Christ (be) with y o u all.

3:1, 2. For the rest, brothers, pray for us, that the word of the Lord may run its race.

The expression "for the rest" (cf. I Thess. 4:1; then II Cor. 13:11; Phil. 4:8) is certainly very appropriate when a letter is drawing to a close; though it is not restricted to this use (see, for example, I Cor. 1:16; 4:2;

---

[130] Or simply: *be glorified.*

7:29; Phil. 3:1). It is as if Paul, having finished chapters 1 and 2, read what he had written, and then decided that there were a few important matters which must not be left unmentioned. So, to the wish for divine encouragement and strengthening (2:16, 17) he now adds some closing admonitions. In Paul's writings the divine and the human, God's decree and man's responsibility, constantly occur side by side. Thus also here in chapter 3 one series of expressions, stressing the former — "Faithful is the Lord, who will strengthen y o u and guard y o u," "May the Lord direct your hearts," "May he, the Lord of peace, give y o u this peace," "The Lord be with y o u all," "The grace of our Lord Jesus Christ be with y o u all" — is interwoven with another, stressing the latter — "Pray for us," "Stay away from disorderly persons," "We command that they eat their own bread," "Do not become weary in well-doing," "Note that man," "Admonish him as a brother." We hasten to add, however, that in Paul's teaching as in that of Jesus the qualifying power which enables man to do what God commands is ever from God, of whom and through whom and unto whom are all things. Thus also in the present passage the word of the Lord runs its race in answer to prayer. It is ever God who provides the blessing.

As has been noted previously, Paul sets much store by the intercession of fellow-believers for himself and his fellow-workers (see on I Thess. 5:25; cf. Rom. 15:30-32; II Cor. 1:11; Phil. 1:19; Col. 4:2; Philem. 22). It is not improbable that here the present tense has continuative force: "Continue to pray for us," or "Pray constantly for us." Note, however, that the prayer is not so much for personal blessings as it is for the progress of the gospel by means of the work of the missionaries, though the latter does not exclude the former. Paul prays that *the word of the Lord* (called thus because it proceeds from him and refers to him, that is, to the Lord Jesus Christ) *may run* (or *may run its race*) without hindrance and constant interference from the side of the enemy. That this is the meaning is shown by the immediate context. The apostle adds: **and be crowned with glory** (or simply: "and be glorified"). The fact that he is here employing a figure is evident at once, for in the literal sense of the term "the word of the Lord" does not "run." It is surely entirely in line with Pauline usage to suggest that, as in many other passages so also here, the apostle is borrowing a metaphor from the race-track (cf. Rom. 9:16; I Cor. 9:24-27; Gal. 2:2; 5:7; Phil. 2:16). The author of Hebrews makes use of the same figure (Heb. 12:1, 2). However, the verb "and be glorified" which can be somewhat freely translated "and be crowned with glory" also indicates that in his mind the reality emerges out from under the figure. The word of the Lord is glorified when it is accepted by true faith, sothat it begins to adorn the lives of believers. Now this "word of the Lord" had been successful in Thessalonica. Hence, Paul adds: **just as it did among y o u** (see the first chapter of both epistles).

The first object-clause is elucidated by the second: **and that we may be rescued from those unrighteous and evil men.**

Note the definite article: "the" or "those" unrighteous and evil men. Paul has a definite, concrete situation in mind, namely, the situation at Corinth. To say that the reference cannot be to the episode before Gallio, recorded in Acts 18:12-17, because this took place a little later, misses the point. What is described in that paragraph is the final flare-up. But surely, the opposition from the side of the Jews did not *begin* then (see, for example, Acts 18:5, 6). In the light of I Thess. 2:15, 16 (see on that passage), it is immediately clear that Paul is referring to the Jews when he speaks of *unrighteous* (literally *out of place*) and *evil* men. The modifying clause, which accounts for the existence of these wicked men, is a characteristically Pauline litotes: **for (true) faith is not everyone's portion** (or simply: "for not all have (true) faith"). The meaning is: "Most people have and show in their conduct the very opposite of faith, namely, unbelief, vicious opposition to the truth." Lack of faith explains the hostile attitude to Christ, his gospel, his ambassadors.

3. Now over against those who lack *faith* stands the *faithful* Lord (note the play upon the words *faith . . . faithful*), ever ready to protect his people: **Yet, faithful is the Lord, who will strengthen y o u and guard y o u from the evil one.**

By a very natural transition Paul, having dwelt for a moment upon the theme of his own conflict at Corinth, returns to the very similar battle which the Thessalonians are waging. Inwardly the young, struggling church is in need of strengthening. Outwardly — for Satan is surely an outsider! — it needs to be guarded. Paul now assures the readers that what he had wished with respect to them (see on 2:16, 17) will also come to pass. They will be both "encouraged and strengthened" (2:16, 17) or, as the apostle now expresses it "the Lord will both strengthen and guard" them. This *guarding* will prevent the Thessalonian believers from falling into the snares of the evil one, such as fanaticism, loafing, meddlesomeness, neglect of duty, defeatism (see verses 5-8).

It is from "the evil one" that the readers will be guarded. Though the noun used here (τοῦ πονηροῦ) can also be translated "evil," yet in all probability Paul has reference to the personal devil. That is in harmony with the entire trend of the epistle and of the one that precedes it (see on I Thess. 2:18; 3:5; II Thess. 2:9) and also with Eph. 6:16; Matt. 6:13; 13:19, 38 (and see N.T.C. on John 17:15).

Between the *strengthening* and the *guarding* there is a very close relationship. By being positively strengthened in faith, love, every good work and word (I Thess. 3:2, 12, 13; II Thess. 2:17) believers will be guarded against the sin of capitulating to Satan.

In all this the Lord (Jesus Christ) will manifest his *faithfulness* (cf. I Thess. 5:24). His promise never fails. He ever completes that which he began (Phil. 1:6).

But, as already indicated (see above on verse 1), in this process of spiritual strengthening believers are not passive. On the contrary, they become very active.

It is exactly as is stated in the Canons of Dort:

"Moreover, when God accomplishes this his goodpleasure in the elect, or works in them true conversion, he not only provides that the gospel should be outwardly preached to them, and powerfully illumines their mind by the Holy Spirit, that they may rightly understand and discern what are the things of the Spirit of God, but he also, by the efficacy of the same regenerating Spirit, penetrates into the innermost recesses of man, opens the closed, softens the hardened, and circumcizes the uncircumsized heart, infuses new qualities into the will, and makes that will which had been dead alive, which was evil good, which had been unwilling willing, which had been refractory pliable; and actuates and strengthens it, that as a good tree it may be able to bring forth fruit of good works. . . . The will, being now renewed, is not only actuated and moved by God, but being actuated by God, itself also becomes active. Wherefore the man himself, through this grace received, is rightly said to believe and repent" (Third and Fourth Heads of Doctrine, Articles XI and XII, my translation).

4. Hence, turning from the work of God to the action of the believer, which action is used by God as a means for the accomplishment of the divine design, the apostle continues: **Moreover, we have confidence in the Lord about y o u, that what we command, y o u are doing and will continue to do.**

Apart from "the Lord" (that is, Jesus Christ; see on I Thess. 1:1) confidence in the readers and in their future conduct would have lacked a firm basis. One never knows what mere men are going to do. But *by virtue of union with the Lord* (for that is the meaning of "in the Lord") the confidence which Paul has is well-founded, for the Lord perfects that which he has begun (cf. Gal. 5:10; Phil. 1:6). By means of obedience to the commandments (cf. I Thess. 4:11) — those issued before and also those which Paul is about to issue (in verses 6-15) — spiritual strengthening and protection is and will be attained. The readers are doing and are going to do what they are told to do.

Verse 4 does not begin a new section. It is very closely related to the preceding verse, as we have shown. It also prepares for the things that immediately follow. It shows delicate, admirable tact. The commandment will not sound nearly as harsh when those who issue it (principally Paul, but also Silas and Timothy) are kind enough to preface it by saying, "We have confidence . . . that what we command, y o u are doing and will continue to do." Verse 4 is therefore a window through which we can look into the wise, kind, and considerate soul of Paul.

5. But although the missionaries have full confidence in the readers, they realize, nevertheless, that it is only with the help of the Lord that men will be disposed to keep the commandments. Hence, the pendulum swings back once more (see on verse 1 above) from the human to the divine: **And may the Lord direct y o u r hearts to the love of God and to the endurance of Christ.**

When the love which God has for the Thessalonians and which he is constantly showing to them becomes *the motivating force* in their lives and when the endurance exercised by Christ in the midst of a hostile world becomes their *example,* then they will do and will continue to do whatever God through his servants demands of them.

Both "of God" and "of Christ" are to be considered subjective genitives. Not "their love for God" but "God's love for them" is what is meant. That is regular Pauline usage (see Rom. 5:5, 8; 8:39; II Cor. 13:14; cf. Eph. 2:4). This is "the love of God which has been shed abroad in our hearts." It is "his own love toward us." It is "the love of God in Christ from which nothing shall be able to separate us." It is "his great love with which he loved us."

> "Thy love to me, O Christ,
> Thy love to me,
> Not mine to thee I plead,
> Not mine to thee.
> This is my comfort strong,
> This is my joyful song,
> Thy love to me."
>
> (Mrs. M. E. Gates, 1886)

This love is strong, sovereign, unconditional (i.e., not dependent in its origin on foreseen love coming from us, but creating love in our hearts), never-ending, and above all human comprehension. See also N.T.C. on John 21:15-17.

When human *hearts* (see on I Thess. 3:13; II Thess. 2:17) are *directed* (see on I Thess. 3:11) to this love, obedience results; for this love is not only a divine attribute, or that plus a favorable attitude toward believers, but also a divine, dynamic force within them, a principle of life in their innermost being.

The "endurance of Christ" must not be interpreted as meaning the wonderful *longsuffering* which Jesus showed to his friends, for example, to

197

Peter. *Endurance* (ὑπομονή) *is the grace to bear up under.* It amounts to *stedfastness,* no matter what may be the cost. In nearly every case in which the apostle employs the term he also uses a word which indicates the hostility directed against Christ and his followers or the trials and hardships which they have to endure. Note the following examples:

Rom. 5:3, 4: endurance in the midst of tribulation
Rom. 15:4, 5: endurance in the midst of reproach (cf. verse 3)
II Cor. 1:6: endurance in the midst of suffering
II Cor. 6:4: endurance in the midst of affliction
II Cor. 12:12: endurance in the midst of persecution, distress
II Thess. 1:4: endurance in the midst of persecution
I Tim. 6:11: endurance in the midst of "the good fight of faith"
    (see verse 12)
II Tim. 3:10: endurance in the midst of persecution, suffering
    (see verse 11)

See also on I Thess. 1:3. Though the two kinds of patience, namely, *endurance* (ὑπομονή) and *longsuffering* (μακροθυμία, often *slowness to wrath*) are very closely related (cf. Col. 1:11), they must not be confused. See on I Thess. 5:14. We *endure* amid adverse *circumstances;* we show *longsuffering* with (or: we exercise patience toward) *people.*[131] *Endurance* is *the bravery of perseverence* in faith and in all good works even then when all things seem to be against us.

In the present context this mention of *endurance* is very fitting. The meaning is this: just like Christ ran the race with endurance of stedfastness — enduring the cross, despising shame —, so we (in this case, the Thessalonians) in the midst of our afflictions should follow the same course. We should "look unto Jesus," and follow his example. (The idea here in II Thess. 3:5 immediately suggests Heb. 12:1-4.) Hence, there should be no forsaking of duty, no fanaticism or inexcusable excitement sothat one lays down his work, thinking, "What's the use of working, if Christ's return is just around the corner?" *Jesus* persevered. *He* never resorted to idleness, loafing. *He* adhered to his appointed task to the very end. So should *we*.

Paul expresses the solemn wish that "the Lord" (that is, Jesus Christ; see on I Thess. 1:1) may direct the hearts of the readers to this love of God and to this endurance or stedfastness of Christ.

6. By means of this expression of confidence (verse 4) and this solemn wish (verse 5) Paul has prepared the reader for what follows in verses 6-15: **Now we command y o u, brothers, in the name of the Lord Jesus Christ, that y o u stay away from every brother who conducts himself in a dis-**

---

[131] Hence, I cannot agree with the interpretation given by Lenski, *op. cit.,* p. 452.

orderly manner and not in accordance with the tradition which y o u received [132] from us.

The command which follows is given "in the name of" — that is, on the basis of the authority of and in accordance with the teaching (revelation) of — *the Lord Jesus Christ* (see on I Thess. 1:1). He alone is the Anointed Lord and Savior of the Church, and in that capacity has the right to issue commands.

The command has to do with individual cases of "disorderly conduct." The expression "every brother" would seem to indicate that the instances were rather isolated: here one and there one. The congregation as a whole was sound in faith and practice. The "disorderly conduct" probably consisted of such things as:

a. *loafing* (see verse 11: "do nothing-ers"), in view of the conviction that Christ would return any day now;

b. *spreading* all manner of exciting *gossip* about Christ's imminent return (cf. 2:2);

c. *asking to be supported by the church* (see verse 12: "they eat *their own* bread," which implies that this was what they did not want to do); and

d. *meddlesomeness*, perhaps interfering with the business that properly belonged to the officers (see verse 11: "busybodies").

The fact that a rather lengthy paragraph (verses 6-15) is devoted to this sin would seem to indicate that the evil here signalized had grown worse since the first epistle was written (see on I Thess. 4:11, 12; 5:14; then also I Thess. 2:9). Such conduct was certainly far removed from "the tradition" (see on 2:15) which the Thessalonians had received from the missionaries. This "tradition" was the teaching which Paul, Silas, and Timothy, on the basis of the authority vested in them, had passed along to the congregation. It included such instructions as this one: "If anyone does not want to work, neither let him eat" (verse 10). The Thessalonians had received it from the missionaries during their first visit (verse 10), and also subsequently by letter (I Thess. 2:9; 4:11; 5:14). No doubt Timothy, on his visit, had stressed the same thing.

In the case of some individuals all this instruction had been in vain. Hence, somewhat stronger methods must now be used. When *admonition* does not succeed, *segregation* must be resorted to, at least to a limited extent. Note that the severe measure mentioned in I Cor. 5:5 is not yet contemplated here in II Thess. The "brothers" (see on I Thess. 1:4) are told *to stay away* (cf. II Cor. 8:20) from such a "brother" (note that the disorderly persons are still referred to by this name!). Even this *staying*

---

[132] Whether the text as originally written had "*y o u* received" or "*they* received" makes little essential difference. If *y o u* received it, then *they* (the disorderly ones) also received it.

away however, is qualified. It does not imply complete ostracism, for verse 15 states expressly that such a one must be admonished as a brother. It does mean, however, that the rest of the congregation should not "get mixed up with him" (verse 14), that is, should not associate with such a person on intimate terms, agreeing with him and following his example.

7, 8. Not only was the disorderly conduct contrary to *the instructions* which had been delivered to the Thessalonians, both orally and in writing; it was also in conflict with *the example* which the missionaries had given them:

For y o u yourselves know how y o u ought to imitate us, because we did not conduct ourselves in a disorderly manner (when we were) among y o u, neither did we eat anyone's bread without paying for it, but with toil and hardship we were working for a living by night and by day, in order not to be a burden to any of y o u.

In the light of the immediately preceding context (verse 6), the present passage (verses 7 and 8), in which several thoughts have been compressed together in a few words, may be paraphrased as follows:

"Now we command y o u, brothers . . . that y o u stay away from every brother who conducts himself in a disorderly manner and not in accordance with the tradition which y o u have received from us. We have a right to remind y o u of the teaching which we transmitted to y o u, for y o u know, of course, what that was; also y o u know how y o u ought to *imitate* (μιμεῖσθαι cf. our "mimic," used by Paul only here and in verse 9; also in Heb. 13:7; III John 11; cf. I Thess. 1:6; 2:14) the manner in which we practiced what we preached. We feel free to add this because we did not conduct ourselves in a disorderly manner when we were among y o u. Specifically, we did not eat anyone's bread *without paying for it* (gratis or "as a gift" δωρεάν, adverbial accusative) but with toil and hardship we were working for a living (or "were working at a trade") by night and by day. We did this in order not to be a burden to any one of y o u."

The clause "With toil and hardship we were working for a living by night and by day, in order not to be a burden to any of y o u" occurs also in I Thess. 2:9; see on that passage.

Truly, what the disorderly persons were doing was the very opposite of what the missionaries had done. The latter had been preaching the gospel and working at a trade besides! The former did not do a stitch of real work in either direction. They were loafers and spongers! Instead of being a help they were a hindrance to the progress of the gospel.

9. Why did the missionaries "work for a living by night and by day"? One reason has already been given, namely, "in order not to be a burden to any of y o u." Another reason, closely connected with the first, is now added: "in order that we might offer ourselves as an example for y o u to imitate." The statement which contains this second purpose clause is as follows: **not because we have no right (to be supported by y o u) but in order that we might offer ourselves as an example for y o u to imitate.**

Again and again Paul insists on his rights, but again and again, in the interest of the kingdom, he is willing to waive the use of these rights. This (in connection with his stand on the question of received remuneration) has been discussed in detail; see on I Thess. 2:9 (the ten propositions).

The desire of the missionaries was that the Thessalonians, each in his own way and with the opportunities given him, might *imitate* (see on verse 7) the example of *unselfish devotion* given by those from whose lips they had heard the glorious message of salvation. Since the example of Christ had been imitated by Paul, he now in turn feels free to ask others to imitate his example (and that of his associates). For this thought (specifically for the concepts *to imitate* or *to become imitators* and *example*) see on I Thess. 1:6, 7. Not only in "welcoming the word with Spirit-imparted joy amid great tribulation" but also in whole-hearted self-surrender, the example given by Paul and his fellow-workers must be imitated. That the great majority of the readers had done the former is the thought expressed in I Thess. 1:6, 7. That some refused to do the latter is implied here in II Thess. 3:9.

10. The Thessalonian "irregulars" could not excuse their conduct by saying, "Y o u never taught us any different." They knew the way, because the missionaries:

a. had given them *an example* of unselfish devotion (verses 7, 8, 9)

b. had *also* (note καί at the beginning of verse 10) given them a definite *precept,* namely, "If anyone does not want to work, neither let him eat" (verse 10).

Hence, the conjunction *for* in verse 10 really refers back to verse 7, the thought being, "Y o u yourselves know . . . *for* when we were with y o u (in addition to teaching y o u by means of example) this we used to command y o u," etc. In a sense this *for* refers all the way back to verse 6: "the tradition which y o u received from us."

For also when we were with y o u, *this* **we used to command y o u, If anyone does not want to work, neither let him eat.** No true parallel to this word of Paul has been found anywhere else. A maxim such as, "If they do not work, they have nothing to eat," is no parallel. That is a mere truism, an axiom so obvious to all except the rich that its very expression seems a bit superfluous. But what Paul had been saying again and again while in Thessalonica, and what he reaffirms here, is something else. It concerns the pious (?) sluggard *who does not want to work,* and who proceeds from the idea: "The church owes me a living." Substitute "world"

or "government" for "church" and the passage would fit many people living today, both inside and outside the church!

The command which Paul, by inspiration of the Holy Spirit, was constantly issuing was this, "Do not permit such a person to eat," that is, "Do
not supply his material needs." If he refuses to work, let him go hungry.
That may teach him a lesson.

Paul keeps perfect balance. While, on the one hand his heart goes out
to those who are really in need, and he is the kind of a man who is even
willing to undertake a missionary journey that will have as one of its
purposes the energetic promotion of a collection for the needy saints in
Judea (see II Cor., Chapters 8 and 9; cf. Rom. 15:26-29; Gal. 2:10), on the
other hand he has no sympathy whatever with the attitude of people who
refuse to do an honest day's work. It is necessary to grasp the deep root
of this labor-philosophy. As we see it, the apostle is not (at least not
merely) "borrowing a bit of good old workshop morality, a maxim applied
no doubt hundreds of times by industrious workmen as they forbade a lazy
apprentice to sit down for dinner," [133] but is proceeding from the idea
that, in imitation of Christ's example of self-sacrificing love for his own,
those who were saved by grace should become so unselfish that they will
loathe the very idea of unnecessarily becoming a burden to their brothers,
and, on the other hand, that they will yearn for the opportunity to share
what they have with those who are really in need. While it is certainly
true that every man in whom any sense of justice is left will assent to
the justice and wisdom of the maxim here expressed ("If anyone does not
want to work, neither let him eat"), it is nevertheless also true that for the
believer this maxim has added force, for selfishness and the truly Christian
life are direct opposites.

11. The apostle now states the reason for being under the necessity of
saying these things: **For we hear that some among y o u are conducting
themselves in a disorderly manner, not busy workers but busybodies.**

Though it is hardly possible for us who are living in a day of fast trans-
portation and air-mail and of telegraphic, telephonic, and televisic
communication to imagine the difficulties connected with the very slow
method of receiving and conveying messages which prevailed in the first
century A. D., nevertheless we must not exaggerate this contrast. Messages
did come through even in the days of Paul. The highways and sea-lanes
were often crowded with travelers. Tidings kept reaching Paul and his
associates. Hence, by this time he was well aware of one fact, namely, that
some "among" the readers (let them take note of the preposition "among,"
in the deepest sense not really "of" unless they repent) were conducting
themselves in the manner outlined above, in connection with our discussion

---

[133] Thus A. Deissmann, *op. cit.*, p. 314.

of verse 6; see on that passage. Paul says that these disorderly individuals were "nothing working but working (i.e. gadding) about." In the original there is here a play upon words. We read μηδὲν ἐργαζομένους ἀλλὰ περιεργαζομένους. In order to retain the flavor of the original, at least to some extent, we have translated this: "not busy workers but busybodies." It is easy to picture these persons — there were *some,* not many — laying down their tools, running from one "brother" to another with fantastic stories about Christ's immediate Return — the "day" had already arrived! — making extravagant claims for the truthfulness of their thrilling tales, returning home without the day's wages to buy food, then attempting to sponge on others or even on "the benevolence-fund" of the church, meddling in the affairs of the authorities, etc.

12. Now such people we command and urge in the Lord Jesus Christ that by quietly working for a living they eat their own bread.

For such irregular people Paul has a formal, objective *command,* a *message* sent *along* or transmitted (the first verb is παραγγέλλω, just as in verses 4, 6, and 10; cf. I Thess. 4:11) from the Head of the Church, who is the Chief Commander. This command, moreover, is at the same time a warm, personal *admonition* (the second verb is παρακαλέω: *admonish, urge,* I Thess. 2:11; 4:1, 10; 5:14; cf. a slightly different sense in I Thess. 3:2, 7; 4:18; 5:11: *encourage, comfort;* and see N.T.C. on John 14:26).

The missionaries do their commanding and urging "in the Lord Jesus Christ," i.e., by virtue of union with him, his Spirit speaking through them. For the full title "the Lord Jesus Christ" see on I Thess. 1:1.

The substance of the command and admonition is that by "calmly working for a living" these irregulars shall "eat their own bread." Instead of gadding about feverishly, running in circles and agitating, spreading excitement and alarm on every side, these people must work *calmly* (literally "with calmness"). This last expression immediately recalls I Thess. 4:11 ("be ambitious to live calmly"); see on that passage and also on I Tim. 2:2.

If they will obey this commandment and heed this admonition, they will not only be doing *themselves* a favor, and this both spiritually and materially, but also *others.* No longer will they be annoying other people. They will be "eating their own bread," providing their own sustenance.

13. Over against the irregular conduct of the few, Paul urges the many to persist in doing whatever is excellent: **But as for y o u, brothers, do not become weary in well-doing.** They must not *begin to behave badly* or *become weary* (ἐγκακήσητε, aorist subjunctive ingressive, cf. Luke 18:1; II Cor. 4:1, 16; Gal. 6:9; Eph. 3:13) in the matter of *well-doing.* As a compound verb (here nominative plural, masc. present participle καλοποιοῦντες) *well-doing* (one word) or *well doing* (two words) makes little, if any, difference. The two words (three if the article is counted when it occurs: τὸ καλὸν ποιοῦντες) occur in II Cor. 13:7; Gal. 6:9; Rom. 7:21. The point to note is that in each of these passages the meaning is general; that is, it is not specifically "giving to the poor" that is meant, but performing what accords with God's will in every walk of life. Doing the *excellent, honorable,* or *beautiful* (καλός-ή-όν) thing (hence, the *good* deed, cf. Mark 14:6) simply stands over against doing *(the) evil.* Note the following:

II Cor. 13:7: "Now we pray God that y o u may not do evil . . . that y o u may do the good."

Gal. 6:9: "And with respect to doing the good (or simply: "in well doing") let us not grow weary."

Rom. 7:21: "I find then the law that to me who would do the good, the evil lies close at hand."

It is probably not necessary to depart from this general meaning here in II Thess. 3:13. It is true that something can be said for the idea favored by several leading commentators, that what Paul meant in the present context was this:

"Do not become so exasperated by the troublesome conduct of a few loafers that y o u will begin to tire of exercising charity with respect to those who are deserving." But nothing in the context forbids us from interpreting the meaning to be:

"Do not be misled. Do not let a few people who neglect *their* duty keep *y o u* from doing *y o u r s.* Never grow tired of doing what is right, honorable, excellent."

Since this interpretation, in addition to fitting into the present concrete situation and context, is also the one demanded in the other passages (as has been shown), we accept it to be the right one.

For the concept *brothers* see on I Thess. 1:4.

14, 15. Doing the good and honorable thing means obeying the will of God as revealed by his servants. Some, however, refuse to obey. Hence, Paul continues: **Now if anyone does not obey our word expressed in this letter, note that man for yourselves, do not get mixed up with him, in order that he may become ashamed.**

Paul and his associates provide for the possibility that there will be those who refuse to obey "our word expressed in this letter." The writers are probably thinking especially of those members who were making themselves guilty of disorderly conduct: laying down their tools, rushing away to spread Parousia-gossip, and sponging on (as well as meddling in the affairs of) other people.

These members had been repeatedly warned with respect to these matters: first, during the personal presence of the missionaries when the gospel was brought to Thessalonica (II Thess. 3:10). No doubt Timothy, on his mission, had reiterated the warning. Then, by means of the first letter (both by implication, I Thess. 2:9; 5:14, and directly, I Thess. 4:11, 12) and now in this second letter they had been admonished again, in clear and forceful language (II Thess. 3:6-12). They had been called "busybodies, not busy workers" (3:11). One might expect that Paul would long ago have lost his patience with them, and would now advise their excommunication. However, we find nothing of the kind. The apostle still regards them as "brothers" (see verse 15), though *erring* brothers. To be sure, Paul and his fellow-workers are conscious of their authority, and they believe in discipline, personal, mutual, and church (discipline). But they do not believe in harsh intolerance, rash action, precipitate decision which cannot tolerate the light. They believe in honesty and integrity, and in the exercise of genuine love and patience! Hence, what they desire — and they are speaking by inspiration! — is this, that if all previous admonitions fail to effect their purpose, sterner measures must be resorted to. But even these measures are reformatory in character. They aim to reclaim, to lead to repentance, to save; not to destroy:

The person who persists in his disobedience must now be *marked* or *noted*. "Note that man for yourselves" (second person plural, present imperative middle), he says. This is addressed to *all* the faithful brothers at Thessalonica, not only to the consistory of the church. Or shall we assume that though the pronoun y o u in verse 13 and again in verse 16 refer to *all*, yet the similar y o u (implied in the verb) in the intervening verses (14 and 15) does not apply to the congregation but only to the consistory? The idea of some, namely, that what the writers have in mind is this: "Let the consistory display this disobedient person's name on a blackboard or bulletin-board" is simply *read into* the text. One cannot find it there, not even when reference is made to certain papyri where the verb ("note" or "mark" or "signify") does occur, but in connections that shed little or no light on its use here in II Thess.

What is actually meant is probably this: The congregation, having listened carefully to the public reading of II Thessalonians, a letter in which the character and conduct of the disorderly members are clearly indicated, must take definite notice of the persons described. In the future these individuals must not be treated as if nothing had happened. On the contrary, to a certain extent *the obedient members* must "withdraw themselves" from such disobedient ones. That the writers have this in mind is clear from the fact that it is exactly what they have already said in verse 6 (see on that verse). Writers should be allowed to explain their own words! Here in verse 14 the command is, "Let there be no intimate association with him" (i.e., with such a recalcitrant member) or "Do not get mixed up with him." [134] The disobedient members must not associate with such an individual *on intimate terms*. They should not welcome him into the company of *close friends*, agreeing with him, approving of his conduct, etc.

The purpose of this limited segregation or ostracism is "in order that he may become ashamed" (cf. I Cor. 4:14; see on Titus 2:8). Clearly this purpose is reformatory. It springs from love, from the desire to heal, not from the desire to get rid of an individual whom one does not happen to favor.

The *shame* will probably result when the individual in question begins to reflect on the patient and loving manner in which, in spite of his own grievous error which is pointed out to him (see verse 15), this "discipline" is being exercised. This man is not being excommunicated, at least not yet and probably never. That will depend on *his own* subsequent behavior. The writers' approach to the subject (here in II Thess. 3:14, 15) is not that *the person* in question *should be barred or banished,* but that *the obedient members* should withdraw themselves from him! It is exegetically unjustifiable to superimpose I Cor. 5:13 ("Put away that wicked man") or I Cor. 5:11 ("do not even eat with him") upon II Thess. 3:14, 15. The present case is different. To be sure, it *may develop* into something analogous to the stern disciplinary measure demanded in the fifth chapter of I Corinthians, but that stage has not been reached here. And even with respect to the Corinthian passages one should bear in mind that, according to what many regard as the most probable interpretation, the stern disciplinary measure there imposed had its wholesome effect, sothat Paul was happy to follow up his earlier commands by saying, "Forgive him, comfort him . . . confirm y o u r love toward him" (II Cor. 2:5-11).

That the "shunning" of the disobedient person was not intended to be absolute is shown by the words: **And do not consider** him (or "Do not regard him *as*"; ὡς is pleonastic, perhaps a Hebraism; cf. Job 19:11) **an enemy, but admonish him as a brother.**

This beautiful exhortation which affords an insight into the fatherly heart of Paul — and into the Father-heart of God! — immediately reminds

---

[134] Whether one adopts the imperative or the somewhat better attested infinitive makes little difference. It cannot be denied that, from Homer down, Greek at times carried on an imperative by means of an infinitive with imperative meaning. See Gram.N.T., pp. 943, 944. Here in II Thess. 3:14 (συναναμίγνυσθαι) we probably have an instance of such an infinitive in which the imperative sense of the preceding verb (σημειοῦσθε) is carried on. That would seem to be the simplest explanation. Basically nothing changes when the weaker reading (συναναμίγνυσθε) is adopted, for this is an imperative. But even if one should agree with some interpreters who favor the infinitive but who regard it as an infinitive of *purpose* ("note that man for yourselves *in order not* to have intimate fellowship with him") or of *result* ("note that man for yourselves *so as not* to have intimate fellowship with him"), the basic idea — namely, that either directly or by implication, the readers are here ordered not to have intimate fellowship with such a disobedient person — remains the same.

one of Rom. 12:20 ("If your *enemy* is hungry, feed him; if he is thirsty, give him to drink"), and via Paul leads the mind back to Christ in Matt. 5:44 or Luke 6:27 ("Love y o u r *enemies*"). In all these cases the same word is used, namely, *enemy* (ἐχθρός, which according to some is derived from ἐκτός; hence, basically *an outsider, stranger;* then, a person with a hostile disposition toward one: *an enemy;* cf. the Latin *hostis, a stranger, foreigner,* and finally *enemy*).

But though Rom. 12:20, Matt. 5:44 and Luke 6:27 have as their starting-point the actual existence of an enemy, II Thess. 3:15 warns against positing an enemy where there should be none. The person in question, though heedless with respect to all previous admonitions and even with respect to the earnest counsel given in II Thessalonians, must *not* be placed on the list of enemies . . . no, *not yet* at least! It is as if we hear the vine-dresser say, "Lord, let him alone this year also" (cf. Luke 13:8). "And do not consider him an enemy, but *admonish* (νουθετεῖτε) *him as a brother.*" See on I Thess. 5-12, where the verb *to admonish* has been discussed. For *brother* see on I Thess. 1:4. That this work of *admonishing* must be performed by *the entire congregation* is clear from I Thess. 5:14 (and cf. Rom. 15:14; Col. 3:16). That *the elders* take the lead is clear from I Thess. 5:12, 13.

The question is asked, "But what happens when the person whose conduct is here criticized persists in his refusal to give heed to loving counsel and admonition?" No doubt, such a one would finally have to be excommunicated, for he would be revealed in his true character as a factious person (cf. Titus 3:10). Christian tolerance has its limits (cf. Matt. 18:17; Rev. 2:14-16; 2:20-23), yet, until it is absolutely necessary it is well for the congregation not even to think of this possibility. Hence, Paul here in Thess. 3:15 says *nothing* about it! The erring one must be looked upon and treated not as a possible *reprobate* but as an erring *brother!*

16. Thoroughly convinced that in their own strength the readers cannot fulfil the precepts contained in the preceding verses, the writers add: **Now may he, the Lord of peace, give y o u this peace at all times in all ways.** The Lord of peace is the Lord Jesus Christ. It is he who established peace through his cross. It is he who not only pronounces it but actually *imparts* it. Hence Paul writes, "Now may he . . . *give*" (δῴη, 3rd. per. sing., aor. optative active). This *peace* or spiritual *prosperity* will prevail when the disorderly persons begin to live calmly, attending to their duties both earthly and heavenly (that is the immediate context here), when the faint-hearted go to the depths of God's promise, no longer worrying about their departed friends and about their own spiritual condition, and when the weak gain strength through sanctification. It is needed "at all times, in all ways," that is, in every circumstance of life. The peace here indicated is of a very special character. Note the article in the original (literally, "Now may he, the Lord of *the* peace"). Objectively, it is the condition of being reconciled, God's wrath having been removed. But here the subjective must not be dissociated from the objective. It is the reflection of God's smile in the heart of the believer who, by sovereign grace, has received the blessed assurance of this state of reconciliation. This, truly, is prosperity! Note also the similar expression toward the close of the first epistle (see on I Thess. 5:23; also on I Thess. 1:1, for the meaning of *peace;* and see N.T.C. on John 14:27).

Implied in *the peace* is *the fellowship*, which, however, because of its superlative worth, merits special mention. Hence, there follows **The Lord** (i.e., the Lord Jesus Christ) **with y o u all** (with the verb "be" understood). Note: *y o u all*, not even the disorderly ones are excluded! Did not the writers proceed from the idea that the censored persons were, after all, *brothers?* Cf. I Cor. 16:24; II Cor. 13:13.

17. An autographic conclusion follows, as a token of the fact that the letter is an authentic product of the mind and heart of the great apostle: **The greeting by the hand of me, Paul,** which **is a token of genuineness in every epistle; so I write.** It was customary in those days that the man who dictated a letter — as Paul, no doubt, dictated this one — would add a few words of greeting, etc., with his own hand, as a sign of authenticity.[135] That this was also Paul's habit is clear from the present passage and from I Cor. 16:21; Col. 4:18. Cf. also Philem. 19. The apostle never failed to do this. It was, indeed a *token of genuineness* (σημεῖον) in *every* epistle. This, of course, does not mean that Paul always *called attention* to it! Often he did not. But that does not change the fact. Thus, we may assume that the benediction at the close of II Corinthians was written by Paul's own hand, even though he does not there expressly state this.

The words, "which is a token of genuineness *in every epistle*" are not difficult to understand if one bears in mind the following facts:

a. Paul had already written I Thessalonians and probably also Galatians.

b. He no doubt intended to write many more letters. Moreover, in God's wise providence, not all the letters written by Paul have come down to us (see I Cor. 5:9). Perhaps, the apostle had even now written more letters.

Why did the apostle, here in II Thess. 3:17, call special attention to this mark of genuineness? The following reasons have been suggested and may well point in the right direction:

a. To prevent the disorderly persons from being able to say, "We admit that the letter which was read to us during the service (II Thessalonians) contained some rather uncomplimentary things with respect to us, but we

---

[135] See A. Deissmann, *op. cit.,* pp. 171, 172.

do not believe that it actually represents the thought of Paul. We deny that he either wrote or dictated it."

b. To discourage the spread of spurious epistles and/or the claim that someone had in his possession (or had seen) a letter from Paul stating that the day of the Lord had already arrived; see on 2:2.

18. The closing benediction **The grace of our Lord Jesus Christ (be) with y o u all** is exactly the same as in I Thess. 5:28 (see on that passage), with the sole exception that here, at the end of the second epistle, the word *all* is added. Was this word added in order to make sure that the individuals who had received a rebuke would feel that, in Paul's great and loving heart, there was room even for them?

Synthesis of Chapter 3

See p. 192. *The Revelation of the Lord Jesus From Heaven is a firmly anchored hope whose contemplation should result not in disorderliness but in calm assurance, stedfast endurance, and strength-imparting peace.*

Verses 1 and 2. *Request for intercession*

Being a firm believer in the power of intercessory prayer, Paul requests that the Thessalonian brothers will remember in their devotions the men who had brought them the glorious gospel of salvation. He makes this request in order that not only in Thessalonica but also at Corinth, where Paul, Silas, and Timothy are staying while this letter is being written, the word of the Lord may run its race and be crowned with glory, and God's servants may be rescued from "those unrighteous and evil men," which expression probably has reference to the Jewish opponents.

Verses 3-5. *Calm assurance and stedfast endurance required*

Over against faith-*less* men stands the ever faith-*ful* Lord, who will inwardly strengthen and thus (as well as in other ways) guard the readers from the evil one. Paul expresses his complete confidence in the obedience of the group which he is addressing. He expresses the hope that the Lord may direct the hearts of the readers to the love which issues from the heart of God, and to the endurance which was shown by Christ in the midst of his own bitter suffering. When this love becomes the motivating force in the lives of the Thessalonians and when that endurance becomes their example, spiritual victory is assured.

Verses 6-15. *Directives with respect to "every brother who conducts himself in a disorderly manner" (Disorderliness condemned)*

Reminding the readers of his own example (and that of Silas and Timothy) while at Thessalonica, an example of bustling activity and industry ("with toil and hardship we were working for a living by night and by day"), and of the order which he had repeatedly issued at that time ("if anyone does not want to work neither let him eat"), Paul rebukes the "busybodies" who refuse to work. He commands and urges them in the Lord Jesus Christ "that by calmly working for a living they eat their own bread." He counsels the congregation not to copy their evil example, that is, not to fall behind in doing whatever is noble and honorable. If "disorderly" individuals disobey the word expressed in the present letter, they must be shunned, but not entirely. The other members must contact them for the purpose of admonishing them. However, as long as the idlers continue in their sinful course, the rest of the membership should refuse to associate with them on intimate terms. The purpose of admonishing them and of the refusal on the part of the others to get "mixed up" with them and their deeds is that the erring ones may become ashamed and thus brought back to a healthy outlook upon life.

Verses 16-18. *Conclusion*

The apostle expresses the ardent wish that upon the struggling church at Thessalonica, oppressed by persecution from without and plagued by fanaticism from within, the peace established by Christ may rest, that peace which alone is able to impart strength and courage. He continues, "The Lord be with y o u *all*," that is, not only with those who are not in need of special instruction or admonition but also with mourners, with those who are on the way to become martyrs, with the weak, yes even with fanatics, busybodies, and loafers, who repent of their sins.

In order to add weight to the contents of the divinely inspired letter, to prevent the spread of false rumors, and to pronounce upon the readers, assembled for worship, the most precious of all gifts, there follows, "The greeting by the hand of me, Paul, which is a token of genuineness in every letter: so I write. The grace of our Lord Jesus Christ be with y o u all."

SELECT BIBLIOGRAPHY

An attempt has been made to make this list *as small as possible.*

Calvin, John, *Commentarius In Epistolam Pauli Ad Thessalonicenses I et II, (Corpus Reformatorum, vol. LXXX)*, Brunsvigae (apud C. A. Schwetschke et Filium), 1895; English translation (in *Calvin's Commentaries*), Grand Rapids, 1948.

Frame, James E., *A Critical and Exegetical Commentary on the Epistles of St. Paul to the Thessalonians* (in *The International Critical Commentary*), New York, 1912.

Milligan, George, *St. Paul's Epistles to the Thessalonians*, London, 1908; reprint Grand Rapids, 1952.

Van Leeuwen, J. A. C., *Paulus' Zendbrieven aan Efeze, Colosse, Filemon, en Thessalonika* (in *Kommentaar op het Nieuwe Testament*), Amsterdam, 1926.

GENERAL BIBLIOGRAPHY

Only those books and articles are listed to which reference has been made in this volume. Many more books have been used, but these are not listed.

Aalders, G. Ch., *De Profeten Des Ouden Verbonds*, Kampen, 1918.

Alford, H., *The Greek New Testament*, Boston, 1878.

Alger, W. R., *A Critical History of the Doctrine of a Future Life*, New York, 1866.

Ante-Nicene Fathers, The, ten volumes, reprint Grand Rapids, Mich., 1950.

Auberlen, C. A. and Riggenback, C. J., *The Two Epistles of Paul to the Thessalonians* (in *Lange's Commentary*), reprint Grand Rapids, 1950.

Bacon, B. W., *An Introduction to the New Testament*, New York, N. Y., 1900.

Barnes, A., *Notes on the New Testament, Explanatory and Practical*, reprint Grand Rapids, 1951.

Barnes, A., *Scenes and Incidents in the Life of the Apostle Paul*, reprint Grand Rapids, 1950.

Barnett, A. E., *The New Testament, Its Making and Meaning*, New York, 1946.

Baur, F. C., *Paulus*, Stuttgart, 1845.

Bavinck, H., *Gereformeerde Dogmatiek*, third edition, Kampen, 1918.

Bavinck, H., *The Doctrine of God* (translated by William Hendriksen), Grand Rapids, Mich., 1951.

Bengel, J. A., *Gnomon Novi Testamenti*, London, 1855.

Berkhof, L., *New Testament Introduction*, Grand Rapids, 1915.

Berkhof, L., *Systematic Theology*, Grand Rapids, 1949.

Bible, The Holy. In addition to the original for both Testaments, various New Testament translations have been consulted (the familiar English modern-language translations; also translations in Dutch, both old and new, French, German, Latin, Swedish, and Syriac).

Blackwood, A. W., *The Fine Art of Public Worship*, Nashville, 1939.

Blair, E. P., "The First Epistle to the Thessalonians," *Int.* vol. II, No. 2 (April, 1948).

Bornemann, W., *Die Thessalonicherbriefe*, Göttingen, 1894 (translation in *Meyer's Critical and Exegetical Commentary on the New Testament*), London, 1928.

Calvin, John, *Commentarius In Epistolam Pauli Ad Thessalonicenses I et II* (*Corpus Reformatorum*, vol. LXXX), Brunsvigae (apud C. A. Schwetschke et Filium), 1895; (English translation in *Calvin's Commentaries*), Grand Rapids, 1948.

Conybeare, W. J., and Howson, J. S., *The Life and Epistles of St. Paul*, reprint Grand Rapids, 1949.

Deissmann, A., *Light From the Ancient East* (translated by L. R. M. Strachan), New York, 1922.

Denney, James, *The Epistles to the Thessalonians* (in *The Expositor's Bible*), reprint Grand Rapids, 1943.

Dijk, K., *Het Rijk der Duizend Jaren*, Kampen, 1933.

Eadie, John, *A Commentary on the Greek Text of the Epistles of Paul to the Thessalonians*, London, 1877.

Ellicott, C. J., *St. Paul's Epistles to the Thessalonians*, London, 1880.

Erdman, Charles R., *The Epistles of Paul to the Thessalonians*, Philadelphia, 1935.

Fausset, A. R., *The First and Second Epistles of Paul the Apostle to the Thessalonians* (in Jamieson, Fausset, Brown Commentary on the Old and New Testament), reprint Grand Rapids, Mich., 1945.

Findlay, G. G., *The Epistles to the Thessalonians* (in Cambridge Greek Testament), Cambridge, 1904.

Frame, J. E., *A Critical and Exegetical Commentary on the Epistle of St. Paul to the Thessalonians* (in the *International Critical Commentary*), New York, N. Y., 1912.

Free, J. P., *Archaeology and Bible History*, Wheaton, Ill., 1950.

Gesenius' *Hebrew Grammar* (edited and enlarged by E. Kautzsch, second English edition, revised by A. E. Cowley), Oxford, 1910.

Goodspeed, E. J., *Paul*, Philadelphia and Toronto, 1947.

Greijdanus, *Bizondere Canoniek*, two volumes, Kampen, 1949.

Grosheide, F. W., *De Handelingen der Apostelen* (in *Korte Verklaring der Heilige Schrift met Nieuwe Vertaling*), Kampen, 1950.

Hahn, H. F., *Old Testament in Modern Research*, Philadelphia, 1954.

Harris, J. R., "A Study in Letter Writing," *The Expositor*, Series 5, volume 8 (September, 1898).

Hawkins, R. M., *The Recovery of the Historical Paul*, Nashville, 1943.

Hendriksen, W., *More Than Conquerors, An Interpretation of the Book of Revelation*, Grand Rapids, Mich., seventh edition, 1954.

Hendriksen, W., *Bible Survey*, Grand Rapids, Mich., fourth edition, 1953.

Hendriksen, W., *The Meaning of the Preposition ANTI in the New Testament* (unpublished doctoral dissertation submitted to Princeton Seminary), 1948.

Hendriksen, W., *Lectures on the Last Things*, Grand Rapids, 1951.

Hendriksen, W., *New Testament Commentary, The Gospel of John*, two volumes, Grand Rapids, Mich., 1953-1954.

Hepp, V., *De Antichrist*, Kampen, 1920.

Heyns, W., *Liturgiek*, Holland, Mich., 1903.

Hooper, J. S. M., "Translation of Biblical Terms: An Illustration," *BTr.* vol. 4, No. 3 (July, 1953).

International Standard Bible Encyclopaedia, The, five volumes, edition published in Grand Rapids, 1943.

Kepler, T. S. (editor of) *Contemporary Thinking About Paul*, New York, Nashville (no date).

Knap, J. J., *The Resurrection and Life Eternal*, Grand Rapids, Mich., 1928.

Knox, John, *Chapters in a Life of Paul*, New York and Nashville, 1946.

Kuyper, A., Sr., *Onze Eeredienst*, Kampen, 1911.

Kuyper, A., Sr., *De Engelen Gods*, Kampen, 1923.

Kuyper, A., Sr., *Het Werk van den Heiligen Geest*, Kampen, 1927.

Kuyper, A., Sr., *Dictaten Dogmatiek*, five volumes, Kampen, 1910.

Lenski, R. C. H., *The Interpretation of St. Paul's Epistles to the Colossians, to the Thessalonians, to Timothy, to Titus, and to Philemon*, Columbus, Ohio, 1937. Other volumes in the series of Lenski's Commentary have also been consulted.

Loeb Classical Library, New York (various dates). The Latin-English volumes have been consulted for the translated writings of Augustine, Cicero, Horace, Lucretius, Pliny, Tertullian, and Virgil; the Greek-English for Aeschylus, The

Apostolic Fathers, Diogenes Laertius, Epictetus, Euripedes, Eusebius, Homer, Philo, and Plato.

Machen, R., *The Origin of Paul's Religion*, Grand Rapids, 1947.

Milligan, George, *St. Paul's Epistles to the Thessalonions*, London, 1908; reprint Grand Rapids, 1952.

Moffatt, James, *An Introduction to the Literature of the New Testament*, New York, 1917.

Moffat, James, *The First and Second Epistles of Paul the Apostle to the Thessalonians* (in The Expositor's Greek Testament), reprint Grand Rapids, Mich. (no date).

Moulton, W. F., and Geden, A. S., *A Concordance to the Greek New Testament*, Edinburgh, third edition, 1950.

Moulton, J. H., and Milligan, G., *The Vocabulary of the Greek New Testament*, New York, 1945.

Neil, William, *The Epistle of Paul to the Thessalonians* (in Moffatt Commentary), London, 1950.

Perry, A. M., "Translating the Greek Article," *JBL* 68 (December, 1949).

Plummer, A., *A Commentary on St. Paul's First Epistle to the Thessalonians; . . . Second Epistle to the Thessalonians*, London, 1932.

Pieters, A., *The Lamb, The Woman, and The Dragon*, Grand Rapids, Mich., 1937.

Postma, F., *Paulus*, Pretoria, 1949.

Quimby, C. W., *Paul for Everyone*, New York, 1944.

Ramsay, W., *St. Paul the Traveler and the Roman Citizen*, reprint Grand Rapids, Mich., 1949.

Ramsay, W., *The Cities of St. Paul*, reprint, Grand Rapids, Mich., 1949.

Richardson, A. (editor of) *A Theological Word Book of The Bible*, New York, 1952.

Robertson, A. T., *The Epistles of Paul* (in Word Pictures in the New Testament), New York and London, 1931.

Robertson, A. T., *Grammar of the Greek New Testament in the Light of Historical Research*, New York, 1923.

Robertson, A. T., *The Minister and his Greek New Testament*, New York, 1923.

Smith, David, *The Life and Letters of St. Paul*, New York, N. Y., 1920.

Stewart, R. W., *The Epistle to the Thessalonians* (in The Speaker's Bible), Aberdeen, 1951.

Trench, R. C., *Synonyms of the New Testament*, edition Grand Rapids, 1948.

Van der Vies, A. B., *De Beide Brieven aan de Thessalonicensen*, Leiden, 1865.

Veldkamp, H., *In de Schemering van Christus Wederkomst*, Kampen, 1928.

Vos, G., *The Pauline Eschatology*, Princeton, N. J., 1930.

Vos, G., *The Self-Disclosure of Jesus*, New York, 1926.

Warfield, B. B., *Biblical and Theological Studies* (edited by Samuel G. Craig), Philadelphia, Pennsylvania, 1952.

Westminster Dictionary of the Bible, by J. D. David (revised and rewritten by H. S. Gehman), Philadelphia, 1944.

Westminster Historical Atlas to the Bible (edited by G. E. Wright and F. V. Filson), Philadelphia, 1945.

Wuest, K. S., *Golden Nuggets from the Greek New Testament*, Grand Rapids, 1939.